First Due:

Baltimore

by

Michael Kernan

dmc associates
Dover, NH

published by
dmc associates, inc.
PO Box 1095
Dover, NH 03820

ISBN: 1-879848-15-5

Printed in the United States of America

First Printing

Dedication

More years ago than I would care to admit, fate took me to the Ocean City, Maryland boardwalk looking for a summer job. For three summers at Edwards 5 & 10 cent store, I worked for one of the finest men I ever met. My boss was Al Harmon who had recently completed twelve years as the volunteer fire chief in his community.

Mr. Harmon came into my life at a time when I wasn't sure which fork in the road to take. He inspired me with his uncompromising work ethic, incredible energy, deep sense of community, genuine dedication to family, and abiding love of the fire service. He became the mentor whose wisdom and encouragement helped me shape my life immensely. We remained friends many years after I had moved on and taken a job in the Baltimore City Fire Department. Always he was there when I went to the shore to visit, listening patiently to my youthful exuberance for the job. He never failed to tell me how proud he was of what I had become. I still miss him.

On the day of his funeral I told Mr. Harmon's wife and daughter that some day I would write a book and dedicate it to him. I'm sorry it has taken me so long. I hope it would make him proud.

Acknowledgments

No undertaking of the magnitude of book writing would be possible without the help of many people.

Foremost, I must thank my family. They have often had to endure my less-than-pleasant demeanor as I worked on the manuscript. At least I could blame the pressures of writing for those times. Their encouragement and sacrifice have made this book possible.

My thanks to all the others who have contributed by furnishing pictures, reading chapters, offering their constructive criticism, and providing their support and encouragement. I deeply appreciate their help. I will refrain, however, from listing names lest I offend someone I would surely miss. They know who they are.

To Dennis Campbell, my publisher, thanks for having faith and patience. I am grateful you decided to take a chance.

My appreciation to Commissioner Leo Stapleton (ret.) of the Boston Fire Department who strongly encouraged me to write. Thank you for your confidence and support.

Finally, to all the men and women of the fire service, particularly the Baltimore City Fire Department, my admiration and heartfelt thanks. I am honored to be one of you. I hope the book pleases you; it's for all of us.

Author's Note

During my career in the fire service I've heard dozens of my coworkers say "Some day I'm going to write a book." Most of us never get around to it. There are undoubtedly plenty of my fellow fire fighters who could do a finer job, but here is my rendition of our story.

To describe what the book is, I have to begin by telling you what the book isn't. **First Due—Baltimore** is not a journal. That would bore me, let alone you, so the book is not strictly in chronological order. Rather the book is more like our lives that mix today with memories of yesterdays and hopes of tomorrows. It's not a critique of the fire department in my city or anyone else's. There are more than enough critics, consultants, and analysts to go around. **First Due—Baltimore** is certainly not a training manual, and definitely not a safety course for fire fighters.

My book is not a great literary work. My wonderful high school English teacher, Father Sheridan, is probably rolling over in his grave. I can't imagine any of his writing guidelines that I've failed to break. Some of the writing uses past tense. Other parts are written in the present tense so that, I hope, you can feel as though you are there with us. Some passages are in the first person, which I hate, but which sometimes feels the only right way for me to describe what's here. They are *my* experiences. At other times I have used the second and third person for the narration, but all is intended to inform, enlighten, and entertain.

Please don't confuse my inattention to politically correct conventions with chauvinist attitudes. If I inadvertently offend some person who resents being lumped in with "the guys", I apologize. I find the whole gender issue a little too much to grapple with each time. My firefighter daughter will testify to my position on females in the fire service.

First Due—Baltimore is actually a collection of writings, some from years ago, some more recent. Much was taken from note I've made over the years. With the exception of some very minor changes we've made for the sake of privacy, all of it is true.

When you've finished reading the book, I hope you'll feel that you have shared with me the emotional roller coaster we fire fighters experience. I think you will laugh; maybe you'll cry. That's the same way our days go.

For all those who never got around to writing this book, I offer this look into our world.

Mike Kernan
March, 1999

Contents

First Due: Baltimore

1
Worlds Apart

The warm, southerly wind ruffles the hair that I have left and dries the salt on my skin. The surf has been whipped to a frothy, pounding, sand-filled tempest. As far as I can see only a brave few have ventured into the ocean, and yet, the Kernan boys can't resist.

My sons, David and Tim, have just spent twenty minutes with me fighting the waves and wind here on the Delaware coast. Now we sit watching the seagulls comb the sand for the day's leftovers. We laugh as we watch them fight over the scraps of french fries left by a family who has headed for the showers. The gulls scream at each other and chase and pull and tug, not unlike the kids who just left the fries.

The clouds are spectacular as the sun begins to dip westward over the Bay. Layers of pink and blue alternate with the now graying, cottony clouds that have been so brilliantly white all day. I hate to see the day ending.

My wife, Diana, reads contentedly as the boys get up to run on the beach. The surf pounds its relentless tune that soothes and cleanses the soul. For my entire life it is here I have come to rejuvenate. The ocean possesses a unique healing quality for me. My mind clears of all the usual adult pressures and I can be a kid again. My worries recede temporarily, and life seems so much nicer in this world.

Though it is only 150 miles from here, *my* world is truly light years away. It's hard today to relate to my world of urban decay, poverty, crime, suffering, and fire. This week is different, but next week my life resumes. Next week it's back to doing what I do, being what I am—a Baltimore City Fire Fighter.

Baltimore is a great city. Situated on the shores of the Patapsco River, an estuary of the famous Chesapeake Bay, the city is ideally located for conducting commerce. Baltimore boasts one of the country's busiest seaports. Around this port has grown a region that is home to iron and steel, machinery, food processing, printing, chemical, and numerous other industries.

The port is not only a great place to work; it's a great place to play. The port and the city are teeming with marinas and pleasure boats of all sizes. The waterfront that once was filled with endless rows of ramshackle warehouses, ship repair yards, and rotting wooden piers is now a modern, beautiful, urban success story. The National Aquarium, the Science Center, the World Trade Center and Harborplace, filled with shops and restaurants, line the banks of the Inner Harbor. Moored proudly near the modern yachts and tour boats is the *USS Constellation*, arguably the oldest US warship afloat. She was launched here in Baltimore in 1797 and has returned to her home. Tourists flock to these and numerous other attractions in the area.

Just around the bend from the inner harbor area sits Fort McHenry. During the War of 1812 it was here that the British were repulsed in a battle remembered many times each day around the nation. As Francis Scott Key observed the battle from a British warship where he was seeing a prisoner, he was inspired to write the "Star Spangled Banner".

The city is also home to the world-famous Johns Hopkins Hospital, the Walters Art Gallery, Pimlico Race Track (home of the Preakness), and so many reminders of our heritage that it has been dubbed "the City of Monuments."

Baltimoreans are rightfully proud of their great city, but there's another side to the city that the tourists don't frequent. That's my world. Together with about 1500 others, I am sworn to protect the city from fire and other calamities.

The Baltimore City Fire Department is a full-service department. We provide inspection of all buildings for violations of the Fire Prevention Code, the Building Code, the Electrical Code, and the Housing Code. We teach public fire safety programs to community groups, neighborhood organizations, and our schools. We patrol a harbor teeming with commercial shipping and pleasure boats. The department provides high-rise rescue, confined space rescue, structural collapse rescue, and trench rescue.

When any of the many thousands of hazardous materials that fill our modern world cause a problem, we respond. If you are unfortunate enough to be involved in an automobile accident while in our city, we will disentangle you from the wreck, we will treat you with the latest in medical care, and we will transport you to the hospital. And, almost overlooked in these days of diversification of services, we fight fires.

Any city the size of Baltimore keeps its emergency services pretty busy. Philadelphia, New York, Boston, Washington, Baltimore—the cities are much the same. Tough budgets, difficult crime problems, heavy fire activity, and dedicated fire personnel are common to us all. This book could be set in any of those cities or in countless others, for in all of those places fire fighters risk their lives while the city sleeps, blissfully unaware, sometimes uncaring.

"Truck 22 on the scene—two story brick—heavy smoke showing," the radio crackles as I respond toward the Cold Spring Lane address.

No fire fighter can shake the concern that grips us at 3:00 A.M. as we respond knowing that a family who had been sleeping peacefully moments before may be struggling for their very lives. There is a heightened sense of urgency that accompanies a middle-of-the-night dwelling fire and we cannot shake that until we know that everyone is out.

"Truck 22. Dispatch a medic unit. Injured civilian," Lieutenant Mike Jenson radios as I near the scene. My mind considers the possibilities—somebody has escaped, but is injured; the fire fighters have rescued someone from the house; somebody has jumped from a window before the fire department arrived.

The big questions remain unanswered: How many may still be trapped inside literally sucking up their last gasps of terrible, hot, smoke-filled poison? Can we get them all in time?

Heavy smoke fills the street and the distinctive smell of burning wood greets me as I arrive. As I park my chief's car out of the way I note the hoseline Engine 29 has stretched into the front door. The attack is underway. Sounds of breaking second floor windows crashing in response to the "truckies'" axes tell me that the ventilation we need is being performed.

Those two steps—the advancement of the interior attack line and the coordinated ventilation of the fire building—may help us get to the occupants in time. Smoke and heat usually kill trapped occupants before the fire actually burns them. One gulp of superheated air can sear the lungs and cause fatal injury. Every second counts.

If any people are unconscious down on the floor, where the relatively cooler air may be, they might still be alive. Ventilation begins to allow the worst of the smoke and heat to escape from the top of the building, and cooler, fresh air begins to replace it from below. Of course, with the increased oxygen now available, the fire intensifies, so the hoseline must be ready.

Fortunately, the engine company has positioned their line properly. Poorly-timed or incorrectly-performed ventilation could cause the fire to spread, and our chance for rescue will be lost.

Engine 29 has no trouble locating the seat of the fire within the building. Fire has completely engulfed the kitchen and dining room, and has begun to enter the hall The deep red glow of a fire seen through dense smoke guides them right to it. The fire has not yet reached the stairs to the second floor. The open stairway, however, acts just like a chimney to spread the terrible heat and toxic gases upstairs. Had we been a minute longer, the fire itself would have followed. The captain and the fire fighter on the hoseline know the importance of protecting the stairs. Truck company members are searching upstairs with no hoseline. Terrific heat and zero visibility force them to crawl on their hands and knees as they search quickly for any remaining occupants. Without the engine company there to protect the stairs, the fire could race upstairs in an instant and turn the would-be rescuers into victims. Few jobs are as dangerous as searching above a working fire.

From the hall the engine crew begins to beat the advancing fire back into the kitchen. Outside the rear of the house another hoseline is now in position, but the engine crew there does not open up their nozzle. Heavy fire blows from the back door and windows and the temptation to hit it is great.

Crouched down to avoid the worst of the heat, the lieutenant coaches the nozzleman to be patient. Their job is to keep the fire from spreading across the wooden back porches to involve other houses. Having been on the initial attack line plenty of times himself, the lieutenant is keenly aware of the need to be patient. A stream of water directed from outside here would endanger the crew inside and possibly drive the fire through the rest of the house. Improper tactics could prove disastrous.

The sounds of the hose stream inside and the expulsion of smoke, fire, and steam soon reassure the lieutenant that he has made the right choice. Engine 29 is knocking the fire, driving it right out the back windows and door where it will do no harm.

Out front the scene is different. Billowing, ink-black clouds of smoke belch from the second floor windows where the truck company members have entered to search. Smoke oozes from the eaves of the rowhouses on either side of the fire building.

On the front lawn two fire fighters are performing CPR on a child. Frantic family and neighbors scream hysterically and are being restrained by others and by police officers.

The driver of Truck 22 has positioned the 100 foot aerial

ladder to gain access to the roof and is scurrying up the ladder. At a fire like this it is crucial to get the top opened up to release the pent-up heat and smoke. Skylights over the interior stairs are common in this kind of construction and provide a quick, easy method of vertical ventilation.

As the third engine company arrives, I assign them to stretch a backup line inside to assist in controlling the fire and to help in the search operation. Meanwhile, the second truck company is carrying ladders down the narrow alley in the rear. The ladders will allow the crew to vent the upper areas of the rear of the dwelling and to gain entry to the second floor to search. These ladders will also serve as an emergency exit for any fire fighters who might become trapped above the fire.

When the fourth and last engine company arrives, I direct them to check the adjacent houses on either side of the fire building. Smoke is visible at the roof line of each. Fortunately the quick attack and the brick walls have held the fire to the original building.

"Chief, there's nobody else in the dwelling," comes the report I want to hear. This confirms the information the hysterical family members have given us out front. Fire fighters learn early in their careers not to rely on such information. Terrified, confused civilians frequently provide inaccurate information, so we absolutely must check for ourselves. This time the information is correct. Only the one little girl was trapped upstairs. Everyone else had made it out. Truck 22 made a valiant rescue attempt. They were able to locate and remove the young victim from the second floor, front bedroom almost immediately after they arrived.

For fifteen minutes the paramedics attempt to get a sign of life from the tiny, broken body in the front yard. After consulting with the doctors by radio the paramedics make the decision. Fire fighters help the paramedics carry the young victim and all the medical equipment over the hoselines and around the fire apparatus to the medic unit. As the medic unit pulls away with its siren wailing, we all silently hope that she will survive. We've all seen the signs too often to be optimistic. Non-breathing, full arrest, burns to the respiratory tract—these are terms that leave little room for optimism.

The investigator from our Fire Investigation Bureau finishes talking with those who have escaped the burning house and enters the house to begin the search for the cause of the fire. Extensive training and much experience have made our investigators experts in their field. At this fire the cause is readily apparent—a late-night snack turned deadly. Unattended cooking is one of the leading causes of fire nationwide, and Baltimore is no exception.

Until the investigator finishes, we move nothing within the dwelling unless absolutely necessary. Any evidence, any clue must be preserved at a fire of this nature. The police department's arson squad and their crime lab eventually arrive and, together with the fire department investigator, they photograph the scene and document evidence. Only after all these important steps are complete can the companies begin the task of overhauling.

While controlling the fire took only a short time, we will spend several hours on the scene. After the investigators have completed their tasks, the long, tedious job of overhaul begins. We remove every bit of burned furniture from the house. We separate the burned clothing from the pieces that can be saved. Anything burned goes outside to be wet down. We will leave nothing inside that could possibly cause a rekindle.

The truck guys pull down the plaster ceilings and tear open the walls throughout the burned area searching for any hidden sparks. The officers inspect the area with their handlights and supervise the removal of wooden window and door frames that could conceal leftover fire. One ember left undiscovered, one spark hiding inside a partition, could mean a new fire after we leave.

Finally the time comes for the engine company to do a final wetdown of the most heavily burned areas, but before that I do my last walk-through inspection. After all these years I am still amazed at how quickly fire can move. I look at the charred stove and picture the pot overheating as the fire turned from friend to foe. Up the wall to the cabinets, across the ceiling, the fire went. Heat and smoke, the silent killers, were already finding their way upstairs like predators drawn inexorably to prey. How long had it taken, I wondered, and turned away.

"OK, Twenty-nine, wet it down and let's get going."

Outside the investigator informs us that the hospital has been unable to revive the patient we sent to them. Another of Baltimore's children has fallen victim to fire. I don't even know her name. Tonight I don't want to. I tell the investigator that I'll get the information needed for my report tomorrow night, but not tonight.

Back at the fire station I enter only the barest pieces of information regarding the fire in the battalion journal. Time, box number, location, time out of service—the rest can wait until tomorrow, make that *tonight*, when we'll be back in.

I hear the engine backing in as I flop onto the bed, clothes and all, to try to get a half hour's sleep before my relief reports for day shift. Like so many nights, sleep will not come. Instead I lie awake staring at nothing and replaying all that has happened.

Satisfied that nothing else we could have done would have made any difference, I get back up and head across the apparatus floor to the kitchen to get a coffee. It comes as no surprise that the engine crew is in there already, the television playing unwatched in the corner.

An hour later I head home. The lead story on the morning radio newscast is the fatal fire overnight in northwest Baltimore. I wonder if my family will hear the news report later in the day and figure I was there. Probably not, I guess. The kids are getting ready to leave for school when I get home.

"Hi, Dad, how was your night? Have anything?"

"Just routine," is my answer as I head upstairs.

2
What's It Like

Every once in a while somebody will ask me, "What's it like to be a fire fighter?" Or somebody in the fire service somewhere else will ask, "What's it like to be in the fire department in Baltimore?"

After all these years the answers should come easily, but it seems as time goes by it becomes harder for me to reply with some clear-cut, short, simple answer. With the years and all the experiences they've brought have come dozens of feelings, hundreds of scenes on which to reflect, thousands of frozen moments that complicate the answer.

What's it like? It's dirty. Every fire fighter can tell you of the lousiest, smelliest, dirtiest job encountered. By its very nature firefighting's not the cleanest of pastimes. It's the smell of fuel oil that defies every effort to remove it from your gear, your clothes and your skin. After a particularly bad fire in an oil company long ago, before we were better educated about the hazards of doing so, many of us spent months trying in vain to remove the smell from the oil-saturated heavy firefighting clothing. No matter how many times we scrubbed the coats, the smell was there. Each time any of us put the coats back on, we smelled like something dragged from the oil changing pit at the local gas station.

Dirty and smelly are relative terms. Any serious discussion must inevitably turn to a comparison to the known. For those of us who have been around awhile in Baltimore the litmus test is usually "Yeah, well how does that compare with that fish meal?" Fish meal looks somewhat like oatmeal, which I've never particularly liked even before my introduction to the foulest smelling goo ever invented. Nobody involved in fighting the fire that day will ever forget the joy of wading knee-deep in the quagmire of wretched glop that clung like a scared baby to everybody and everything. Imagine a carcass that has sat rotting in the sun for a month covered with maggots. You would gladly rub that on you to remove the smell of fish meal. That fire forced even us to discard many, many sets of firefighting gear. And I thought pig crap smelled bad!

But more common to all fire fighters are the distinctive odors of burned, wet wood and of melted plastics and foam rubber that before we arrived were someone's home and toys and clothing and furniture. Even with the protective clothing and the air masks that today's fire fighters wear, the smells come away with us from every fire. Sometimes it's the biting smell of smoke created by burned food left on the stove, a smoke so thick and stinking that only a drunk or a teenager could sleep through it. Sometimes it's the smell of a burning mattress (one of my early lieutenants used to call them workbenches) that fills the house. Amazing how the shift from natural to synthetic materials over the years has caused the odor and the colors of the smoke given off to change. And always the smoke gets deadlier. The poisons put off by a burning foam rubber chair cushion can kill a sleeping family.

Gone are the days of my early career when leather-lunged fire fighters would crawl along the floor toward the burning furniture with reddened eyes burning and running, noses pressed to the floor for the remaining available oxygen. Thankfully today's fire fighters don't stand outside afterwards coughing and spitting up the black globs they didn't suck all the way into their lungs. The carbon monoxide-induced headaches that afterwards made me feel like my head would explode or my eyes would bulge right out of my head are distant reminders of how firefighting has changed.

But today as then firefighting is a dirty job. Whether it's a brush fire that has put the sweaty fire fighter in clouds of grimy ash or the house fire that leaves the clothing and the person inside of it contaminated with the airborne particles of the burning substances, there isn't yet a clean way of fighting dirty fires. For days afterwards, the fire fighters are still sometimes reminded of the earlier fire when each hot shower brings out more of the embedded odors and gases from their pores and especially their hair.

Yes, it's a dirty job and any fire fighter who has scrubbed down the hose and readied the apparatus for the next fire can tell you. After a back-breaking effort extinguishing the fire, pulling apart the ceilings and walls, throwing out the burned and water-soaked furniture and other contents, the work really begins.

The excitement has long gone. The adrenaline-filled first moments of the fire long since have given way to the non-glamorous but important tasks remaining. Find all the tools that were used on the fire. At a serious fire tools of all shapes and sizes may have been employed, especially by the truck companies. Sometimes members of other units grab tools from a closer fire truck. Many times tools get used, passed on to someone else in another part of the structure, set on the side so something else can be used, etc. Debris falls, ceilings collapse, even walls come down. All of these things make it tough to account for everything on the scene, but the company doesn't leave until it has sorted through the piles and uncovered every tool.

For the engine companies remains the chore of retrieving all the hose stretched hundreds of feet to the hydrants possibly through mud or snow or polluted with the black stinking runoff of charred debris and water from the fire building. Dirtier by far is the removal of the hoselines that carried the water from the engine's pumps into the building. Snaking throughout the building's burned interior, lines may run to various floors, into the burned out shells of rooms where everything was consumed but the soggy, stinking, waterlogged remains. Often covered with soot and wet plaster, pieces of broken glass, wood splinters, and other debris, the wet hose must be pulled outside, rinsed off, drained of any water remaining inside it, and rolled up or carefully re-packed on the engine, ready for the next use.

The spectators have long since gone, the media is already reporting the stories about the fire if it was newsworthy, but the work of the fire fighters goes on. Back at the station the vehicles need to be checked over. Keeping the truck full of fuel is necessary; the next fire might be the one that lasts all night. The booster tank that contains the water initially used to fight a fire must be checked and refilled, and each tool that was used needs to be cleaned and checked.

Each of the air masks that was used must be cleaned and checked thoroughly. Soot-soaked shoulder straps must be washed and left outstretched to dry; each air bottle must be replaced with a full one. Every facepiece must be carefully washed and disinfected so it is ready for the next run. A single small piece of fire debris hidden down in the diaphragm could cause the facepiece to malfunction next time. Operating in atmospheres where one breath of superheated, toxic smoke could spell serious injury or death, fire fighters stake their very lives on this equipment. Before the fire fighter gets to clean up and rest or grab something to eat, the dirty work must be completed. Many times a fire that was controlled in just a couple of minutes means hours of work. That's the side of the work that few people even *know* about.

A fire fighter's work is indeed about dirt and soot, but it is also about clean and cleaning. Every fire fighter has spent considerable time—many would argue way too much—cleaning.

The fire engines and trucks that sparkle in the sunshine don't get that way by themselves. Fire departments take pride in the appearance of their stations and their equipment. Many, many hours are devoted to cleaning the vehicles. Fire fighters clean inside the compartments where water could lay and rust tools or the compartments themselves. They climb up in the hose beds (the places on top of the engines where about two thousand feet of hose of various sizes is stored) to sweep out the cinders and other debris that inevitably accumulate there. The windows and the shiny painted surfaces get water and soap and polish as one might expect. All those surfaces visible to the casual observer receive the loving care lavished on them by proud fire fighters. But the underside of the vehicle and the motor compartment get large chunks of attention as well.

Constantly wiping away grease and oil, mud and road salt, and the grime that commonly cakes the working parts of the average car is not a matter of pride, but of necessity. The small leak that might signal a mechanical problem with the motor or the suspension or the brakes is much easier to detect on an otherwise unblemished, sparkling clean surface. Left undiscovered, the problem could jeopardize the safety of the members responding on the vehicle and endanger the public. A disabling failure while responding could mean delay in help arriving at a serious incident. A fire vehicle thrown out of control by a mechanical failure while responding could cause a new tragedy. Obviously, neither is acceptable, and so the fire fighters spend hours making the hidden parts of the fire apparatus cleaner than many of the restaurants we all visit.

Cleaning the windows of the fire station, stripping and waxing office and dormitory floors, scrubbing and squirting out the apparatus bays, removing the windblown trash from around the outside of the station, cleaning the toilets and the sinks, mopping, sweeping—all the jobs mom couldn't get them to do at home—the new fire fighter soon learns are part of what it's like to be a fire fighter.

Polishing the brass takes special skill. Baltimore, rich in tradition in so many ways, is filled with fire stations adorned with the fascinating poles that allow a fire fighter on the second floor to descend quickly to the apparatus floor for an alarm. Many a kid of all ages has stood wide-eyed as we've demonstrated this skill. When the big wall-mounted brass gong echoes through the station, fire fighters, one behind another, magically appear from the ceiling clinging to the shining brass poles and sliding to the floor below. It's a sight that has fascinated firehouse visitors throughout this century.

"Brass day" for the fire fighters means meticulously polishing the long poles from top to bottom. Careful to have at least one pole ready for use at all times, the fire fighters coat the metal with the creamy liquid that is allowed to semi-dry. Rags are then used to remove the polish that has evolved into a darkened glaze, somewhat like removing car wax. Once the job is completely done the poles will shine like new and sliding them will be smooth and easy. A key step to removing the last remnants of the polish, however, is occasionally omitted, sometimes by accident, other times by design. The finishing touch to a well done pole requires that someone wrap an old sheet or something similar around the pole and slowly slide down. One day early in my career I learned the consequences of somebody's sliding the pole before the job was completed. During the pole polishing process, the gong struck signaling a response for us. In my eagerness to get to the engine I didn't think to yell out to anyone to avoid the pole I was working on as I ran to another. I can still remember the truck lieutenant swearing up a blue streak as he angrily displayed his khaki pants which we wore at the time for us all to see. What a mess! Of course, the other guys thought it was a riot that the rookie screwed up the lieutenant's pants.

What's it like being in the fire department? It's about extremes and superlatives. Being in the fire department is witnessing the ironies in life, marveling at the coincidences, and abhorring the cruelties. It's about straddling the line between old and new, seeking the innovations so vital to the job and trying to assimilate them into a culture so steeped in tradition. Fire fighters are only half-kidding when they claim that we'd still have the horses if we could. Yet these same fire fighters today explore the world of computers, satellite technology, and infra-red heat sensing devices in the hopes of improving their ability to help people.

Being in the fire department is about rage. Forced to confront the atrocities man can bestow on others, fire fighters are often the first to react. "How can anybody possibly think it helps to burn out the community library? What kind of a statement does that make?" lamented the baffled fire fighters as we watched the reaction to the Rodney King verdict a country away. Meanwhile, in another part of our district other companies were battling a Korean grocery store fire. And from this fire, I would soon be responding to yet another intentionally set fire that destroyed two frame houses.

It's about the rage that fire fighters choke back when more innocent kids die trapped in a fire because their junkie mother left them alone while she was down the street buying or selling, or as she usually reports, "Goin' to the store a minute for medicine."

Being a fire fighter is about the rage felt when the very people for whom they risk their lives attack the fire fighters with bitter words. Or worse, rocks and bottles. Or worse yet, gunfire. When ten year olds stand and taunt fire fighters with hate-filled eyes, it's hard to be optimistic about their future, and it's hard not to feel your blood boil.

But more than the rage, being in the fire department means experiencing the absence of feelings, the hopelessness and the indifference we see too often. It is this emotional void reflected in the glazed expression of that mother who thinks nothing of leaving the kids alone or using the welfare check for drugs rather than food or heat. Resigned to a fate of jail or early death, too many of the neighborhood's young spend the days avoiding school and the nights on the corner.

While so many of the decent people huddle scared inside their homes and the truly brave struggle tirelessly to stop the scourge, this lost generation intimidates and terrorizes. In some places violence has become so common and expected that it desensitizes even the best of people. Kids in the city learn very young to recognize the sound of gunfire. Far too many have been the unintended victims of drive-by shootings and drug related gunfights. Fire fighters called to such incidents often deal with the shattered families while the perpetrators callously move on, oblivious or indifferent to the horror they leave in their wake.

In too many of our schools, hard-working, dedicated educators face an almost insurmountable struggle as they fight the parental indifference that has fueled the decline of the educational system. Fire fighters feel the frustration of trying to relate fire safety tips and home fire escape programs to kids whose only meal might be the one they get at school and whose bed is a corner of a trash-littered, roach-infested, drafty room. I remember seeing that abstract triangle thing, that Maslow's Hierarchy of Needs. Being in the fire department is like taking that college lesson out to the streets where it means something. Indeed, being in the fire department is about taking all those hypothetical, theoretical, upper-crust postulates that fill academia and dragging them into reality. Keep me safe, make me warm, end my hunger, then we'll talk.

What's it like to be in the fire department? It's like seeing life for the first time without the filter; it's like finally opening your eyes all the way; it's like focusing the camera. Being a fire fighter is like learning to read; it opens before you a new way of looking at life. You haven't felt life, truly *felt* life, or seen it in color until you've:

delivered a healthy, crying baby in the back of the medic unit or in someone's living room and been able to hand the newborn to mom for the first time.

or tried in vain to save a stillborn baby wedged half inside a screaming fifteen year old mother.

breathed life back into the smoke-stained limp body of a child you've just pulled from a burning house.

or failed to revive them no matter how hard you tried or how loud the anguished family screamed.

watched with unbridled pride as a co-worker received a much deserved award for valor.

or stood unashamedly with tears streaming down your

face among some of the strongest people you'll ever meet as you bury a fallen fire fighter.

The experiences of a fire fighter uniquely provide a glimpse into the hell my sixth grade teacher, Sister Godfrey, regularly promised to the wicked young men of the parish. Being a fire fighter is about heat—incredible, terrifying, excruciating heat. In temperatures that instantly incinerate everything combustible, where one breath will irreparably sear the respiratory tract and send poisonous super-heated gases into their lungs, fire fighters willingly risk themselves to find those trapped by the fire. Protective equipment provides some protection, but nothing can protect the fire fighter caught in a flashover for more than a few seconds. In temperatures of 1400 degrees nothing survives.

There can't be a worse way of dying. And yet fire fighters crawl through zero visibility—absolute *total* blackness—where a flashlight beam goes absolutely nowhere. With their bodies hugging the floor, knowing that the temperatures in the area just above them are unsurvivable, they'll crawl through a stranger's house, praying not to become disoriented and run out of air or become hopelessly entangled in the wires, light fixtures, and dropped ceiling grids as they crash down on them from above. Fire fighters look into the hell of my religion and go in willingly so long as there's the slightest chance that a life can be saved.

But if Sister Godfrey was wrong and hell isn't the heat, it must be the cold. Being a fire fighter is about being so cold you honestly wonder if you'll ever be warm again. Fighting fires is hard, dangerous work under the best of circumstances. In the depths of winter, nature ups the "degree of difficulty." On those nights when any sane person stays inside cuddling, fire fighters fight some of their nastiest battles. On those coldest nights, water leaving the nozzles freezes on contact with everything except the flames themselves. The walls and the roofs of buildings shimmer and reflect the flashing lights of the fire engines in an eerie display. Cascading water freezes in little waterfalls-like molds that form on the ledges and sills of windows and doors. Ice coats the stark, jagged remains of broken buildings and the remnants of a family's possessions now strewn on the sidewalk.

Climbing the metal ladders coated with ice is about like trying to climb naked up a greased telephone pole. Tools quickly become coated, and an axe flying out of someone's hands could become a terrible surprise to those working underneath. The sight of fire fighters trying to pull heavy hoselines into place or position additional ladders would be comical if it weren't so serious and dangerous. Looking like first-time ice skaters, they struggle with every step. And at least the skating rinks are level.

Hell, indeed, could be the biting north winds which heap misery on the tired, wet fire fighters as a reward for all their hard work. Fingers and toes that long ago lost all feeling refuse to do the simplest movements. Ears which sting unbearably at least remind you that you're still able to feel something. Hoselines spew water continuously adding to the constantly growing layers of ice that slowly fill the sidewalks and the streets and embed the hose in the process. In one of those ironies, the water can't be shut off or the hose will freeze solid in a matter of seconds, so it's left running until the last possible second and then the fire fighters scramble to uncouple and drain the hose as quickly as possible. Time seems to stop as the fire fighters huddle behind anything that will break the frigid winds and stomp their feet instinctively. That's usually about the time that some wise guy photographer type headed back to his warm car quips, "Isn't it all so beautiful?"

Being a fire fighter isn't about not being afraid...it's about being afraid and doing it anyway. It's about climbing the aerial ladder one hundred feet up into the sky for the first time with your knees shaking and knowing that everybody is watching you. It's about jumping out of the fire training academy building into a life net held only by a group of your fellow probationary fire fighters. It's about leaning backwards off the top of the six-story fire training tower held only by a rope your instructor claims will hold you as you begin your first rappel down the outside of the building—and watching the nearby seagulls flying lower than you are.

Being a fire fighter is about learning that the absence of fear can be a dangerous thing and that a healthy respect for the perils we face helps keep us alive. It's about meeting fear head on and accomplishing the task, whether it's getting up in front of the local middle school assembly to speak or advancing a hoseline on a burning gasoline tank truck in the hope of rescuing the trapped driver.

For a fire fighter one of the most terrifying situations is to become lost within a burning building, totally disoriented in the blinding dense smoke, unable to find anything to show them the way out, unable even to tell someone where they are to guide their potential rescuers. Cut off above a raging fire, running out of the precious life-sustaining air on their backs, feeling the heat building to the point of flashover when certain death awaits any who remain, fire fighters must be at their best. Only clear thinking and good decisions can help the fire fighters survive. The instinct to stand up, tear off the mask facepiece and run is great. Only training and courage enable the fire fighter to do what does *not* come naturally. Being a fire fighter is learning the instincts on which to act and the instincts to suppress. The difference can be fatal.

What's it like being a fire fighter? It's boring. No fire department fights fire constantly. Even busier departments have slow periods when the time can drag endlessly. When the required work has been done and the fire fighter's time is his own, the differences in personalities become evident. To some, these are the perfect times to read a good book or the paper. It's fascinating to observe one fire fighter engrossed in a crossword puzzle, another in the sports section of the newspaper, one with the latest Tom Clancy novel, and yet another doing his daily Bible study. What a strange mix we are.

Quiet times are opportunities for phone calls to the wife or to the girlfriend, or for some of our braver guys, to both in succession. I never was *that* brave. Television is a constant companion in the fire station, sometimes droning on ceaselessly as background music might in the finer restaurants, seemingly ignored by everyone there. Other times it becomes the focal point of activity as the fire fighters occupy their time. Some fire fighters are painters, some do calligraphy, some assemble models.

And then there are the thinkers, those who sit and stare off somewhere the rest of us never quite seem to reach. Idle time sometimes breeds discontent and often aids in the hatching of some of the most hair-brained schemes and practical jokes you can imagine.

What sensitive guys we are. Take a guy who's scared of his own shadow. Add the middle of the night watch in a darkened, creaky, eerie firehouse to which he has been sent for the night to work. Throw in the allegedly mysterious death of the truck captain the month before—a popular man who had seemed healthy to everyone who knew him. Build the mystery and the reported "strange" events since throughout the evening's discussions around—but never overtly at—the unsuspecting dupe. "That Captain Davidson was such a dedicated guy, you know. They say he's been down there roamin' around all night watchin' over the truck." The stage is set.

In the wee hours, watching through the pole holes in the floor from above in the darkness, the fire fighters almost give it away as the unexplained footsteps and whispers from the shadowy apparatus floor slowly drive the poor victim to near-panic. Pacing, scared to sit down, unable to ignore the growing uneasiness, the target sweats. Calls of "Who's there?" go unanswered. The final ingenious trap has been carefully laid. Unseen in the darkness, the long cord runs down from above and connects to the clapper of the bell we had on the old fire trucks of that era. One tug on the cord, one full clang on the truck's bell which shattered the pre-dawn stillness and the guy's fate was sealed. Screaming, he ran upstairs at full throttle like a man who had truly seen a ghost. That story was good for years. Idle time between runs can be fertile "mind time" indeed, even for those not acclaimed as intellectually gifted.

But while being a fire fighter is about the boring and the quiet times, it's also about the hectic, frantic pace of the emergency service. One severe thunderstorm or tornado that sweeps through the city in fifteen minutes could result in eight hours of non-stop running. Trees blown down onto houses, live power lines down and burning, exploding transformers that illuminate the night, flash flooding that traps people in their cars or sweeps them into swollen streams—the calls can quickly overpower any department. A lightning bolt crashing into the top of a building carries phenomenal force and heat. Many buildings have burned during and after such violent storms as the thinly stretched fire units responded frantically to call after call. Finally, it's over and the fire fighters can breathe a sigh of relief.

The stresses from this pendulum swing of relaxation to intense, often physically and emotionally taxing bursts of activity are well documented. Hearts and blood pressures suffer. Personalities and relationships are affected. Muscles thrown into heavy strain without any warm-up can cause painful injury. The list is long and growing still as researchers continue to study more of the unique demands of the fire service. Much has been written lately about the sleep disturbances so prevalent among those who rest, or try to, while knowing that the next second they could be charging out into the night with all senses at full alert.

Even the most hardened fire fighters feel the emotional rollercoaster of the job. Today they might experience the joy of rescuing another human being, saving a choking baby, or being able to present a crying child with his or her dirty, wet, scared puppy feared lost in a fire. Tomorrow the world turns over on them as the best they've got isn't good enough to save the toddler found at the bottom of the swimming pool, left alone for just a minute by the now inconsolable mother. Fire fighters feel the pain too when they have to come tell those who've escaped a fire and are huddled outside the fate of their not-so-fortunate loved one still missing. And how do you tell a mother why she can't see her child when you know the sight of her baby with arms and legs burned off and its stomach exploded from the heat would never leave her? Some days it is a damn lousy job.

What's it like being in the fire department? After all these years, I'd probably have to answer that it's not *like* anything else. It's so different from the mainstream as to be unfathomable at times. It's so different from day to day, hour to hour, run to run as to be incomparable. I'm not sure what it's *like*, but I do know I wouldn't trade it for any job in the world. And I know I'm not alone.

3

In the Beginning

Every fire fighter remembers his first assignment. As fire academy progressed and the end was in sight I began to think seriously about where I would be stationed. Would I go downtown to the high-rise district? Would I be assigned to some busy truck company in the heart of the ghetto? Maybe I'd be going back to the old neighborhood and work the streets I once used as playgrounds. As the day grew near I tried to envision my assignment.

I just knew that somehow I would get a great place to work. Location meant nothing to me. Any part of the city would be fine. All I knew for sure was that I wanted a busy spot—and preferably a truck company. Throughout our months at the fire academy we had been regaled with stories of the exploits of Truck 5, Truck 10, Truck 13. I could hardly wait.

"Kernan, Engine 45," the voice announced unenthusiastically. My heart sank.

The department thought that they had done me a favor by placing me close to my home. I would be able to drive there in about ten minutes.

Engine 45—also known as the "Country Club"—was located at the very outskirts of the city. Going to Engine 45 and Truck 27 was definitely *not* what I had hoped for. How would I ever learn in a slow station?

Still, the anticipation of being out in the field made the next few days fly. Graduation came and went. Family and friends shared in my pride. Sworn to protect the citizens of Baltimore, I was eager to do battle with the "red devil."

My dress uniform hung ready for the first day of day shift when the call came to my house. "Honey, it's a lieutenant from the fire department," my mother announced.

"Fire Fighter Kernan, this is Lieutenant Mueller from Engine 45," began the solemn voice.

I haven't even been there yet. What could I have done wrong already?

"Yessir."

"You're on vacation tomorrow."

"Excuse me?"

"Tomorrow, don't come to work. You have been assigned vacation."

Totally bewildered I hung up the phone and tried to explain something to my parents that I did not even understand myself. How the heck could I be on vacation when I haven't even worked there one day yet? In retrospect this should have provided some insight into government efficiency.

As I was to learn later, the battalion chief had too many men assigned to work and had ordered the company to assign vacation to someone. Since I was the rookie, I was that someone. As the budget cuts and shorter work week thinned our ranks, this situation soon disappeared forever. How times change!

One day later than I had planned, I reported to Engine 45 for my first day. Up Falls Road, alongside the rushing Jones Falls, across the Kelly Avenue bridge I drove, thinking all the while about what lay ahead. The guys—will the guys be good to work with? And the officers—I wondered how I would measure up in their eyes. During our entire time at the academy we were cautioned that officers were akin to God and should be afforded the same respect.

It was still pitch dark as I drove along Cross Country Boulevard lined with stately trees and statelier homes. Around the bend and there it was. Built in 1950, the same year I was built, the two story red brick fire station sat in the triangle in the road ahead. My heart pounded as I parked my car in the rear. The station was completely dark and quiet. The only sound was the bubbling of Western Run just across the road. I was obviously the first to arrive.

Although I had been to the station before to get my locker and drop off my gear, this was the first time I was actually reporting for work.

"Kernan," I announced to the man who sat illuminated in the halo of light at the watch desk.

"Who?" came the startled reply.

"Fire Fighter Kernan," I said from the shadows.

"Oh, the new guy," he muttered somewhat disdainfully. Begrudgingly he entered my "time in" on the watch desk sheet and pointed to the engine. "You're on the pipe today."

My heart raced. The new guy was almost always assigned the "lead off" position. The lead off man is dropped at the hydrant to make the hose connection and await the pump operator's instruction to turn on the hydrant. Only then can he join the rest of the crew in attacking the fire.

The "pipe man"—that's the action spot! When the engine company attacks the fire it is the pipe man, or nozzle man, who controls the stream of water. The pipe man, under the direction of the officer, will lug the hose up the stairs, down the hall, and feel the power surge in his arms as water fills the line.

It is the pipe man who meets the enemy head-on. One hundred gallons of water per minute, more if it's a big fire, would be at my fingertips today. *They must really have confidence in my abilities. Maybe they've talked to the fire academy instructors.* I walked on air as I ascended the stairs, confident that today I would *make a difference.* All that training would be put to the test today.

In the front office I was greeted by the off-going officer, the man behind the voice, Lieutenant Mueller. He seemed friendly enough, not nearly as formal as the other night's phone call. The usual welcome speech followed and an explanation of why I had been assigned vacation the day before.

"Your lieutenant's off today, so Shake's in charge. He'll fill you in on everything."

Shake, the first acting lieutenant, was to be my mentor.

"They don't come any better," I was assured. "You stay with him at all times and you'll be all right."

Shake began to take form in my mind. What a man this must be, I thought. A cross between John Wayne and Superman—the image grew.

CRASH went the short-lived picture as First Acting Lieutenant Thomas Schanberger waddled into the office. My John Wayne was fiftyish with dark, somewhat greasy-looking, thin and receding hair, and had skin that appeared not quite clean. His imposing 5'6" frame was the same in any direction. *And what,* I wondered, *is it in those brown eyes that seem not quite awake?*

"I'm on the pipe today," I blundered into my first mistake of the day.

"Yeah? Well, kid, just remember one thing. You don't do a *damn* thing until I tell you. You understand?"

For the next half hour Shake and I discussed the company and some of the procedures I would be expected to learn. I had been assigned to the engine. Good thing for me, I was informed.

"We get some fires down in Pimlico, but the truck doesn't go down that far on first alarm—bunch of *prima donnas*," Shake informed me. Several members passed by the office and I got some cursory introductions.

"Come on, kid, let's go to the kitchen."

"Yessir." I couldn't catch myself.

"Kid, I told you don't you ever call me sir," I was again sternly warned.

Nervously, I fell in, a respectful two steps behind my leader. We headed for the back of the engine house through the bunkroom where several fire fighters slept peacefully.

"There is absolutely no sleeping allowed between 6:00 A.M. and 9:00 P.M." I remembered automatically from our endless hours of *Rules and Regulations* instruction at the academy. Deciding to postpone my second blunder of the day, I made no comment nor inquiry.

My hands were sweating as we neared the kitchen. I could hear the people inside talking loudly, and I wondered if the day would ever come when I would be accepted into the group.

"Hey kid, have you met 'the Ghoul' yet?" Shake asked with deadly seriousness as we came to the doorway.

Again my heartbeat increased as we entered the narrow kitchen filled with coffee-drinking, arguing men. They didn't even seem to notice us. We stood there a minute and Shake slowly shook his head in disgust. He reached into the dish rack and pulled out a well-worn saucepan which he clanged with a heavy spoon.

"Hey! Hey! Where's your manners?" he chastised. "This here's the new kid, Mike Kernan."

One-by-one I met the members of the group and nervously shook hands or nodded to those in the back of the table. Only one man had not looked up from his coffee. Sitting farthest away from me, he would be the last of the introductions. I couldn't help but notice the silver collar pins which indicated that he was a lieutenant of the truck company.

"And this is the Ghoul," Shake delivered with absolute sincerity. "I ask you, kid. Have you *ever* seen an uglier human being in your entire life?"

The kitchen exploded with laughter and people slapped the table. All eyes shifted to the figure in the corner anticipating the reaction.

"Up yours, you little bowlin' ball son-of-a-bitch," Lieutenant Gilbert Randall retorted... And the ice was broken forever.

4
Initiation Rites

When I found out that I had been assigned to Engine 45, one of my major concerns was that I would be bored. During the year I served there, however, boredom was never a problem. While the level of fire activity was exceeded by many of the city's stations, the cast of characters assigned to Engine 45, Truck 27, and Ambulance 14 was unsurpassed. Each day I spent there was an adventure.

In addition to the Ghoul, who, I had to admit, *was* unquestionably one of the "ugliest human beings I had ever seen," the shift included Cliff Vogelein. Cliff was a veteran fire fighter who had spent his years in busier companies, most recently Truck 12. He had chosen to spend the last few there at Engine 45 in a more relaxed setting.

Cliff's weathered, perpetually-red face and bulbous nose fit well with the slow motion, Santa-like laugh that he inevitably gave before he delivered his favorite line—"Fuuuckin' goooof!" This was Cliff's most frequent description of those he encountered, but it seemed to be delivered with special emphasis when used in describing officers.

Cliff was handy to have around, not only to give commentary on the department's leaders, but because he was the shift barber. Every couple of shifts the upstairs large bathroom was transformed into Cliff's barber shop. Using one of the wooden chairs from the bunkroom, and covering his "customers" with a sheet from the linen locker, Cliff opened shop. At one time Cliff had cut hair professionally—at least that's what some of the guys claimed. The others, however, swore he had been a butcher. Others described his haircuts as "bowl style." According to them, he just put a bowl on top of your head and cut around it. Those arguments raged the entire time I was there, surfacing most frequently and loudly on haircutting day.

Even the most vociferous of his critics took their turns, however, complaining the whole time. Cliff would just laugh his goofy laugh and keep on cutting amid his usual "oops" and "uh-ohs."

Even with his somewhat questionable skills, Cliff offered what fire fighters universally crave—something for nothing. Many of us were then able to pocket the money our wives had doled out to us for our haircuts. All Cliff ever asked in return was an occasional case of beer. I suspect that contributed to his ruddy complexion.

Another of the characters who kept me laughing was Tom Fallon. The pump operator of the engine company, Tom was the one responsible for getting us to the fire safely and running the pump to provide us with the water we would need. Tom was actually quite competent and conscientious, but he loved to keep us all guessing.

Often, when the truck or ambulance would get a run without us, he would exclaim for all to hear, "Man, I'm sure glad that wasn't for us. I don't have the faintest idea where that is." He said this with so much sincerity that I was never quite sure he was kidding. Invariably, though, when the call was for us, Tom took us there unerringly.

Tom, or "Tubby Tommy" as Shake loved to call him, was a mild-mannered man with a keen sense of duty and an even keener sense of humor. He delighted in lightening the mood with some half-crazed performance. I remember one night when a motorcycle cop stopped by the station to use the bathroom. Tom volunteered to watch the officer's bike for him after getting the okay to sit on it. Now Tom couldn't just *sit* on it. He had to get the best laugh of the shift, so he darted back into the station for a hastily improvised "uniform."

When the police officer returned from the bathroom his

eyes nearly popped out. There on the front ramp of the station where all could see was his official Baltimore City Police Department motorcycle straddled by a 250 pound man wearing a bright blue bathing cap, a crazy pair of horned-rim sunglasses, and a white scarf thrown back ready for his ride. More than one motorist did a double-take at the police department's latest motorcycle cop.

Another quiet, summer evening Tom—our pump operator, or "the pilot on the ship of fools" as the truck guys referred to him—decided that things were a little too slow. Beautiful days and gorgeous evenings inevitably resulted in firehouse conversations relating to where we'd all rather be. Some of the guys lamented missing the opportunity to go chase the golf ball around the course. Others complained about a great beach day being wasted. A few with guilty consciences would even chime in with, "I really should be home cutting the grass."

That particular evening Tom Fallon added, "I think I'll go fishing."

Nobody thought too much of it when he got up and left the kitchen a few minutes later. The scuttlebutt continued until Shake stuck his head into the kitchen and exclaimed, "Come 'ere an' look at Fallon. I think the sumbitch's finally gone off the deep end!"

Down the black, metal, spiral staircase we all paraded. I could only wonder at what was ahead. We took turns looking out the window of the side door in amazement.

On the side lawn of the firehouse sat Tom in a beat-up beach chair. He was dressed in his turnout boots, a fishing vest, and sunglasses. On his head sat a big, straw hat, and in his hand was a fishing rod.

"Look at him. I tell you he's crazy," Shake said solemnly as he shook his head.

Tom was fishing in a bucket placed at his feet. Every so often he bobbed the rod up and down a little. Each time a car passed and the occupants made eye contact, Tom would smile broadly and wave, usually evoking a somewhat tentative half-wave in return. Some of the drivers honked their horns and obviously enjoyed the spectacle.

Occasionally Tom tipped his straw hat to the passersby as we all watched in amazement. People hollered, "Catchin' anything?" from open windows as they whizzed by. Leave it to Fallon to liven up the evening. At least nobody complained. During the time I served at Engine 45 it was not unusual for citizens to register complaints about one thing or another. One of the neighbors had a particular pet peeve about our flag.

High atop the engine house was a flagpole which proudly displayed the Stars and Stripes, but only from dawn to dusk as prescribed by the flag protocol of that time. If our flag wasn't lowered at the proper time or was left flying in the rain, this woman called headquarters to complain. Soon we would get the phone call from downtown chewing us out.

To reach the flagpole a fire fighter had to enter the hose tower at the rear of the apparatus floor, ascend the vertical, wall-mounted steel ladder about forty feet to a catwalk. There a door opened onto the roof. From there, at the rear of the station, the fire fighter then had to walk the entire length of the building across the station's flat roof to the front wall. At the base of the flagpole the fire fighter then attached or detached the flag and operated the halyard to raise or lower the flag.

Wind, frigid temperatures, or ice on the roof were no excuse. Religiously, the flag went up early and came down at sunset. You may have guessed that this was definitely a job for the rookie.

Anytime I was working on the engine or truck, the flag duties were mine. I had been warned by the guys of the dangers of being too far from the engine when the gong hit. I had only been there a short while when, flag in hand, my horror was realized. Responding to the gong, I came charging the entire length of the roof to the rear, through the door, onto the catwalk. I descended the narrow, vertical ladder as quickly as I could, convinced that I had been too long. I was scared to death that I had missed the run and that they had left me. Missing a response was—and still is—considered a very serious offense.

As I hit the floor of the hose tower at the rear of the station, I could hear the pumper running in the front part of the station. I still had a chance! Running across the apparatus floor I heard "Reds" Wilson hollering at the top of his lungs, "Geeeeezus Keeee-rist, where's the kid?"

My mad dash to the back step ended when I realized that everybody was standing at the back of the engine waiting for me, trying to keep from laughing themselves to death. Not content to settle for just one hilarious time at my expense, the guys made sure to tell the other shifts how proud they were to have a "fast rookie," always loud enough for me to hear. As each guy feigned ignorance with a "Wadda ya mean?" the story would be retold to a resounding chorus of laughter. Thankfully, I'm not thin-skinned and enjoyed the laughs with everyone else. It was a kind of "welcome" to the shift.

The process of being assimilated into the group is a ritual in the fire department. With much fervor the more senior guys formulate elaborate plans on how to "screw with the rookie."

Pump Operator Tom Fallon was an expert in initiation rites. On my very first shift he presented me with a list of instructions or "Rules for the Rookie." In addition to my flag duties, I was given the privilege of performing several other less than desirable duties. As I went about my daily activities I had to be ready to react to certain questions in the prescribed fashion.

For instance, whenever I heard, "Hey kid, what's your name?" I was instructed to respond, "Sir, Probationary Fire Fighter Michael Kernan, Engine 45, badge number 1778, sir," in a military style while standing at attention. I was informed that this was the only proper way for a rookie to address the other members.

Another kind soul, whose identity I was never able to positively ascertain, had a special way to mess with the rookie. At that time, fire fighters wore the old style three-quarter length boots to fight fires. These thigh-high boots were normally kept in a folded down position which allowed a fire fighter to step into them and, when ready to fight the fire, pull the tops of the boots up to protect about three-quarters of each leg.

At the beginning of each shift I would dutifully position my boots on the floor near the back step of the pumper so that I could quickly kick off my shoes, jump into my boots, and step up onto the engine. There I would don my coat and helmet.

Doing this rapidly was an essential skill for a rookie to master, and I secretly practiced to improve my time. Occasionally, some helpful co-worker decided to increase the "degree of difficulty" on me. Sometimes I would slide the pole and race to my boots only to find them turned, one forward, one backward. Other times the left and right boots had been switched. These variations certainly caused some momentary confusion.

Undoubtedly the most difficult time in quickly donning the boots was encountered when the "phantom" pulled my boots up for me ahead of time. I was quite a sight half-sitting on the back step struggling to get my feet all the way down into the extended boots. If you've ever tried to put on your jacket with the sleeves pulled inside out, you've had a small test. Doing this with your feet is a tad more difficult unless you can balance yourself on one foot, jump around, and are fortunate enough to have arms that are five feet long. Another good laugh at the rookie!

The prime suspect in this and many other crimes was "Reds" Wilson. He was a man who certainly enjoyed a good laugh and sometimes went to great lengths to get one. It was Reds who was to be my partner on the back step of Engine 45 on my first night of night shift, an event I will never forget.

During my first day shift at Engine 45 I had spent much time preparing for the time I would stand watch alone. We were trained in watch desk duties at the fire academy, but the real thing was definitely a place for the rookie to be nervous.

When the phone rang it was absolutely imperative that it be answered on the first ring. Fire department tradition held that a phone ringing a second time indicated neglect. The fire department phone was used to give the ambulance its runs and, occasionally, to give unusual or specific information to the company officers on responses for the engine or truck.

Many times the phone calls were from the battalion chief or other officers calling for our company officers. The man on watch answered all phone calls. Then he pressed a doorbell-type button which rang upstairs to summon the correct person. One ring—engine officer. Two rings—truck officer. Three rings—ambulance run. The fire department phone is always answered with the rank, name, and company of the person answering. "Fire Fighter Kernan, Engine 45," I officially answered each time the phone rang.

As important as the phone answering job was, the man on watch had an even more important duty. It was his responsibility to properly alert the units for response to emergencies. Under the glass on the surface of the desk were listed all the boxes to which we were automatically assigned on the first alarm. Next to some of the box numbers and locations a red **E** indicated that only the engine from our station was due on the box. All the other boxes called for both our engine and truck to respond.

A large metal drawer in the desk held the assignment cards for every fire alarm box in the entire city. Every company in the city was listed on every box in the order of their proximity to that location. While the boxes we normally ran on first alarm were listed under the glass, we would also be called to other boxes if the normally assigned units were out. So, it was very important to be able to look up the correct assignment card quickly.

In addition to announcing the box number and location over the speaker, headquarters would also send out the signals over our "joker." This was a ticker tape device that was mounted at about eye level on the watch desk. Counting the holes punched in the tape saved many a poor guy who had snuck back to the bathroom in the middle of the night only to hear the clanging of the little bell on the watch desk and the chop-chop of the joker going off. From the rear of the station it was impossible to hear the voice information, so counting the holes provided the only means of checking the number of the box that had just been struck out.

It would be a while before I learned the other use of the joker. On those long, quiet times, when everybody else was asleep upstairs, the man on watch sometimes became irresistibly sleepy. Though it was absolutely forbidden by department regulations, sometimes the person on watch dozed at the desk, nodding off in the chair. I was never able to close my eyes for fear I would miss a run, but some guys became quite adept at sleeping while sitting straight up in those hard, wooden chairs.

Before nodding off they would place a pencil in one of the little, triangular holes punched in the tape from the previous alarm. The tape stretched horizontally between the full reel and the take-up reel and moved sideways as the box number was chopped out. By bringing an eye half open, these "experts" could check to make sure the tape had not moved. This seemed a little too risky to me so I learned to read, study, and get up and walk around when I got sleepy on watch. However, I did borrow this trick as a backup during those dashes to the bathroom.

Sleeping on watch was forbidden for good reason. The person on watch desk duty was the only one who could hear the alarms coming in with the system we had in those days. It was his responsibility to write down the location, throw the switch that activated the big, brass gong to alert the others, turn on the bunkroom lights if it was nighttime, and open the apparatus bay doors. His actions determined whether the companies responded promptly and accurately.

All that responsibility made sleeping an impossibility for me as I awaited my turn at the watch desk that first night. I didn't even try to lie down when the other guys went upstairs for the night.

Night shift brought with it a certain anticipation and uneasiness. More serious fires seem to occur at night when fires have greater opportunity to burn unnoticed. Fire burns so quickly and early detection is crucial. In those days before smoke detectors were used in homes, people were even more vulnerable than today.

The little wooden board indicated "1:40—3:20" next to my badge number. Each night the senior fire fighter on duty set the watches, supposedly by some progressive rotation system, though the *system* was often questioned by fire fighters detailed in from other stations for the night who swore they somehow always got the middle-of-the-night watch.

Not wanting to appear too overly anxious or eager, I read and watched television in the back room rather than come down to the watch desk too much before my scheduled time. Reds Wilson turned over the watch to me after cautioning me to pay attention for the umpteenth time. Sleepily he headed upstairs and I was alone—I mean *really* alone.

The firehouse had a ghostly quietness that instantly surrounded me. The stark watch desk light was the only break in the eerie blackness that filled the apparatus floor. Barely visible in the shadows, Engine 45, Truck 27, and Ambulance 14 stood waiting—waiting for me to tell them to come alive. I moved and the squeak of the chair legs on the raised, watch desk platform reverberated like thunder. I was sure that I had awakened everybody sleeping upstairs in the bunkroom.

After a while, I walked idly to the map hanging on the wall beside the engine and flipped on the light over it. So many streets to learn, so many boxes to commit to memory, I thought. The awesome responsibility weighed on me that first night as I waited for my first call on the watch desk. A couple of runs were dispatched for other units, but nothing in our area. And then it happened!

"Alert. Box 8858. Pinkney Road and Hopeton Avenue," the disembodied voice announced over the communicating set. I quickly scanned the list of boxes on the watch desk looking for these totally unfamiliar streets.

BANG! BANG! BANG! The large, brass gong shattered the quiet as it reacted to my tripping the switch. "Engine and truck, turn out!" I hollered as I turned on the lights. Reds had taken great pains to remind me that our gong switch did not activate the house lights as was the arrangement in most stations.

My heart pounded as I waited for the others to slide the polished, brass poles to the apparatus floor. Seconds seemed like hours. I soon sensed that my eagerness and excitement were not characteristic of the general sentiments toward this middle-of-the-night run.

"Box 8858. Pinkney and Hopeton," I reported to the officers as we mounted the apparatus. My excitement overcame the cold that bitter night, but the others knew what we would face when we hit the outside air. Unlike the truck company, which had a new enclosed cab, the engine had no roof, no shelter from the biting cold.

Shake took his time donning his turnout coat and a warm hat with ear muffs before he squeezed up behind the steering wheel. Jim Pearce, the acting lieutenant of the truck company was even more prepared. I didn't understand the system at the time that dictated that if both companies were responding and only one officer was working, the officer rode the truck. This meant that our lieutenant got on the truck and their acting lieutenant rode the engine. Poor Jim now wrapped himself up in a heavy scarf as well as his gear as he climbed up into the front seat. The frigid air struck me full in the face as I hung onto the grab rail on the back step.

Not another car was in sight as we silently made our way through the residential neighborhood until we reached a deserted street corner. My eyes took in everything—trees, darkened houses, parked cars, trash cans...but no fire. Reds protested the cold as we stood on the back step doing—what?

Up front I could see Shake and Jim talking animatedly. Both doors opened and they both stormed back to me.

"Are you sure they said Pinkney and Hopeton, kid?"

"I think so. Yeah. That's what they said," I managed, now scared to death. My first run while on watch and I screwed it up. *Oh God!*

"What was the box number?" came the next question.

"I don't remember," I admitted sheepishly.

Suddenly it dawned on me that the truck company was not here. Come to think of it, *nobody* was here. Three engines, a truck, and a chief—*How come I don't even hear a siren? Uh oh!*

"Maybe it's Pinkney and Pierce," they decided, and we drove—no, sneaked—to that box a few blocks away. Nobody!

"Good job, kid," shivered Reds.

Finally the radio blared, "Okay, Truck 27. Units on Box 8858, Engine 46 and Truck 27 will handle."

My career was over! The very first time that I was entrusted with the watch and I sent my company to the wrong location. My heart was broken. *How could I have done such a thing?*

The whole way back to the station I replayed the alert in my mind. It was so simple—box number and location, announced twice. How could I have messed it up? I dreaded what was in store for me when we returned.

Finally, the truck returned and the story unfolded. A new procedure had been used. Headquarters had sent us all out, giving only the closest box number and location over the communicating set. Then, on the radio, they informed everybody that the box had been "struck out" for a fire reported at a certain address in the area. Nobody had ever physically pulled the fire alarm box on the corner.

Unfortunately for us, we were a little slower starting up the engine. Our old-style radio had not warmed up yet and we missed the radio instructions. I felt like the world had been lifted from my shoulders. I was very glad when, shortly afterwards, headquarters began giving all the information when the companies were initially dispatched.

One false alarm later and my watch was over. The letdown had finally left me very tired. After my relief had taken over the watch duty, I trudged up the front stairs and quietly entered the pitch-dark bunkroom. Careful to walk as quietly as I could on the old wooden floor that squeaked so easily, I inched toward my bunk, feeling the way in the blackness.

I carefully removed my shoes, trousers, and uniform shirt. When I went to hang my clothes on the chair by my bed, the chair had mysteriously vanished. Undaunted, I hung my clothes on the rails at the foot of the bed, pulled back the top of the blanket and sheet, and climbed into bed.

Ugh! My legs were stopped about halfway down the length of the bed by a sheet wrapped tightly around and under the mattress. Afraid to make any noise in the silent bunkroom, I slept curled up in the top half of the bed. This short-sheeting was another little greeting to the rookie as the muffled laughter from the darkness proved. It was Reds who made a point of asking me in the morning how I had slept.

"Fine!" was my quick response.

5
Going Downtown

In my early days in the fire department I spent much of my time on duty waiting for an alarm. In retrospect, I should have savored the quiet times. As my duties and the nature of the fire service changed, idle time became scarce.

At Engine 45 it hadn't taken me long to learn the sporadic nature of the fire business. The fire service has sometimes been described as "interminable periods of inactivity and boredom interrupted by unbelievable events of phenomenal stress and exertion." Instantly accelerating from rest or routine duties to heart-racing, frenetic action contributes greatly to the increased rate of heart disease among fire fighters.

The start of night shift brought the usual exchange of personnel on Engine 45. With my helmet, coat, and boots poised for action at the back step of the pumper, I began the great waiting game. The day shift guys headed home and we settled in for our fourteen hours at the station. First on the list of duties tonight for some of the guys would be planning tonight's dinner. I listened to the discussion with only mild interest since my dinner sat in a brown bag in the refrigerator upstairs.

After the change-of-shifts information exchange had ended, I took up my place at the pool table. Before going to Engine 45 I had played pool only a handful of times. Now, with a beautiful, full-sized, Brunswick table tempting me, I found myself spending many hours learning to play. Our shift included some very good players. By far the best was the truck lieutenant, the Ghoul, who spent a lot of his spare time at the pool hall. I enjoyed watching him play and learning from him.

It wasn't long before the clanging of the bells and the chop-chop of the ticker tape at the watch desk caught my attention. "Second alarm. Downtown," was the report from the man on watch. When you are stationed on the very outskirts of the city, a fire Downtown might as well be a fire on Mars. It hadn't taken me long to realize that we were not exactly at the hub of activity. After the watchman looked up the assignment card in the drawer he added, "Engine transfers on the third." In those days, the assignment cards indicated which companies were to move into the vacated stations as a fire escalated. In this way, no area of the city would be left without protection. Now that I knew we might transfer, I was suddenly more interested. I stayed there at the watch desk and waited in case the fire grew. After a few minutes of no activity, the other guys drifted away with apparent disinterest.

"Alert, third alarm ..." the speaker announced. The fire had obviously gotten worse and more help was being summoned Downtown. I looked with anticipation at the other guys walking back to the watch desk as the companies who were due to respond were announced.

How could they contain their excitement?

"What are we waiting for?" I asked.

"Kid, in this fire department you don't go *anywhere* until they tell you to," was the answer. "Even though the card calls for us to transfer, headquarters can change that if they want to."

Great.

This could be my first chance to get to a busy station and move Downtown during a big fire, and now they tell me that we might not be the ones to go. The minutes seemed to drag forever.

"Engine 45, transfer to Engine 7. Acknowledge."

Yes!

"O.K. Engine 45," replied the man on watch as he tripped the switch to activate the big brass gong. "Engine company," he yelled, for the benefit of any who had not already heard.

I dashed to the back step of the engine with the noise from the gong still ringing in my ears. I displayed my finest gear-donning style as I quickly kicked off my shoes, stepped into my boots, pulled on my heavy, black turnout coat, and snapped all the fasteners. As I put my black, shiny, metal helmet onto my head, I stepped smartly up onto the back step in record time. My practice had paid off.

Proudly, I looked to my right at my partner on the step tonight, Bobbie Williams. Nothing! Bobbie's gear still sat untouched on the floor. And Bobbie was nowhere to be seen. In fact, now that I thought about it, Shake and Tom Fallon had disappeared as well. There I stood, fully dressed, anxious to go, and there wasn't another member of the engine crew to be found. I knew I had heard correctly. I was totally baffled.

Soon, the voices behind me reassured me that I had not totally lost it. "Hey, kid, you better take your dinner," Tom suggested. "We're gonna be there a while. And don't forget to take your shoes or your going to be pretty uncomfortable spending the night in those boots."

There's something to say for experience. The other guys knew that once we arrived at Engine 7's station we could be in for a long night of waiting in a different place. In my haste to get going I hadn't even thought about how we might spend the next hours. Feeling pretty stupid, I took off the gear that I had so quickly put on and went up the black, metal, spiral staircase to retrieve my bag from the refrigerator. "Don't worry about it, Mike," Bobbie comforted me, as we left on our trip downtown.

Transfers, or relocations of apparatus to other stations, are considered non-emergency responses, and are handled without using the warning lights or siren. Driving along with all the other traffic can take quite a while, and this time it seemed to take forever. What made the journey seem endless was the radio blaring in the cab of the engine. On the back step, Bobbie and I could hear that the fire was getting worse. Headquarters could reach us by radio if they needed us, but the procedure of that time was to remain "out of service" until we had backed into our destination.

During our trip Downtown the fire had grown to six alarms. The radio was non-stop chatter the entire time. I didn't know what was on fire, but it was obvious that the fire was a big one. "Might be your first big one tonight, Mike," Bobbie offered as we strained to hear the messages coming over the radio.

I stood in the street stopping traffic so Tom could safely back the pumper into Engine 7's home. Huge clouds of gray and black smoke reached above the Downtown buildings.

"Engine 45 in service at Engine 7 and off the air," radioed Shake.

Now we were ready. Here at the northern fringe of the downtown district, we were only about a mile away. Any more calls for help could summon us to the big fire.

Even though we were "off the air" and would be dispatched over the house communicating set if needed, Tom kept the apparatus radio turned on so that we could listen to the action.

In those days, only headquarters transmitted on that frequency, so we could hear only one side of the conversations coming from the fireground. The dispatcher was swamped with messages from engine companies trying to tell other companies to charge their lines or to increase pressures. The dispatcher had to relay every one of the messages and grew frustrated by the volume of requests barraging him.

"All units stand by. Come in Aide to Deputy Chief, First Division," the dispatcher said anxiously.

"OK, Aide to Deputy Chief, First Division," the dispatcher continued after the message that we could not hear had been completed.

"What do you think he asked for?" I asked of the others expectantly.

"Could be anything," was the disappointing answer I received.

I watched the little bell on the watch desk and stared at the speaker as if watching them would somehow trigger their action. When nothing came over, I reluctantly understood that the chief had not asked for more equipment.

From the windows next to the parked apparatus we watched the clouds of smoke drifting westward. The radio continued to talk, but not as often, and the smoke turned more gray than black.

"They've got it," proclaimed Shake as he walked away from the window. He promptly took up a position next to the watch desk and opened the newspaper abandoned by the crew of Engine 7 when they had responded.

"Yeah," agreed Tom Fallon as he sat down in the watch desk chair and leaned back.

I couldn't believe their cavalier attitude. Even Bobbie drifted away from the window.

"I'm going up to the hose tower for a better look," I announced with sudden inspiration. I took off my boots and put on the shoes I had been reminded to bring, but I held off putting my dinner in the refrigerator. It occurred to me that nobody had put their bags into the refrigerator, and Shake and Bobbie still had their boots on. *Humph.*

Imitating the "smoke watches" that once were a part of life in the old firehouse, I scaled the long, vertical, metal ladder to the catwalk fifty feet above. From there I could see over many of the buildings that had obscured our view downstairs. I was still too far away to actually see the fire, but I watched the huge mushrooms of smoke billowing into the evening sky.

I was mesmerized by the changes I witnessed from my perch as the fire fighters battled for control. I followed the ebb and flow of the fight by the changes in the color and intensity of the smoke.

Down the ladder I came, careful not to fall in my haste. "I don't think they've got it," I reported to Bobbie as I emerged from the bottom of the hose tower. "The smoke's getting wider and blacker than before," I added.

"That doesn't sound too good," Bobbie answered sincerely.

"Come in, Deputy Chief, First Division," the radio halted

our conversation. "OK, 2-10-4."

A holdover from the pre-radio days when officers used the telegraph key inside of the fire alarm boxes to summon help, a "2-10-4" was the signal for four additional engine companies. We all heard it.

I walked quickly the twenty feet to the back step of the engine, put on my gear, and got onto the back step. But I was the only one who moved.

The little bell that I had watched so intently now gave the familiar four dings that preceded every verbal message over the watch desk speaker.

"Special call. Signal 2-10-4. Box 524. The following units respond . . . "

I couldn't believe it. There were four engines closer to the fire than we were. I tried to look nonchalant as I once again took off my gear and put it on the back step.

"For God's sake, kid, will you relax. I'm getting tired just watching you," Shake quipped wryly without even glancing up from the newspaper. Ten more minutes passed.

"Now, kid, get on the damn engine," Shake said as he shook his head. The chief had just requested the adjacent box, the terminology used for a seventh alarm in those days.

In seconds we were on the street. I clutched the rail for dear life as I hung onto the back of the engine. Tom expertly navigated the old Ward LaFrance pumper through the congested city streets, never missing a gear. The siren screamed and eerily echoed off the walls of the tall buildings, furthering the sense of urgency in our response.

"Well, Mike, it looks like you're going to your first big one," Bobbie shouted over the siren.

As we grew nearer, the clouds of smoke loomed ever darker and more ominous ahead of us. The fire was obviously getting worse.

The radio blared instructions that Bobbie and I couldn't make out from the back step. Even though I had tried to imagine the scene we would face, I was overwhelmed at the sight of the Federal Tin Company ablaze. Federal Tin wasn't just a building; it was a huge turn-of-the-century, seven story factory building. The heavy wooden, paint and turpentine-soaked floors inside the old building had fueled an incredible fire which tore through the building, leaping from floor to floor and bursting from window after window. Some of the first companies on the scene were lucky to have escaped the inside of the building with their lives as the fire took off. They abandoned their hoselines and ran for their lives.

"Lead off two lines from Engine 6," Shake instructed as he stood up in the front seat and turned to face us. We were going to lay additional lines from an engine already connected to a hydrant. At last, we were going into the battle.

"Oh my," said Bobbie as we stood on the back step again, making sure to stay away from the hose "flop-flopping" off the back of the engine into the street. I couldn't say anything. The scene in front of us was incredible.

We arrived just in time to see the top of the building in front of us erupt in huge fireballs that blew vertically into the clouds of pitch black smoke and horizontally over the narrow street causing the fire fighters below to scramble. I honestly thought the top of the building would blow right off.

At the corner of the building directly ahead of us, the crew from a ladder truck was running away as the aerial ladder swayed dangerously in response to their desperate attempt to yank it away from the inferno. The truck shook and rocked, but did not fall over.

In front of the ladder truck, a pump operator flattened himself on his belly and crawled under his pumper to escape the bricks falling in the street.

"Oh my" was quite an understatement.

We took our position next to a large building directly across the street from the fire. With the fire intensifying, this building was now in grave danger, and we were assigned to protect it. I had no idea what it was, but the building was tall and old.

"Grab the hose rope and the two and a half inch pipe and let's go," Shake instructed us after conferring with a chief's aide. "Bad news. The standpipe's not available. We'll have to haul a line up the side of the building."

I didn't fully realize the implications of that tidbit as an employee led us to the freight elevator. I also didn't know that the building we had just entered was the McCormick Company Annex. The McCormick Company made the aromatic spices that normally scented the entire area. Tonight was not the norm.

At the top floor the elevator door opened and we got our first real glimpse of the dangerous task ahead of us. The whole side of the building that faced Federal Tin was filled with windows typical of that type of older construction that relied heavily on natural lighting.

Through every single window we could see a boiling cauldron of angry, orange flames that seemed close enough to touch.

When we stepped from the elevator, the temperature inside the area was noticeably warmer and smoke drifted lazily throughout the entire floor—the entire heavy, wooden-plank floor packed with stacks of flattened cardboard boxes as far as we could see.

"Oh shit," was Shake's size-up of our situation. He walked over to the windows, took off a glove and felt the glass with his bare hand. "Oh shit."

"The stairs to the roof are right there," the McCormick Company employee pointed out from the elevator he hadn't left.

We started toward the narrow stairway as Shake hollered to the frightened man, "Hey, you stay right there with the elevator in case we need to get out of here quick."

"You guys are crazy," was his chilling reply as the elevator doors closed.

We threw the 125 foot long rope over the side away from the fire after tying off our end. The rope uncoiled just like it was supposed to as it went all the way down, down, down to *the second floor*. Now I knew we were really up there. Our rope didn't even reach the ground. I fervently hoped that we would not have to escape down that rope if the fire entered the building under us and cut us off.

Fortunately, Tom Fallon saw the problem right away and got a helper to raise the pumper's ladder against the building. He took the end of the hoseline up to the bottom of the rope and secured it.

Then began the tortuous task of hauling the heavy hose up ten floors. There is a device that fire fighters can use to put over the edge of a roof. Equipped with rollers, it allows the rope and the hose to slide over the edge of the roof more smoothly. I never understood why these hose rollers were carried on the *truck* companies. Doing the job without one was a formidable task. Fear helps. The softball-size fire brands bouncing all over the roof were also great motivators. I tried not to think about the conditions on the floor beneath us. At any minute a window could fail and the fire would leap into the waiting fuel stacked beneath us. No ladder could reach us. Another comforting thought.

The three of us tugged on the rope until we had pulled enough hose onto the roof to have a workable line with some hose to spare. Once Tom put water in the line we wouldn't be able to pull up any more.

In those days before we had portable radios, it was difficult to communicate ten floors to the ground. Tom couldn't see us and couldn't hear us. I waved and hollered but there was no response from below. *Uh oh.* Shake calmly pulled out the heavy-duty handlight he had stuffed in his pocket and signaled to Tom to charge the line. Soon, 250 gallons of water a minute would surge from our nozzle. Thank God for experience.

With water in our hoseline, our first job was to drench the roof itself hoping to keep it from igniting. Chunks of burning debris rained down on us like a misdirected fireworks display. Plink, plink. What a strange, hollow sound my metal helmet made when the red-hot embers bounced off it. I crouched and tried to make my neck disappear into my shoulders. A burning ember down the collar could produce a very painful burn. We used the water from our hose to wet each other as added protection against the brands that danced like thousands of fireflies around us.

Finally, we were able to direct our stream across the street into the inferno. Not too difficult to hit the target. Just pick a spot. It was more a symbolic gesture than a meaningful tactic, somewhat akin to spitting into a hurricane.

After an eternity or two, a familiar voice greeted us from behind and I looked around to see our battalion chief, Pete O'Connor. His bent-up white, metal helmet and Irish red face were a welcome sight.

"I've got more lines coming up and one of those new, portable monitor pipes," he assured us. The chief knelt beside me and put a hand on my shoulder. That simple gesture helped transform my fear to determination.

Eventually other companies with their hoselines joined us on the roof as more alarms were sounded, and we poured tons and tons of water across the street onto the fire. For hours we could hear the rumbling as floors and walls and chimneys collapsed throughout the dying building. With each collapse a rush of embers and smoke belched from the blaze as the fire refused to surrender.

It was a long night on that roof, but eventually the tide turned. I hadn't yet learned the fire fighters' somewhat cryptic comment, "We haven't left one burning yet."

We had done our small part. The McCormick Building Annex survived the fire, as did many other buildings the fire fighters saved that night.

Hours later, exhausted and drenched to the skin, we re-packed our hose and prepared to go back. My arms ached from the hours of exertion, but I didn't complain. I managed a laugh when I found my brown bag with the filthy, water-soaked contents mashed into an unrecognizable lump. I wasn't really hungry anyway.

As I stood on the back step, ready to go, Shake walked back to me. "You did a good job tonight, kid," he said.

Bobbie gave me his broadest smile, and I knew that I had passed the test.

6

Coming Home

Like most of us, the older I get the more I reflect on the decisions I have made in my life. Good or bad, the decisions we make along the way determine the course of our lives. I certainly have made a few poor decisions, ones that I would take back if I could. One of the career decisions I made as a young man would have profound impact. It was a decision I would never regret.

Life at Engine 45, my first assignment, had been interesting, but I wanted more—more experience, more fires, more opportunities to learn, more contact with those wanting to advance in the department. Actually, I also wanted less—less time riding the ambulance. In Baltimore the fire department provides the emergency medical service. Much of my time at Engine 45 had been spent riding the ambulance housed in the station—a job I quickly determined was not for me.

Thank heavens that some of the most dedicated people in the fire service prefer the medical end of the job. Today, that has become a huge part of the daily activities of most fire departments in this country. The developments in EMS (emergency medical service) have resulted in tremendous improvements in the pre-hospital treatment phase of emergency medicine. Day in and day out, nobody works harder or trains more in many departments than the paramedics.

For me, though, and for many fire fighters, it is the firefighting side of the job that holds the most allure. While Engine 45 was a wonderful place to work, the only way I would ever learn to fight fires well was to go to plenty of fires, and that meant a transfer to a busier station.

Consistently in our fire department the majority of promotions come from the busier stations. With all the studying required to do well on promotional exams, the opposite would seem to be more logical. Slower stations should provide more available time for studying, logic would dictate. Invariably, though, the fire fighters most interested in advancing through the ranks gravitate to the busier stations where the opportunities to learn abound. Often studying together, frequently competing against one another, endlessly quizzing each other on the thousands of possible test questions, the kindred spirits motivate each other to devote the long hours necessary to prepare themselves for advancement. That was the atmosphere I sought—a place to learn, a place to get experience, an opportunity to be around others who could help me advance.

They say you can never go home? I had the chance to test that theory. The long, narrow fire station on Greenmount Avenue seemed a natural choice for a transfer. Home of Engine 31 and Truck 7, the old, dark-red brick firehouse had once held the horse-drawn rigs of a bygone era. As a child, my grandmother had thrilled to the spectacle of the magnificent horses lugging the smoke-spewing steamer to the next alarm—a scene straight out of the Currier and Ives books I read so often on their living room floor. Growing up not far away near Engine 28, my grandfather told me often of his childhood delight at watching the fire fighters exercise the horses on Sunday mornings as all the neighborhood kids watched. Indeed, several generations of my family and I had grown up in this working class neighborhood.

The firehouse was always a place of fascination for me even from my earliest days when my dad dragged me to the barber shop across the street. I tolerated Mr. Al, the barber, who scared the crap out of me by shaving the back of my neck each Saturday with the straight razor he so lovingly stropped on the thick, leather, black belt attached to the intimidating barber's chair. I even endured the indignity of spending the time with all those "old" men, boring and smelling of cigars, who filled the small shop with talk I didn't understand.

The potential payoff of the Saturday ordeal and my not-too-secret hope was the chance that watching from the barber shop window I would get to see the members of Engine 31 and Truck 7 spill out onto Greenmount Avenue on their way to some heroic battle I could only imagine. The magical age of horse-drawn apparatus might have vanished, but the response of the neighborhood fire apparatus still drew observers as passersby stopped to watch. Hands held to their ears to protect them from the sirens, people often paused from their walk through the shop filled blocks of Waverly, sometimes pointing, sometimes waving.

When the fire station doors began to open and the khaki-clad fire fighter dashed into the street with the flag he would use to stop oncoming traffic, I would watch fascinated. From the single apparatus bay always came the engine first. The traditional Baltimore red and white adorned with that funny gold leaf emblem on its front fenders and the big brass bell gleaming in the sunshine, the engine would nose carefully into the street, turn and disappear in one smooth motion. From the barber shop window I could see the fire fighters standing on the back step, clutching the handrail, sometimes pulling on their black fire coats as they headed away.

It was the second piece out of the station that left me spellbound, however, and I would silently hope that the truck company would also be responding to the call. When the monstrous, mile-long ladder truck poked out into the street, I always held my breath. The truck was so long that the front was almost to the curb right in front of me when the back end was just coming out of the station. The fire fighter who drove the front end cut the steering wheel like a madman to make the ninety degree turn; these were the days before power steering. But the guy in the back (the tillerman I learned years later), perched high above the long aerial ladder at another steering wheel, had the trickiest part. The wheels that he controlled were in the very rear of the truck, the part that was being drawn near the side of the firehouse door opening as the truck turned. I watched with youthful admiration as he would lean to the side, look down, and deftly steer the wheels in the opposite direction to keep the truck from smacking the wall. As soon as the back end of the truck was in the clear, he would quickly turn the wheel the other way so the back end would now follow in the same direction as the front end. Incredible! They made it look so easy.

The truck arced slowly toward the direction of travel as the fire fighter who had been standing in the street to stop traffic now angled toward his riding position on the side of the truck back near the tillerman. As the truck slowly began its trip to the fire, the man with the flag timed his grab for the side of the truck and fluidly pulled himself onto the side step where he would ride. Thankfully, today's fire fighters utilize much safer riding practices learned the hard way after many years of clinging to the outside of moving vehicles, but those scenes made for great excitement.

When I got a little older, the fire station became a solemn ground into which I made brief pilgrimages. Riding my bike through the streets of Waverly, I frequently found myself passing by the firehouse, pausing briefly to say hi to any of the men sitting outside or near the watch desk. And any time the apparatus screamed through my neighborhood on the way to a response I stopped to watch in awe.

For me, this was coming home. Only a few short years before, I had been the neighborhood kid who had run errands for the fire fighters of Engine 31 and Truck 7. For pocket change I made the "food runs" to the Little Tavern, the White Coffee Pot, or to Harry Little's sub shop. With each glimpse into the mystical world of the fire fighters I tried to learn everything I could.

The price for using me to run to the store always included having to answer the inevitable questions I brought. "What's that? How does this work? Why does the truck company carry those? What does a 2-10-3 mean? How come some boxes get two trucks and others only get one? It wasn't until after I worked there that I learned from one of the guys my nickname. He shared with me how the guys would see me coming and groan, "Oh man, here comes 'Twenty Questions.'" I guess I've been called worse.

"What the hell do you want to transfer there for, boy? Have you lost your mind?" growled an annoyed Captain Frank Brown when I initially discussed the possibility of a transfer with him. "They don't get any more fires than we do, you know. All they do is run false alarms all night long."

"You're makin' a big mistake, kid," cautioned Shake. "The pay's the same, and you'll never find a better house to work in than here. Besides, if you stay here you'll have the chance to move up into driving in a few years."

Only Tom Fallon, always the clown, told me privately with an uncharacteristic serious tone, "If you're going to get ahead in this job, get outta here before you get too comfortable like the rest of us."

Torn between my desire to get to a busier station and my comfort with my current assignment, I waited for a sign to guide me, something to nudge me in the right direction.

Riding the ambulance for four straight shifts was the sign. Having ridden the ambo—not too affectionately dubbed "the gut bucket" by the guys, for four days then four nights then four more days, I was less than thrilled when the man on watch informed me I was on the ambulance again as I reported for work that night. Call it a sign, or maybe the straw that broke this fire fighter's back, that was the night of decision.

At that time, the Third Battalion was the only battalion that didn't have an ambulance in any of its stations, and since fire fighters almost always worked within their own battalions, it sounded like the perfect answer. Transfer to Engine 31, in the Third Battalion, no more ambo!

Walking through the firehouse doors in Waverly the first night was like coming home—but not. It was different now. The mystical place of my youth would gradually take shape as another fire station, another workplace. Tonight, I was no longer the kid on the bike to run the errands; tonight, I was one of them. What a proud moment it was when we headed out the door on our first response not fifteen minutes after I had reported to work. Someone had pulled a street fire alarm box on the far side of our first alarm district. It could be anything.

Down Greenmount Avenue we headed, and now I was the one pulling on my heavy, black turnout coat and clutching the handrail on the back step. Down the familiar street, past the corner where my family had bought fresh vegetables from Johnny Butcher's shop, past the barber shop I had chosen when old enough to escape the dreaded Mr. Al. With the air horns blaring, we turned and headed across the familiar 29th Street of my youth. How many tackle football games I had played on the narrow grass strips alongside the school. Grass was a scarce commodity in my neighborhood—one to be savored and utilized, but never exploited. We rotated the exact location of the games, sometimes moving to the Barclay Street side of the school, so we didn't wear the strips down to bare ground.

On the right as we responded came the playground that had backed up to my house. For most of my growing years, the large, mostly open area behind the school had exuded the delicious summer smells of hot asphalt and provided the backdrop for city life. In this typical Baltimore blue-collar neighborhood of brick rowhouses and tiny back yards the playground had provided all the harried moms their only breaks from the kids that seemed to overflow all of our good Catholic households.

Baseball had been the passion in the neighborhood. "Baseball" for us was a game with twenty-five cent rubber balls from the corner drug store, or sometimes the smaller, ten cent balls when our pooled resources weren't enough for the full-size balls. The bats were often broomsticks, but sometimes a real bat. Even a cracked bat would work with the rubber balls. Stick ball, wall ball, curb ball—we played them all. A strike was a pitch that hit inside the white box painted onto the wall. In the air past the little fence in front of the swings was a double. Hit the big fence in the air and that was a triple. Over the big fence in the air was a home run until we lost too many balls to the cranky old lady who lived on the other side of the alley; eventually over the fence was an out and the batter got to go sneak into her yard to try to retrieve the ball.

All year long, the playground was our meeting place, the place we all literally grew up. In fall and winter, hearing the cheers rise from the stadium on Sunday afternoons as John Unitas connected on a last minute game-saver to Raymond Berry somehow inspired us to greater touch football on the sandy asphalt which hurt more than any astro turf burns. And it was here that I had carved out a rectangle from the hard-frozen snow and filled it with buckets of water from my house until we had an ice rink. Dad didn't share our enthusiasm for this ingenuity and initiative, however, when he realized they were his golf clubs we kids were using to smack the peanut butter jar lid around in our "ice hockey" game.

We passed by Dee's house where the neighborhood kids had all put on "West Side Story" in his sweltering rowhouse basement—quite an accomplishment for a bunch of neigh-borhood kids. No wonder he went on to New York and the theater. Dee's basement had been the site of so many things most parents never wanted to know about. Hypnotized by the ever creative Dee, my brother's best buddy, Larry, had sat oblivious to the pain while pins were shoved into his hands and the rest of us gawked in disbelief. My brother still reminds me of the zaniness of it all. And the concoctions (he called them magic potions) that Dee mixed in the basement were legendary. Fortunately, most of them weren't toxic or explosive. Of course, the ones that did blow up their containers made for some pretty interesting experiments. It's a wonder any of us survived.

With the wind hitting me in the face I grasped the handrail harder by reflex as we passed Calvert Street and then St. Paul Street, busy intersections where I had seen many an accident growing up. It would help to be so familiar with the streets in the neighborhood. That would be an edge in learning the district.

Then the familiar shape of Saints Philip and James came into view. Church of my youth and of my marriage only a few months earlier, the church held so many memories for everybody in the neighborhood. It was S.S. Philip and James that had exposed me to the solemn novenas, the Way of the Cross, and May Processions. Here I had learned to hate incense that assaulted the nostrils, and to love the renewal of faith that Christmas midnight mass always brings to me. It was here that I had learned to recite the smattering of Latin required of us altar boys and to mouth the words to the hymns that so melodiously filled the cavernous house of worship. I say *mouth* because the nuns had early on decided that I would always have the privilege of being a "listener" while the others sang, a move no doubt appreciated by all. My voice didn't sound that bad to me.

This had been the center of so many of the neighborhood activities. From the somewhat dubious honor of serving many a 6:00 A.M. mass to the experiences of summer club activities, bus trips and Catholic Youth Organization dances, the church had been a large part of my life. It was this parish that sponsored the Phil-Jays Little League baseball team, a team who undoubtedly would have been creamed by the Bad News Bears. Our small parochial school (my eighth grade had twenty-three girls, but only eight boys) didn't even have enough boys to field a team in the right age groups, so we always had to recruit some of the younger kids. In the six years I played for the various age group teams we never won a game, but we had a lot of fun.

It was here at S.S. Philip and James that I learned some of life's unforgettable lessons—some cerebral, some practical, some moral, some comical. I learned from Monsignor Duggan the sedating qualities of Sunday sermons and that not all priests had great singing voices no matter how distinguished looking and proper they were. Father McGuire showed me that sometimes the quiet ones really are the deep thinkers. Father Zorbach, brother of a city fire fighter, taught me, among many things, that good pasta is essential to a good life. And Father

Lippold repeatedly showed us that when the guy with the basketball looks left, don't assume that's where the pass is going. Man it was embarrassing how that old guy always whipped us on the outside basketball courts at Johns Hopkins University. Of course, *old* was a lot different to me then.

Some of the lessons were a bit confusing, like how one week we were hurting God by eating hamburgers on Fridays. I forget exactly when it was that God said it would now be OK. And the dreaded confessional where another priest solemnly warned all of us adolescent boys that touching ourselves for sexual gratification was despicable in the eyes of God and, as a mortal sin, put us in the "most likely to go to hell" category. This was the same priest who later left the priesthood and married one of the high school girls he had been "counseling."

Here, too, I learned that girls weren't so bad after all. They smelled sweet and were so soft to dance with. Kathy even taught me to cha-cha, but slow dancing was always easier as long as you didn't step on the girls' feet. And it was here that I learned that boys and girls thought so differently. I didn't understand them then; I still don't.

Clearing the Charles Street intersection, we zoomed past Wyman Park where my dear great aunt had taken us as kids to play and picnic. It was here that I first played on some of the monuments that have caused many people to refer to Baltimore as "the Monumental City." Civil War heroes or resident poet, Edgar Allen Poe, the monuments in those days were just a place to climb and run and picnic. With age comes appreciation.

It was hard to believe it was all true—a childhood dream come true. How fortunate I was.

Captain Brown wasn't right about this one, I thought as we were released from the small woods fire in the park off Huntingdon Avenue that had been the reason for the box having been pulled. The first run wasn't much, but it wasn't a false alarm either, I gloated with smug satisfaction.

"Hey, rookie, get up here. You're driving back."

I was flabbergasted. My new lieutenant, Fred Rafferty,

introduced himself with the admonition, "If you're gonna be on my shift you're gonna learn how to do everything."

What a difference! At Engine 45 seniority had been everything. Live long enough and you too can drive and maybe, someday, even learn to act lieutenant.

That set the tone for what was to become a pivotal time in my career. Working with highly professional and motivated people and learning how and what to study gave me the shove in the right direction that I was looking for. "Book learning" is one thing; actually learning and doing the job well is something else entirely. The fire department, like most walks of life, has its share of those good at one or the other. Fortunately, Engine 31 provided the opportunities for both. As I quickly learned, there would be plenty of opportunities to fight fires and to learn from some top-notch people.

"Coming home" for me to a station of semi-strangers was unique. Though I had seen a lot of these guys before, and some of them remembered me as "That kid who used to run to the store for us," I didn't really know them.

"Hi, Mike," said soft-spoken Otto, the pump operator, as he held out his hand in greeting. I'd seen him many times over the years sitting and reading the newspaper, sometimes out front, often by the big map on the wall just a few steps from his spot behind the wheel.

"Ugh" or something like that was the greeting from the big guy, Scottie, one of the loudest men you'd ever not want to hear yell at you. Gruff, abrasive, obnoxious at times, he was actually just a little worse once you got to know him.

Dick Miller and Dick Gessner, I'd confuse the two initially. They both rode the truck; both were soft-spoken and friendly. I mixed them up for awhile, much to my embarrassment, until one day Dick Miller reminded me with his dry humor and loud enough for all to hear that he was the one whose feet could reach the pedals. That's why he was the driver.

Next was Ernie Johnson, the tall, thin truck lieutenant who put us all to shame by running or riding his bike back and forth to work each day—about a thousand miles or so. There must've been an ounce of fat there somewhere—or maybe a half-ounce.

It was the two senior guys, though, one on the engine, the other on the truck, who were the most familiar. Coming home meant meeting two of my idols, two of the khaki-clad heroes of the neighborhood I had seen riding by for years. "Mr. Frank" and "Mr. Charlie"—that's how they had always been pointed out to me by my parents as they would go by, sometimes hanging on to the outside, sometimes tillering, sometimes riding up front in the officer's seat. If they weren't responding they would often wave to us kids on the sidewalk as they passed, and on special occasions even clang the bell. My mom had grown up in the neighborhood and knew these guys well.

Taking my extended hand reluctantly, Charlie, "Mr. Charlie" of my youth, turned to Frank Schlosser and announced loudly, "Christ, look Frank. It's Brownie's kid."

I could see it would take some doing to be taken seriously. At least Frank was pleasant enough.

"Christ, Scottie, look here. Billy's recruited another young one to undermine us," Charlie observed.

Uh oh. Some imaginary line of young guys vs. old guys had apparently been drawn; no doubt where I had been placed. And who the heck is Billy, I wondered.

"Billy" was the less than complimentary name given to Charlie's lieutenant, now mine. Fred Rafferty, engine company lieutenant, was my new leader. It didn't take me long to figure out that Lieutenant Rafferty and Charlie were firmly entrenched on opposite sides of that age line.

Charlie, the "King of Waverly," was a fixture at Engine 31 and in the neighborhood. I'm not sure there was anybody within a square mile that he didn't know—or at least claim to know. In the evenings, the Rules and Regulations permitted sitting outside the fire station. In the middle of Waverly with its shops and busy sidewalks it was an evening ritual to carry the barrel-type hard wooden chairs out front. Most of the guys in the department agreed that it had to have been one cruel s.o.b. that invented a chair so hard. But they served the purpose well for the evening pastime. Leaning back against the firehouse wall, balanced on the back two chair legs, the guys could begin the people-watching session. I was constantly amazed at how many of those strolling by greeted Charlie by name, often stopping to chat. No wonder he resented what he perceived as a bunch of new guys bent on taking over.

Lieutenant Fred Rafferty represented the opposition. Aggressive, progressive, quick-thinking, hard-working, and perpetually studying, he was one of the new breed of officers. Fred had been in busy companies before he made lieutenant. Promoted into a slower company when he had made lieutenant, Fred sought the activity and challenge of a busier company and so he had transferred to Engine 31. He was working here on Greenmount Avenue because he wanted to be in on the action.

Charlie's slant on that, I soon learned, was "You gotta be some kind of sicko to want to go to fires."

Fred yearned to get out and go, to be the busiest if he could, and have the best company. That drove Charlie and the other older guys nuts. For those of us who shared Fred's desire to learn and to work hard, he was a prince. To those who wanted peace and quiet and to live life at half-speed, Fred was their worst nightmare.

Oh yeah, "Billy." Fred was dubbed "Billy Bust Out" because of his penchant for hollering "Come on, guys. Let's bust outta this place" whenever things got dull—a battle cry to action for the younger guys. To Charlie, it was his cue. "There's something terribly wrong with that man!" was the inevitable reply.

On the contrary, there was something terribly right with this man. It was there at Engine 31 that I first came to know and appreciate the dedicated people in the Baltimore Fire Department. Working with Lieutenant Rafferty and several others like him proved to be a great boost to my career. For the first time, I was surrounded by people who wanted to work hard and to learn everything they could about the job. I learned by their examples how to perform well on emergency scenes.

Between runs, they taught me how to study—I mean really study. I observed guys who were serious about advancement work diligently to prepare themselves. Quite a few of them rose through the ranks.

The assignment at Engine 31 was hilarious at times, grueling at times, serious occasionally, even bizarre and sad. One night when I was the acting pump operator certainly qualified as bizarre and sad.

We had just cleared a response that night when the dispatcher directed us to report to a basketball court on the side of a school not far from Memorial Stadium. I had spent so much time around there as a kid that I knew just about every place you could play ball or goof off. The dispatcher's message to us was unusual and perplexing. "This response has been authorized by the officer in charge of field operations," he informed us over the radio. That usually means that you are about to encounter something outside the usual scope of duties. When other agencies need specialized help or tools, they sometimes ask the fire department to respond. Some odd situations develop in the city, and the fire department is often called to make them right.

Up beside the darkened side of the school we could see the police officers walking around with their flashlights. That's never a good sign. Lieutenant Rafferty walked up to meet them, conferred, and glumly instructed me to drive the pumper up over the curb and alongside the school. In the darkness it was impossible to see what was going on.

"That's good. We'll drag the line down from here," the lieutenant instructed me. In the city it's not all that unusual to have to wash away blood after a shooting. It's not a pretty sight, but you can't just leave it there on the sidewalk either. Most of us have done it. But this was cruelty taken to a new low.

Somebody had rented a pony for the day. Instead of returning it at day's end, they decided it would be great fun to torture it. The culmination of the sadistic ritual included shoving bottles up the pony's rectum and then smacking the animal with a baseball bat to break the bottles inside. Nice guys. The blood and entrails from the dead pony were a horrible red sludge. Washing it with the powerful fire hose helped sweep away the blood from the court. But nothing could sweep away the impression that such a senseless, barbaric act left on us all. There were no funny quips about that one.

Fortunately, most of the time spent at Engine 31 was much better. True to his word, my lieutenant had quickly included me in the driving rotation—as soon as I had proven I was ready, that is. Every run we went on, day or night, rain or shine, the return trip was mine. If we were responding and were returned by a unit already on the scene the engine would pull to a stop and the lieutenant would holler back, "Hey, Rook, get up here." I never did stop being the rookie the entire time I was there, but I never minded. My lieutenant always used "Rook" as a sort of term of endearment toward me. "Wolfie" used it to indicate he was no longer at the bottom of the roster, since he had been assigned there a few months before me. On the other hand, Charlie found it useful to remind me of my rightful place.

I had spent a lot of time driver training and demonstrating that I knew how to operate the pumps before I was permitted to drive on an actual emergency response. We were out on inspections in the district one day with me driving for practice when the run came in. As I started to pull over to switch places and let the real pump operator get up front, Lieutenant Rafferty told me to go ahead and take the response.

Siren blaring, we headed down Greenmount Avenue toward the reported dwelling fire. I silently hoped that I would shift all the gears properly in the big diesel Mack engine. Downshifting at 25th Street to make the turn—OK. A hundred things raced through my mind. Watch for crossing traffic. Listen for other sirens. Upshift. Downshift. Don't ride the clutch. Keep the speed under control. I didn't want the lieutenant yelling at me for going too fast. Every officer I'd ever heard of was always yelling at their driver for going too fast. No sir, not me. I took it nice and slow. I remember well how patiently the lieutenant later informed me that I really could go a little faster. Eventually, that graduated into his patented "Kick it in the ass!" instructions.

For Lieutenant Rafferty being "first in" whenever possible was the goal. I quickly learned his philosophy and adopted much of it. We would be the best company we could possibly be. And on every fire where we could do so, we would be the ones to put out the fire. Being first in symbolized the desire to excel. Actually being the one to make the fire go out is a satisfying feeling. Meeting the fire head on and conquering it is what fire fighters train for; it's what some of the best fire fighters crave. Every serious fire requires a team effort from different companies and people doing a lot of various jobs. Most fire fighters would agree, though, that actually being the first ones in on the blaze is the most satisfying of the roles.

Friendly rivalries have replaced the bitter feuds of the early American fire service. Gone are the days when brawls erupted over whose company was going to extinguish the fire—well, almost gone. "Brawl" is probably a little strong, but competition can get sort of physical at times. My lieutenant relished responding with certain companies because he figured they'd be waiting for us to come in and get it. Nothing delighted us more than to hear a company pinned down on the steps by terrific heat, unable to move forward. "Move over, then" my lieutenant would tell them, and we would squeeze by them, sometimes actually crawl over them to advance on the fire. Doing that didn't always endear us to the "crawlees," but it built confidence in our crew and gave us valuable experience.

Sometimes the more aggressive fire fighters could be a little more tactful. One favorite trick I learned from my lieutenant was that successful firefighting (or taking it away from the other guys) was a lot like real estate. Location, location, location was the name of the game. If we weren't the ones actually advancing our line, we found a way to get in the right spot however possible. Sometimes it meant sneaking around the pinned down hose crew, but other times it meant seeking another stairway, another door, or even a ladder to get in position. With a little creative positioning, and sometimes maybe a tad of trickery and deceit, we could innocently claim to have found ourselves in just the right spot to be helpful: "Hey, pal, I think from here we can get a pretty good shot at the fire, but there's not a lot of room up here. How 'bout passin' the line to us." This ploy was sometimes a barometer of the aggressive nature and intestinal fortitude of the potential dupes. The companies the lieutenant enjoyed taking fires away from usually relinquished the line all too willingly. But the more experienced, busier companies weren't so easily taken in. They invariably responded more along the lines of "Yeah, well if it's so crowded up there, why don't you girls move aside and let us get up in there and put out the fire?" It was always worth a try, though.

Experience is a funny thing. There are fire fighters who have been in the department a long time, and then there are fire fighters who have experience. The two aren't always the same. One way to get experience is to go to fires, plenty of fires. But all experiences are not equal. Being the third or fourth engine to arrive on the scene of a fire will get a fire fighter some experience based on the size and complexity of the fire. Sometimes, though, the later arriving units pull up to see the steam starting to roll out of the windows as the first in companies attack the fire. In time to help with all the overhauling, the guys on those companies didn't get too much of a challenge.

Being first in almost guarantees more learning opportunity. Company officers learn more quickly when they regularly make important early fireground decisions. The pump operator of that first in company will most likely have the most lines off and will be the center of the fireground activity. And the guys on the first in engine company will do battle with the unchallenged fire raging inside. Those first truck company guys will be in a position to make or break the operation by their precise entry, ventilation, and search activities. Being first in is the way to learn the fastest.

With each fire we fought together at Engine 31, our crew became better. Working together well meant learning each other's strong points and idiosyncrasies. In the fire department, where a fire fighter's safety often rests with his coworkers, it is important to build the trust of a team. Each serious fire met and beaten back helps solidify that team. As with most teams, a newcomer has to prove himself worthy to gain acceptance. Add the generation gap, and earning acceptance from Charlie, the King of Waverly, would take real effort.

Charlie grudgingly admitted that we young guys weren't all that bad when we fought some pretty nasty fires together. He even got to admit that we weren't doing a bad job of driving when the regular pump operator was off. Slowly, we were blurring the age line.

Old firehouses in Baltimore are *old* firehouses. I loved being at Engine 31 where my grandmother remembered the horse-drawn apparatus. The gloomy, long, narrow, single-bay station was a holdover from the glorious days of the steamers and gallant fire horses. The inside walls of the firehouse still contain the outline of the stalls that held the horses. Years of licking the stone window sills have worn them smooth and wavy, forever etching the horse drawn era into the history of this firehouse. A number of the old fire stations still contain the outlines where coal chutes carried the fuel of the day into the heating plants of the time. And the top portions of some of our stations are the old hay lofts. I can't help but think what life must have been like in the stations. Living in a barn with coal burning for heat and keeping the boiler on the steam fire engine banked and ready to go at a moment's notice—ah, they must have been the good old days.

The old firehouse in Waverly contained the typical black metal spiral staircase to the second floor. Coming down from the second floor for a response meant sliding the brightly polished brass poles, a sometimes challenging feat. Jumping up from a dead sleep (and I swear some of the guys do sleep like they're dead) to the clanging of the gong, many a fire fighter has limped across to the pole hole with a leg or arm asleep. Hanging onto the pole the right amount of time when part of your body refuses to cooperate can be dangerous. Fortunately, most of the time it's just plain hilarious to watch. Another factor which ups the degree of difficulty is water. Anyone dashing from the shower to the pole had best be prepared for the trip down. If it weren't so dangerous, it would be funny. It's kind of like jumping from the second floor and, oh yeah, I'll touch this pole a little on the way down.

For me, the trickiest conveyance was the other "stairway" at the back of the station. To call it a stairway is to do it gross injustice. If you've ever watched linemen climbing an electrical pole in the field, you're closer to the picture. The stairs were actually just a series of metal rods embedded at regular intervals into the rear wall of the station. Like giant, heavy duty staples, the steps reached all the way from the apparatus floor into the opening in the kitchen floor above. Spaced just the right distance from the steps was a brass pole like the others throughout the house. To climb the stairs, more appropriately a ladder, you had to walk on the metal rods with your back centered on the pole behind you. Somewhat like trying to climb out of a narrow shaft by forcing your body against both sides, balance and coordination were strongly recommended. It was awhile before I even tried it. I was amazed by the guys who routinely descended from the kitchen with a cup of steaming coffee in one hand and never spilled a drop.

The middle of the night watch in Waverly was sometimes pretty interesting, especially on the weekends. The neighborhood bars made for quite an atmosphere of loud music, parking complaints in front of the firehouse and drunks. Some of the drunks who came in were pleasant, some were loud and nasty, but one pattern seemed pretty common: "What'd you guys do with my car? I know I left it right there." One guy even swore he had ridden his bike to the bar but parked it in our hose tower. He was convinced that one of us had stolen it.

Other nights the local working girls provided the entertainment as they cruised up and down Greenmount Avenue. Some of them were actually pretty friendly. I guess that helps in that business. But it was the gay guys who cruised the sidewalk across the street that sometimes caused the most stir in the firehouse. It took me a while to catch on. I wondered why it seemed that as soon as I came downstairs to assume my watch one of the guys would come in to visit. Young and a bit naive, I hated to be rude, but my hospitality only went so far. Eventually, the visitors would leave but sometimes with hurt feelings or loud comments about how they had "wasted a half hour." Finally, somebody tipped me on the game. When you're just about to go off watch, motion one of the guys over and tell him your buddy's coming down in a minute, but he's pretty shy. He likes guys, but most of the other guys don't know it, so don't mention that you heard it from me. Then you go upstairs, tap your relief's bunk, and listen at the pole hole in case there's a run while he's getting dressed. With him sleepily on the way downstairs, you can rest well knowing he won't be lonely.

I just knew that I shouldn't have tried to sneak a cup of coffee from the kitchen while I was on watch. There, all the way at the rear of the long, long station, perched precariously on the vertical stairs with my back against the pole, I heard the bells start. The quiet of the sleeping firehouse was always a concern of mine, so I hadn't turned up the speaker too loud on the watch desk, now about a thousand clanking, thudding, running footsteps away. It's tough to listen to something at low volume and run like your life depends on it. Oh man, I know I heard St. Paul Street in there somewhere. My fingers reached the gong switch and silence was a distant memory. "Turn out!" I yelled, "Everybody goes."

Upstairs, the guys rolled sleepily from the warm beds they had occupied and slipped into various arrangements. Some of the guys jumped right into turnout pants folded down over their short boots. These guys yanked up the pants and threw on the trademark suspenders. Others opted for their trousers and would don their three-quarter length boots downstairs. When the boots were pulled up, they provided some additional protection to the upper legs, but they weren't perfect by any stretch.

"Dwelling fire, 2920 Saint Paul Street," I yelled to the officers as I hurriedly jumped into my boots. From the back step I watched the familiar streets of my youth, now dark and deserted, go whizzing by. At this time of the morning, we could make good time. I knew we were first due, the first companies listed on the assignment card, the closest units. I knew we would be first in, so I prepared myself for my job ahead. The familiar smell of wood burning greeted us even before the actual fire came into view.

Charlie, acting lieutenant for the night, had barely yelled "Lead off!" when I was in the street dragging the hydrant connection and the hose to the fire hydrant on the corner. Acrid, gray smoke hung lazily in the front street forming a haze in the street lights. From one of the large, three-story brick homes that lined the old neighborhood, smoke gushed from the front door.

Flip-flopping the hose up the street, the engine pulled to a stop just past the house on fire. Right behind was the truck from our station, Truck 7. From their position in the front of the fire building, the truck began the practiced routine. Aerial to the roof so the guys can vent the fire vertically and draw the fire and heat out the top of the home. Portable ladders to the second and the third floors would provide the access to begin the search for trapped occupants. The early morning hour and the quantity of smoke pouring from the door didn't bode well for the safety of the residents. Truck 7's crew swung into action as Charlie and Wolfie dragged the one and three-quarter inch hose toward the front door. Nobody from the home greeted them out front, another bad omen.

As soon as the line from the hydrant was connected to the pump on the engine, I swung the hydrant wrench round and round until water filled the hose as it snaked up St. Paul Street.

Grabbing a mask from the engine, I quickly joined the other members of the engine now just inside a hallway filled with dense smoke and punishing heat. Only a few feet inside the door it became obvious that the fire had gained considerable headway, but the location wasn't apparent. Only impenetrable smoke filled the hall. Our flashlights shone only an inch before they disappeared in a fruitless attempt to light the way. Inching forward, crawling and dragging the hose now swelled with water, we advanced cautiously, pausing to listen. No screams, no crackling of flames, no sounds to lead us to the fire.

Even through the heavy firefighting gear the heat of the serious unseen fire was causing us great discomfort. Oven like temperatures in the hallway enveloped us and nearly drove us back out the door. From the doorway, the acting lieutenant, Charlie, urged us on. If the situation were this bad for us, the upstairs had to be worse for anyone still inside. We needed to find the fire quickly and cut it off if the occupants were to have any chance. Those truck guys were entering upstairs in their search, counting on us to control the fire before it could reach upstairs.

Further into the hallway we pushed, each foot bringing more heat until we thought the area might suddenly erupt in flame trapping us. Fire fighters are taught not to open the nozzle and actually shoot water until they can see the fire itself, but some circumstances require otherwise. If we were going to be able to stay in the hall, much less advance, we needed to reduce the temperature, and fast. Wolfie turned the nozzle toward the ceiling and opened up with a few bursts. Steam replaced dry heat as the water met the superheated blackness just above our heads. The trick was to use just enough water to reduce the temperature a little bit. Too much and the hallway's thermal balance would be upset driving the now moisture-saturated mess onto us.

Through our boots we could now feel the heat from the floor. The fire was below us, in the basement of the long rowhouse. Basement fires are among the worst fires we fight. With limited ventilation possibilities, fire fighters often face punishing conditions. The heavy combustible loading in many basements make for serious fire conditions. And the danger that surrounds basement fires is well known. The ceiling of that basement burning furiously is that floor we're crawling over. Many fire fighters have been lost when they were suddenly thrown into the fury by a floor collapsing under them.

Fire in the basement meant that our job was clear. Find the door that connects the basement to the first floor and stop the fire's upward progress. If we could slow the fire, the guys from the back outside basement door would attack the fire. Working "in the chimney" of the stairs is brutal, but critical. Only stopping the fire here would give the truck guys the chance to find and remove anyone upstairs.

First left, then right, feeling but never seeing, we scrunched deeper into the home, only the noise of our air masks to keep us company. The disorientation of such a situation is amazing. If a fire fighter leaves the safety of the hoseline, he can easily become lost and perish. At least the hoseline offers a map to the exit.

"There!" heaved Wolfie from the impenetrable veil that completely absorbed him even though we were a foot apart. The heat was unbearable as it burned our shoulders, necks, and ears right through our gear. Noises from upstairs confirmed we were near the stairs. Barely distinguishable, a muted orange glow now pointed the way. Around one more bend and we could make out the fire burning through the top part of the door from the basement. If the fire jumped out of there, it had a straight shot up the stairs to the upper floors.

Whoooosh went the water from the nozzle Wolfie held for dear life. Opening the spray wide enough to cover the opening of the doorway, he attempted to contain the fire which blew out like a blow torch. Fire burning up the stairs from below us had now burned through the top half of the wooden door and threatened to keep right on going. For us, pinned down at the stairway, trying just to hold our own, the battle was very personal. The fire resembled some frantic animal darting here, squeezing there, as it tried to get by our stream of water. Move. Counter-move. With each new thrust from the fire, Wolfie adjusted the direction and pattern of the torrent of water we now threw at the blaze. Totally absorbed by our actions, we no longer even felt the heat. Maybe we were having the desired effect.

Here, deep within the house, we saw only the one small portion of the whole picture. What we couldn't see was that out front the fire had now burst from the basement windows and was lapping up onto the front porch. Another engine crew was attempting to beat back the flames. In the back of the house the situation was even worse. Fire belching furiously from the basement door and window had already engulfed the wooden porch and was threatening to enter the second floor windows. The guys from Engine 18 had stretched their line into the yard and fought desperately to contain the extending flames. If the fire entered the upper floors through the back windows, we would face an even worse situation. Upstairs the truck guys were pulling terrified occupants from the windows onto the ladders they had hurriedly positioned.

The battalion chief had immediately seen the need for help and requested the second alarm. Now as the fire continued to rage and threatened to spread to the properties on either side, he requested the third alarm. More fire fighters would be needed to stretch additional lines and to enter and search the adjacent houses. The sounds of low air pressure warning devices on the fire fighters' air masks told the chief that crews would be scrambling back out from the hellish conditions. Fresh crews would need to relieve those exhausted from the tremendous efforts underway.

From his position at the doorway, Charlie had fed us additional line each time we needed it. Like so many of his era, Charlie was never comfortable wearing an air mask. Times had changed, but Charlie had not kept up. During all of our battle, he was able only to advance a few feet into the hallway, and that was a punishing position for one without a mask.

Nobody lost their life that night. Some of the truck guys

even got commendations for some pretty good rescues they had made under terrible conditions. The guys in the back kept the fire from spreading upward, and the guys in front eventually beat the fire back into the basement. For our part, the young guys held the fire in the basement. No fire went racing up the interior stairs. We didn't put the fire out; we had only one place we had kept our line in place, but we had played a critical part in the overall effort. To this day, that remains one of the most physically punishing fires that I have ever fought. It felt great later when Charlie admitted to all the guys that "Billy's kids" had done a hell of a job.

Everything seemed to be turning out to be just about perfect at my new home at Engine 31. Back in the old neighborhood, working with a good solid bunch of guys, learning to study for promotion—things were great. Then it happened. I couldn't believe the news. The guys must be screwing with me.

"The department has decided to increase the number of ambulances in the department," began Chief Webb that fateful morning. "One of 'em will be going to 11 Truck." Eleven Truck was one of the companies in our battalion.

My heart sank. Part of the enjoyment in being here was not having to ride the ambulance all the time. I thought I had heard the worst until the chief held me with the officers after the others had been dismissed: "You know, Mike, we've never had an ambo. in the battalion before, so our guys don't have much experience riding one. We'll be looking to you a lot to ride it since you have all that experience riding one in your previous assignment."

"Thanks, Chief."

7
Finding the Niche

In every successful organization there are good people at all levels. The fire department is no exception. Some of those in the fire service choose never to pursue the promotions that others work tirelessly for years to achieve. Each is a member of the team. Everybody has a niche. Finding that niche is the key to a rewarding and productive time in the fire service.

Undeniably, the best fought fire is the fire that never starts. Over the last couple of decades the American fire service has responded to the challenges to drastically reduce the appalling rate of fire-related deaths and injuries. Recognizing that putting out fires effectively is not the only measure of a successful war on fire, the fire service has shifted much of its efforts to research, prevention, and public education. Scientists, working with those within the fire service, continue to develop new materials which perform better under fire conditions. Many products today have been developed or redesigned with a new awareness. The fire service has individuals and groups who constantly press industry, politicians, and others to build more fire-safe buildings and furnishings, to improve appliances, to strengthen existing laws, and to enact new legislation and codes. Campaigns to expand the requirements for built-in fire protection systems, automatic sprinklers, even smoke detectors have met resistance, but the persistence of those involved is paying off.

Some in the fire department choose to be the enforcers of the codes which try to legislate safety. Fire inspectors pound the streets every day. They check above ceilings to make sure no holes have been poked through the fire walls, holes often made after the fact to install or relocate electrical, plumbing, or air handling equipment. During a fire these holes could mean a huge difference. Instead of a fire confined to one area or one store, fire fighters could face fire spreading unseen through hidden spaces to other areas or down a whole row of stores. Many times solid construction methods and good workmanship have been negated by a later modification done in the name of improvement. Some of these "improvements" have resulted in notable losses. Discovering these types of problems before a fire occurs is far more desirable than suffering the consequences.

Inspectors peek into the closets where improper storage of materials too close to an electrical panel or to a heating unit might cause a fire. They check the fire extinguishers to make sure they have been properly placed and maintained. They check the storage of explosives and of flammable liquids and of poisons. They issue permits that assure certain processes are conducted safely. They interpret and explain code requirements in efforts to obtain cooperation from building owners and occupants. Failing to obtain voluntary compliance with good practice, they can cite violators who may wind up paying fines, even closing their businesses in the most extreme circumstances.

Fire inspectors patrol the night clubs, the dance halls, the banquet rooms, even our kids' schools to prevent the horrors that locked exit doors or overcrowding can bring to a fire. In many ways these are the unsung heroes of the war against fire. Often faced with uncooperative, apathetic, sometimes even belligerent building owners and occupants, the fire inspectors enforce the lessons learned through some of this country's worst disasters.

How do you measure how many fires do not start? How can we document the many fires never reported because they were caught immediately? Which of the many little fires a fire department sees would have been much, much worse if not for the actions of an inspector a week, a month, a year before? To those who perform this part of the fire service mission, the reward must come in knowing that they are making a difference in the country's fire experience.

Another of the big shifts in emphasis away from the traditional fire department duties has been the emergency medical field. In my career alone, the fire department has changed from a first aid giver to a sophisticated, highly professional system capable of delivering lifesaving care to the most critically injured auto accident victim or to the heart attack patient stricken in his home. With a multitude of medications, assorted electronic devices and monitors, state of the art, real time communications with doctors and hospitals, and intense training, today's paramedics look a lot more like doctors than they do the Band-Aid crews of my early career. Many terrific paramedics have no desire to fight fires. However, the service they provide as members of the fire department touches lives every day in the most meaningful of ways.

The fire department also has investigators whose job it is to uncover the causes of the fires that do start. Arson is still a scourge on our cities, but new detection techniques and programs continue to make inroads. In the past, arson hasn't always received the attention from the national law enforcement community that the fire service would like. In Baltimore, the responsibilities for arson investigation bring the police and fire departments together. Each has roles to play in detecting, documenting, investigating, and prosecuting arson cases. Today the "task force" approach that puts various agencies together to fight arson has become a national trend. The well publicized investigations into the burning of black churches briefly brought some attention to the country's arson problem, but we have short memories. Unlike the high profile cases and their accompanying visibility, the average fire investigation is one of on-scene, non-dramatic, quiet, methodical investigating. Much hinges on an investigator's being able to determine correctly where and how the fire started. With bodies in the morgue or a block-long tangle of twisted metal and smoking ruins where a one hundred year old business had been, the ante is raised.

Did someone forget to turn off the stove before falling asleep, or fail to remove the remnants of the evening's romantic fire in the fireplace to the outside? Had the occupant neglected the chimney where flammable creosote and black muck gradually coated the inside until finally igniting? Was an extension cord, asked to do far more that it was designed to do, overheating for hours until it ignited the carpet? Did a furnace or an air conditioner, pushed to the maximum or worn over the years, send the building up in flames? Were blankets placed too close to a portable heater during the frigid night? Did a cigarette slip down unnoticed beside the cushion in a living room chair and smolder for hours until the chair burst into flames? Could the family cat have knocked over a candle left burning? Was an exhaust fan or a motor on some device overheating as it malfunctioned?

Did a curious three year old find mom's lighter, start a fire, and then "hide" from the fire where fire fighters would later find the little charred body? Or was the fire starter an angry tenant who figured that management would surely give him a better apartment if this one were damaged by fire? Spurned lover, disgruntled employee, burglar attempting to cover his tracks, vandal, owner of a failing business attempting to "sell it to the insurance company"—the possibilities are nearly endless.

With little physical evidence remaining, no eyewitnesses, a crime scene "invaded" and trampled through by hordes of hose dragging, water spraying, tool wielding fire fighters, I'm constantly amazed by the job our investigators do. They can often take a single piece of evidence—the nervous tick of a suspect being questioned, an inconsistency in a statement from an occupant, an observation from a first-arriving fire fighter— and build a picture with uncanny accuracy. The good fire investigator—and we have had some good ones—are a joy to behold. It's like watching Columbo with a turnout coat. I always thought it would be interesting being one of the investigators, but I'm too trusting. I tend to believe what people tell me unless faced with considerable evidence to the contrary. My kids, of course, say that's exactly the opposite of the way I treat them.

Indeed, the fire department has many vital parts, some of them unseen and unappreciated. Just as important as the person who puts out the fire is the person who trained him. Training is another area where the American fire service has changed dramatically. The days of "...and here's a coat and helmet. Do what I do" are gone. Today, nationally recognized standards covering everything but the color of your socks have been developed.

Fire fighters undergo vigorous training in the many physical skills required to do the job. Handling hose carrying tons of water each minute is serious business. Not only can the weight cause trouble to those trying to maneuver it, an out of control hoseline whipping through the air is a potentially fatal weapon. Quite a few fire fighters are injured by hose, some even killed. Instructors patiently teach the important skills to new fire fighters. Advancing hose, extending lines by adding additional sections, working the various nozzles in all the many ways that could be needed to put out fires, breaking the lines, draining the remaining water from them, re-coupling the hose, rolling it, repacking it—the lessons are all important.

Instructors carefully teach each recruit how to select the proper ladder for the job at hand. They will hear "Lift with your knees not your back" until it becomes second nature. Carrying the heavy ladders safely over slippery, uneven ground in dark, unfamiliar settings with people screaming to be rescued will require skill and much practice. Raising the ladder quickly and correctly without its getting away and crashing to the ground is critical. A ladder mishap can bring serious injury or death to fire fighters. Fluid motion will be required to place the bottom of the ladder in the right place and bring it upright without hitting overhead power lines or tree limbs. Rotate it with it sticking up straight in the air where the wind can push it over; extend it the correct number of rungs to put the tip in the right place at the window sill; lower the top into the building while keeping the bottom from sliding out, even on concrete or hills or ice. And don't look up from under the ladder to see where it's going or you risk a face full of breaking window glass from above. Check the ladder to make sure the climbing angle is OK, secure the ladder, climb the ladder safely, climb it while hauling a hoseline or a heavy saw, and with an air mask on your back.

The instructors will teach all of these skills each fire fighter must know and many, many more. They will teach fire behavior and the physical laws that govern how and where a fire will develop. And then they'll teach the proper methods to vent and to apply the hose streams with those lessons in mind. Handling hazardous materials incidents, protecting yourself from infectious diseases, effecting rescue in confined spaces or in the raging torrents of swollen streams will all be important lessons.

Instructors will teach fire fighters how to extricate victims of automobile accidents, automobiles with constantly changing technology and features that force the fire fighter to stay abreast. They'll learn about alternative fueled vehicles and air bags, loaded front bumpers that could maim an unfortunate fire fighter. Rescue from vehicles means dealing with steering columns that negate the techniques we used to use to pull them up and away from someone trapped. Fire fighters must learn about the implications of side impact protection, electric windows and door locks, and shock absorbers and suspension systems that without warning could turn a potential rescuer into another victim.

Instructors teach teamwork and communications and organization and coordination, all essential for emergency operations. Managing an incident efficiently and safely means each fire fighter must know their role and how they all fit together.

Thousands of little pieces make up a fire fighter's actions. Some of these things will be done often and will become second nature; others may never be used. The instructors must teach them as much as possible to prepare them for the day their very lives might rest on something they learned. Firefighting is a lifelong commitment to learning, and instructors will continue to be an important part of anyone's time in the fire department.

Lost deep within a burning building, totally disoriented and separated from his crew, enveloped in a blackness like a subterranean cave where even a flashlight's beam is swallowed up in inches, pummeled from above by burning debris that threatens to entangle him in a deadly snare, almost completely out of air—it's every fire fighter's nightmare, and every instructor's. Will something the fire fighter has learned allow him to survive, one little lesson, one little "trick" taught to him long ago? When I first learned to be an instructor, for me a part-time occupation, I heard an admonition I never forgot. Joe Batchler, one of the finest instructors I've ever been privileged to know, passed it along, though I can't remember the exact source: "Don't ever let the ghost of an untrained fire fighter come back to haunt you." A truly awesome responsibility goes to those who choose this as their niche.

From the mechanics who maintain the apparatus to those who make sure each person has the necessary uniforms and protective equipment, from the dispatchers who handle the public's calls for help and send the correct units on their way, to the people who draw the maps or fix the radios, the fire department is made up of many individuals doing their part to make it all work.

For some, being the fire fighter on the end of the hoseline in face-to-face combat with the red devil has no equal. Being a fire fighter on the engine company means meeting the enemy one-on-one, "putting the wet stuff on the red stuff" as it has been so eloquently described. In the inky blackness of a smoke filled building with heat so punishing it forces fire fighters to be "splinter huggers," the most elemental struggles of firefighting undeniably take place. The fanciest tactics and the best-written books, the most scientific mathematical models of fire propagation, the formulae which fill our trade journals and our heads and purport to predict fire behavior and flame spread, the years of training, the endless drills—in the end it all boils down to the gut level battle fought inside the swirling hell of a structure on fire.

Call it the biblical clash of good and evil, or maybe it's just another of man's feeble attempts to master his environment, this is the battle, this is firefighting in its most traditional sense. The war on fire is fought on many fronts, but none is more gripping, more chilling than this confrontation in the trenches. Choking back the human instinct to tear off the mask facepiece and run the other way, fire fighters do battle like this every day across our country. No part of the war is more dangerous or more important. No wonder many fire fighters find this by far the most satisfying part of the job.

For other fire fighters the front line clash with fire comes as part of the truck companies. These fire fighters have chosen the role that brings them to new heights—quite literally at times. The challenges posed by the myriad of tasks the "truckie" might be called upon to perform make this position attractive to many. Each fire presents different problems. How can we quickly reach the occupants trapped in the third floor rear? What ladders should we place to where to use most effectively the manpower on hand? Wasted effort might mean that another critical task is delayed or omitted. Worse yet, a fire fighter suddenly cut off by the fire crawls to a window to escape and there's no ladder in place for him to use.

Where will the engine company need our help forcing entry into locked areas or opening up the walls and ceilings to get out ahead of the fire? Can we ventilate in such a way as to draw the smoke and fire away from the critical areas? Can we do a roof trench cut (a long, narrow cut) farther down this row of stores to keep the fire from spreading beyond? What tools will be quickest for that type roof construction? How far ahead of the fire should we cut? Too far away from the fire and we could draw the fire into areas that might otherwise have been saved; too close and the fire might roar past us before we can complete the cut designed to stop it.

Every serious fire poses a different set of problems and

operating conditions. Often operating without the direct supervision of their officer, who is also quite busy, the truck company fire fighters must accomplish many tasks simultaneously and unerringly. Foremost among the duties of the truck company is the search for those trapped inside the burning building. Often, while the engine company is laying the hose and stretching the lines into place to begin the attack, the fire fighters from the truck have already begun the search. Using quickly placed ladders, adjacent structures, fire escapes, stairways, windows and doors, their mandate is clear. Find anyone still alive within the building and remove them to safety.

Searching an unfamiliar building in zero visibility with fire roaring beneath them, the truckies race the clock. Anyone still inside could be in desperate straits. Unconscious, unprotected from the heat and poisons filling the structure, the life expectancy of a trapped civilian might be measured in seconds. When faced with a possible rescue situation fire fighters push with superhuman efforts into the worst imaginable situations at terrible personal risk. Results are never guaranteed. Some days it turns out that no one was ever in there, contrary to the reports of those screaming outside. Sometimes those inside are beyond help, dead already from the horrible poisonous smoke. On some occasions the fire fighters are unable to reach those inside, driven back out as the area flashes over into an unsurvivable blast furnace. The fortunate fire fighters often bail head-first out of windows with their protective clothing smoking as fire shares the window they are exiting. Sometimes our guys don't get out. But the thing that motivates the fire fighters on the truck is the chance that their efforts will pay off. Finding a child hidden in a closet, a home owner collapsed short of the window, or a baby still lying in its crib and saving that person is the ultimate reward. Literally risking their own lives in the process, fire fighters put it all on the line for the chance to cheat death. It's a risky job for sure, certainly not one for the faint at heart, but it is also intoxicating.

Some fire fighters seek something different still. Riding the heavy rescue company is a sure way to see action nobody else experiences. The fire fighters who ride Rescue 1 in Baltimore respond to fires in their own area and respond to second alarms anywhere in the city as well. While we do have truck companies that carry some hydraulic tools used to free the victims of car accidents, it is the rescue that carries the extensive line of very specialized tools that can be required at times. Anywhere in Baltimore the rescue responds to industrial accidents, auto accidents where people are trapped, elevator mishaps, hazardous materials incidents, plane crashes, water rescues, building collapses, and just about anything else unusual. With their special tools and special training, these fire fighters face some of the most difficult and bizarre challenges on the job. No instructional guide can foresee exactly the circumstances surrounding some of the unique situations they face. Constant training, intimate familiarity with their tools, flawless teamwork, and clever resourcefulness mark the good rescue company. They are an indispensable part of a modern fire department.

For others in the fire department, their real talent and desires take them into the role of the pump operator. In Baltimore, this is a promotion from fire fighter rank with some benefits. In addition to receiving a modest increase in pay the pump operator works almost exclusively in his own company rather than being moved all around the city to fill staffing requirements. Many find this attractive. Even more attractive for some others is the fact that the pump operator doesn't have to take a turn riding the medic unit as the fire fighters do. Those times when the medic unit has only one paramedic working, a fire fighter rides as the acting EMT (Emergency Medical Technician). Some fire fighters like the change and the challenge, others would rather be tortured.

Being a pump operator (P.O.) brings additional responsibilities. Routine maintenance of the engine, cleaning and caring for the vehicle and all the tools it carries, and similar duties are entrusted to the pump operator. The pump operator assists the officer with the training of fire fighters in the company so that they can assume the P.O.'s duties in his absence.

A good pump operator is essential to the workings of the company. Driving safely and promptly to each emergency incident is an important duty. The entire crew puts its safety into the P.O.'s hands whenever they respond. Emergency driving requires special skills. Unlike the high speed, high thrill responses of emergency vehicles portrayed nightly on television, the reality of emergency driving is quite different. Controlled, precise, cautious driving is what is needed.

Driving a fire engine with siren and air horn blaring, it is easy to lose sight of the fact that sometimes other people truly don't hear or don't see us coming. Other drivers may choose to disregard the law or may panic as an emergency vehicle approaches. As incredulous as this may seem, the P.O. must always act with this possibility in mind. A twelve ton vehicle does not stop on a dime with the best of drivers, so anticipating the bizarre actions of other drivers is essential to good driving. I saw a sign in a fire station in another town many years ago that I never forgot: "There is no emergency so great that we cannot drive safely and responsibly." Getting there in one piece is the first step in being able to help someone in need.

Driving well is important, but so is driving promptly to the scene. This requires an intimate knowledge of the unit's response area and the response routes best for that time of day, weather conditions, etc. The P.O. needs to know the location of all the important buildings in the area, the one way streets, any bridges with weight restrictions that might prevent their crossing, and limited access highways' on and off ramps.

Very importantly, the P.O. must be familiar with the water supply system in the area, including the location of each hydrant in their response area. On the fireground, the pump operator becomes far more than the driver who got us there. Obtaining an uninterrupted water supply for the crew is essential. Fire fighters who begin their attack on the fire using the few minutes' supply of water carried on board the engine rely on the P.O. to keep them supplied. Running out of water while battling the fire inside a blazing building could spell disaster for the crew.

We are fortunate in Baltimore to have a good water system and fire hydrants throughout the entire city, but even then problems can arise. Frozen hydrants, broken valves, burst hose, supply lines clogged with debris, .cars running over and shearing the supply hose in the street, mechanical problems with the pump—nothing can stop the P.O. from the mission of obtaining a reliable water supply for those inside fighting the fire. The best pump operators can be very creative at obtaining and keeping water.

To pass the pump operator's exam, a person must have studied hydraulics and other needed information and then demonstrated the ability to operate under a variety of conditions. The operating crews depend on the P.O. to send the correct pressures to the various hoselines depending on the length and diameter of the lines being used, the type of nozzles on the end, the elevation difference between the nozzles and the pump, and other factors. Important decisions, important job.

The truck company needs drivers and tillermen (the guy who drives the back end). In Baltimore these Emergency Vehicle Drivers (E.V.D.'s) are fire fighters who have competed for that promotion. Like the P.O., they are responsible for the vehicle, for the care of many more tools than the engine company carries, and for the safe driving of the vehicle. Unlike the driver of the engine, however, these E.V.D.'s become part of the active firefighting crew once the truck arrives on the fire scene. Not only do the E.V.D.'s swing the aerial ladder into operation when needed, they are the people who place the portable ladders, search for trapped occupants, vent the buildings, cut holes in the roofs, force the locked doors and security gates, open the ceilings and walls for hidden fire, utilize the powerful fans or smoke ejectors, and light up the scene at night. Some of our members prefer this role because it offers them the best of both worlds, the challenge and responsibility of emergency driving and the active participation in the fireground activities.

The teamwork involved in handling any emergency incident requires the fire fighters who do all the many tasks involved and the officers who supervise the actions, calling the shots and putting the resources to work most effectively. Different departments use different terms to describe these positions of supervisor on the engine and truck companies. An engine company or a truck company in Baltimore has a captain on one of its four shifts and lieutenants on the other three shifts. The captain has the overall responsibility for company policy and firehouse life, but on the fireground the responsibilities of the company officers are pretty much the same.

The days when staffing permitted the officer to be an observer who could guide the actions of those under his command are long gone. Years ago, the company officer pointed the handlight and showed the others where to do the work. Today the company officer is another working member of the team, dragging the hose into position and advancing on the fire, or placing the ladders, searching the building, and performing all the other important truck company functions.

But the company officer has far more to do as well. On the engine company, the officer chooses the best approach into the scene and makes the decision of which hydrant to utilize, what size lines to stretch and where to position the apparatus. The unit has to be placed to operate effectively without blocking out the truck companies who need to position for effective ladder placement. One unwisely positioned piece of equipment can hinder an entire operation.

The engine company officer selects the proper attack line for the fire at hand and assists in deploying it. Making the size-up of the situation, the officer considers the type and size of the building, the obvious fire conditions, the probable conditions which cannot be directly observed, the potential fire spread, the wind speed and direction, the easiest access, the vantage point which will place the line between the fire and anyone trapped within the building. The officer, coordinating with the other companies and the incident commander, must accurately predict the results of the hoseline they will operate. Incorrectly placed or operated, the line could drive the fire into uninvolved portions of the building or onto other crews operating within the structure. Timing, experience, and good judgment are all critical in the safe and effective use of the water propelled from the company's line.

On the hose with the fire fighter on the nozzle, the engine company officer guides the placement of the stream. "Hit it here...Bounce it off of there...Shut it down and let's advance around that corner." Feeding the hose and acting as coach, the officer directs the nozzleman and serves as his backup. Tugging the heavy, water filled, stiff hose around the obstructions encountered is physically demanding. Crawling with the cumbersome firefighting gear and the heavy air mask on his back, the officer tries to control his breathing. Each heavy breath sucks more air from the finite amount on his back and makes it more difficult to hear. It's imperative the officer hear the other fire fighters as they try to talk through the mask which muffles sound under the best of circumstances. It's also important to listen for the sounds of the fire or of trapped victims or of other crews as they operate under or nearby. Paramount to the safety of the crew is the ability to hear messages on the portable radio. And being able to talk effectively means controlling the labored breathing and the emotions that accompany such tense and difficult situations.

The truck company officer faces different problems. Even with pre-assigned tools and tasks, the crew faces different circumstances at each fire. At some incidents, forcing entry may be a major problem. Buildings can contain several occupancies. One common arrangement in Baltimore combines a store on the first floor with apartments above on the second and third floors. In urban areas, where store owners take extraordinary methods to protect their properties from burglars, entering to fight a fire can be very difficult. Fire in the store or in the basement immediately endangers those trapped above. Every second counts. Based on the fire conditions and the types of locks and security devices encountered, the truck company officer needs to select the proper spot to attempt entry and assign the right number of people armed with the correct tools to accomplish the task quickly.

Unfortunately, the other very important tasks still require attention. The truck crew still needs to get ladders in place to gain access to the upper floors and the roof. Ventilation still needs to be addressed and carefully timed and coordinated as engine crews enter the building to attack the fire. Areas above the fire need to be searched immediately for trapped occupants, etc., etc., etc. The list goes on. Somebody has to make it all work quickly and efficiently. The truck company officer has his hands full at any serious fire.

Company officers serve as the eyes and ears of the chief as well. Relaying critical information regarding the conditions encountered and the progress being made, the officer allows this incident commander to assess more accurately the entire situation. Unusually heavy combustible loading, sagging floors, higher than normal ceilings, a maze of cut-up rooms and hidden void spaces, increasing heat conditions instead of the progress anticipated, occupants located or not, the need for more lines or more personnel—the information is all vital to the incident commander.

Foremost in the duties of the company officer is providing for the safety of his crew. This means always being aware of conditions not only in his portion of the incident but in the entire operational area. Monitoring the portable radio and observing the changing surroundings, the officer must constantly evaluate the position of the crew and take the correct actions to ensure their safety. Modern protective equipment with its insulating properties has allowed fire fighters to enter and remain in heated areas longer than before. In an ironic twist, however, this technological advance can also lead to a diminished awareness of the surrounding environment, thus posing new potential threats to fire fighters. More than ever the officer must use all his experience and skills to evaluate the threats to his personnel.

Knowing when to advance and when to retreat is a hard earned skill, one obtained the old fashioned way. Training, practice, and experience are the teachers; sometimes the lessons are hard. Experienced fire fighters have felt the almost unbearable heat swallow them up as a room approaches the flashover point. They've felt the anxious moments when the tide of battle had not yet changed and the fire lapped freely over their heads. They've suffered the steam burns that result from the massive expansion of water hitting the fire, even cursed the other crews who sometimes inadvertently drive the heat and steam right onto them. In the awful darkness of a burning building, they've felt the loneliness and vulnerability that scares any sane person. The officer says stay or go. Pull out and any chance of saving a trapped person vanishes, any chance of stopping the fire there is lost. Stay too long in the wrong situation and risk the lives of the crew trying to save the unsavable, attain the unattainable.

The company officer bears a terrific responsibility to those who work with him. Company officers, like the rest of the world, come in a variety of shapes and sizes and abilities. Some do a decent job, others are superb. Working with a superb officer is every fire fighter's desire. To obtain the rank of lieutenant or captain, a member of the fire department must have demonstrated a knowledge of many, many subjects— demonstrated on paper that is. The real tests come, though, when the new officer assumes his command and begins the process of building his team and earning respect.

In the fire department there's respect and then there's *respect*. The first is bestowed, the second is earned. Rank carries with it a built-in organizational respect. In the paramilitary structure of the fire department, a superior officer is owed certain recognition. Authority comes with promotion; the higher the rank, the more the authority. But no badge or title can earn one the respect that the best officers earn from those with whom they work.

Every great fire fighter does not make a good lieutenant. Every good captain does not make a good chief. I've always thought The Peter Principle a little cynical in describing how people tend to rise to their level of incompetency. I prefer to think that many of us stop moving up the ranks when we have found our niche. It makes me feel better about myself and those I work with anyway.

As traditional as the fire service tends to be—and certainly our department is a great example—the thought of change, any change, brings fear to many. I entered the department at a time of great social upheaval. Vietnam, Kent State, civil rights marches, political assassinations, and urban riots were shaking America from its complacency. A heightened effort to include minority groups in the fire service was one result of the new social consciousness. Not long after I was in the fire department, a court ruling dictated some changes in the way the fire department would handle promotions. I was fortunate enough to be in the right place at the right time.

From my earliest days in the fire department I knew that I wanted to be an officer. I made a pretty ambitious goal of reaching captain in ten years. Studying was a habit I never outgrew. Each and every day I read everything I could about the fire department—well, most days anyway. I have to admit to a brief infatuation with the beautiful pool table at my first assignment. I lugged books to and from work every day much to the amazement of some of my early co-workers. Promotions were frozen during the court case and I really didn't pay much attention. The minimum times in grade required to take promotional exams meant that I had five years before I would be eligible to take a lieutenant's exam. Then, a test might not be given for another year or so, since each eligibility list ran two years. Even if I should pass the test the first time round and was lucky enough to be promoted, it could be up to two years then beyond the test for any actual promotion. It seemed an eternity.

Undeterred, I studied and learned everything I could about the job I had and the ones to which I aspired. The gods smiled on me when I transferred to a company where I learned how and what to study. Surrounded by others who were pursuing promotion, I found an environment conducive to learning. My lieutenant was young, energetic, hard-working, dedicated, and quite sharp. Most importantly, he was willing to teach me. His example and that of some of the others there buoyed my spirits and encouraged my tremendous investment in time and effort.

Then suddenly, the guidelines changed. The court had ruled that in order for black fire fighters, woefully under-represented in the officer ranks at the time, to advance more quickly, there would be some changes. Now a fire fighter with three yearson the job would be eligible to take the test for lieutenant. Only one year's experience would be required to take examinations for pump operator and emergency vehicle driver; three years had been the minimum before. Further, only one year in grade would be required for eligibility to take the next exam in line. New tests would be given more often. And tests were to be validated, job-related tests taken from recognized sources of material relevant to the positions sought. There would be no more of the legendary "How many stars are there on the manhole covers for the high pressure system?" questions. To ensure equal access to the study materials, each fire station received a company library for use by its members.

The new rules applied to everyone and were good news to anyone serious about pursuing promotion. New promotional tests were composed and given, and the empty positions that had accumulated during the freeze were immediately filled. The other fire fighter on my shift with whom I had been studying came out thirty-first on the list. Thirty-one lieutenants were made immediately. He had come in the fire academy class before mine and was just eligible; I was just shy of the time required to take the test for lieutenant. There was no way I was ready to be a lieutenant anyway, but I was thrilled when I made the promotion to pump operator immediately.

After a rewarding stint as the P.O. of a busy engine company where I was fortunate to have great officers and to learn a lot, the day came when I could take a lieutenant's exam. Years of studying paid off when I made lieutenant on the first attempt. Finally, I could show my wife why I took books everywhere we went and studied every spare minute. Taking along the studying materials to your in-laws' house, to the doctor's office, even on vacation may sound a bit obsessive but...Well, yeah, actually I guess it is.

That respect that I would get from putting on the badge was the easy part, at least easier. Suddenly young officers were appearing and the organizational culture was threatened. A number of guys from my fire academy class were very smart and highly motivated. Together we formed a new wave of officers moving up the ranks—young officers, very young officers. The day I walked into my first assignment as a new lieutenant I began to understand the threat we must have posed to the established way of thinking.

As luck would have it, I was assigned to Engine 15 at the department's new downtown "superhouse." There would be no little group, no intimate single company of a half dozen guys to accept me. Steadman Station was the city's replacement for a number of downtown fire stations many years past their prime. Those stations had been built when response distances were gauged on how far the horses could pull the heavy steam engines. Modern apparatus would allow one centrally located station to replace four. The huge apparatus bays fronted on two different streets and housed enough equipment to protect the downtown area.

Here, where I would try to blend in unnoticed, were three engine companies, a truck company, a heavy rescue company, a two-man snorkel company, a two-man air cascade/ flood-light/foam unit, a medic unit, and a battalion chief with his aide. My pump operator could have been my grandfather; the senior fire fighter on my shift, the guy who would act lieutenant in my absence had been doing the acting longer than I had been alive. Oh man!

That first morning at change of shifts, wearing my new silver lieutenant's collar pins for all to see, I confidently strode into the kitchen, a kitchen bigger than some McDonalds. Clustered at tables drinking coffee and reading newspapers were many of the strangers I needed to meet. In the U shaped food preparation area lined with sinks, refrigerators and stoves others milled about waiting their turns at the coffee machine. I looked longingly for a familiar face; about all I got were a few stares and raised eyebrows. There among the guys seeking coffee was my target: Battalion Chief Charles "Chicken Neck" Loughlin stood with his head cocked listening to somebody relating an obviously funny story. Crusty, old Chief Loughlin was widely known, sort of a legend, definitely a character, and by all accounts a good chief. It would be an honor to work with him, I was sure.

And then it was time for one of those poignant moments forever etched on my brain. "Chief Loughlin?" I inquired, my hand outstretched.

"Yeeeeaaaaah?" came the drawn out, reluctant, somewhat quizzical reply accompanied by an unmistakable look of disdain and definitely louder than it needed to be.

"I'm Mike Kernan, sir, your new lieutenant on Engine 15." The words just sort of hung out there for an eternity like a bad line in some *Naked Gun*-type movie. My hand and arm felt like they weighed a hundred pounds and pointed out in space as I contemplated a graceful escape.

My new chief turned away ninety degrees, stared at the floor, and shook his head slowly.

"How old are you, Lieutenant?" came the delayed response, louder still.

"Twenty-four, sir." It seemed so inadequate, but hey I would be twenty-five in just a few months.

Slowly the chief offered his hand, obviously mulling his official welcome. He shook my hand silently, took a step back, gave a little "double-take" look and declared, now loud enough for everyone to hear, "Well...I ain't gonna change yer fuckin' diaper!"

Great beginning.

Actually, the assignment turned out to be a good experience where I learned a lot and made many friends still in the department today. We occasionally have a good laugh over the old days at Steadman Station and over Chief Loughlin, whose bark was far worse than his bite. His stories have outlived him. After a few particularly nasty fires, including two in old, downtown warehouses, the chief saw past my youth. I was very pleased when he privately told me he was glad to have me working for him. I was very pleased when he gave me an annual performance rating that was very good and included some nice written comments. And I was honored when Chief Loughlin tried hard to keep me there after the year I was required to stay in my new assignment. Reluctantly, he had to admit that downtown was where the action used to be, not where it was, and certainly not where it was going to be. With all of the urban renewal, the face of downtown Baltimore was changing. Old loft buildings and century-old stores were methodically being replaced by modern high rises and office buildings. The huge, spectacular and challenging building fires were becoming rarer as the bulk of the department's daily activities radiated outwards. Learning means going to fires, and I wanted to learn everything I could about being a good company officer. Chief Loughlin grudgingly accepted my desire to transfer to the third busiest engine company in the city, back on the city's northwest side where I felt at home.

I was equally honored when my new chief, who had also been my first chief, Pete O'Connor, warmly greeted me and told me how glad he was to have me back as one of his lieutenants. I felt I was beginning to earn the silver bugles I wore with pride. My time at Engine 52 would provide me with many, many opportunities to learn and to earn the respect of the guys I worked with. I was blessed with a terrific crew who made it easy for me to look good. Transferring to Engine 52 was a great move, one that made me feel better about my promotion to captain which was to follow the next year.

Almost exclusively riding the engine companies throughout my career, I was a little apprehensive taking over as the captain of a truck company, and a very busy truck company at that. At least I knew some of the guys a bit and was familiar with some of their response area. My new assignment was in a station adjacent to Engine 52 on the city's very busy west side.

Like most of the plans I've made in my life, the first day didn't work out exactly as I had planned. My plan called for me to assemble my crew after the morning line-up and ease my way in. Admitting that I was a transplanted engine company guy, I would listen carefully to how they had worked under the previous captain. Walking around the truck with them, I would learn the location of all the various equipment carried and begin the exchange of information I was confident would prepare me for the trial by fire that would eventually come. Sounded like a solid plan to me.

The gong struck before I had walked twenty steps into the morning stillness of the dark apparatus floor. Lights illuminated the old open cab Peter Pirsch ladder truck as the poles began to shed fire fighters. Runs at the change of shifts can be a little confusing as each guy whose relief has come in scrambles to pull his turnout gear off the truck and the oncoming guys scurry to make sure they have everything they need.

"Hi, Captain, I'm Lieutenant Fryer," came the hurried greeting from the body stretched up into the cab removing his gear to make room for me.

My official greeting to my new driver was even less momentous: "Know where we're going?" I shot in his direction.

"Yessir, but don't worry. We'll follow the engine anyway."

It only took me one long uphill pull to Edmondson Village to understand why the engine didn't want to be stuck behind us.

Listening to the information repeated over the radio as we responded, I tried to anticipate what we would face. I didn't know the area where we were going; didn't know the construction type we would most likely encounter. Didn't know even who was on the truck with me, much less what their individual and collective abilities might be. I didn't know how they operated; didn't know where anything was on the truck.

Oh, this should be a piece of cake.

Heading down the dark Hilton Parkway, following behind the engine and Battalion Chief 7—yet another chief for me now—I sincerely hoped the reported dwelling fire would be nothing. Wrong again. The familiar voice of our fire officers' team second baseman and lieutenant on Engine 53 calmly announced that they were on the scene with heavy smoke showing.

Terrific.

Soon the message followed that there was a report of people still trapped within the dwelling.

Oh great. It just keeps getting better.

Arriving as the second truck company on the scene, our responsibility was to cover the rear of the row house which belched hot clouds of dark gray smoke visible even in the morning darkness. Engine company hoselines were already stretched front and back as we carried the portable ladders by hand down the narrow alley. Getting a hundred foot aerial ladder truck down the rear alleys of many of the city's streets is impossible, but fire fighters still must get to the rear by whatever means possible.

Truck 8, already in the front street, had begun the ventilation of the front and was attempting entry. Fire that had begun in the basement and was blowing from the first floor front was impeding their progress. In the rear, the hose from the engine company disappeared into the smoky blackness of the kitchen doorway, a swirling curtain which separated safety from horror for anyone still inside.

As I finished putting my air mask into operation, one of my new coworkers quickly disappeared into the tempest to join the engine company in their movement toward the fire threatening to spread through the remainder of the house. Above me the sound of breaking glass told me the windows were responding to the actions of my other guys. Removing the windows would help channel some of the heated smoke out of the building and improve the chances we could locate anyone still inside. Ascending the ladder the guys had quickly positioned two of us (I didn't even know the other guy yet) quickly dropped through the window opening into a second floor bedroom. The bedrooms might well contain occupants overcome while sleeping or while trying to escape.

Dense smoke and medium heat met us as we dropped to the floor and began to search. We quickly began the search process that all fire fighters learn. Check just inside the windows where someone may have been overcome just shy of escape. Stay along the outside walls; use a methodical search pattern to avoid missing any areas and to avoid wasting time by covering ground already searched. Time is critical in a situation like this for the safety of those trapped and for the rescuers themselves. They could become trapped if the fire were to spread upstairs before the engine companies could contain it. Sweep everywhere, using a tool to extend your reach. Look on the beds and under the beds where children might be hiding. Look in the closets, in the bath tub where someone might have tried to escape the nightmare.

Meeting up with the other truck guys who had come in through the front windows, we soon determined there was nobody to be found on the second floor. In fact, there were no victims to be found that morning—the best possible outcome. After the usual overhauling and other fireground activities it was back to the firehouse and the start of another experience.

The next couple of years would bring many fires of all kinds and teach me much about operating as the officer on the truck company. It was a challenging and rewarding time and it wasn't long before my truck company felt right. It was a functioning team long before I arrived and I easily fit in. Before long, the place felt like home and I settled in, confident that I had found my niche. Being a captain felt pretty good. Good crew, excellent chiefs to work with, busy company with plenty of action. This must be the niche I've been seeking.

Silly me.

8
Why I Hate Winter: Reason #854

People love to talk about the weather. It's a harmless way of having a discussion with a stranger. Someone might take offense at talk of religion, politics, or our involvement in the latest overseas conflict. Sports or current local events might hold no interest to the other party. But the weather is something we all have in common, and it's a pretty neutral subject. We've all heard the joke: Everybody talks about the weather, but nobody ever does anything about it.

For fire fighters, though, weather is no joke. The extremes of heat and cold which the average citizen finds inconvenient and uncomfortable take on a whole new meaning when fire strikes.

Heat and humidity make just the thought of wearing all the fire fighter's protective gear unpleasant. Performing the stressful, physically intensive labor of an emergency operation in such an outfit is quite a challenge. My cousin from Denver got off the plane at Baltimore-Washington International Airport a few years ago and immediately clutched his hands to his throat. "What did you do with all the air?" he greeted me. Seemed pretty normal to me.

Fighting fires in the bitter sub-zero winter nights is an experience that few fire fighters relish. Each winter I see the pictures from Chicago and the upper midwest, and I'm glad I live in Baltimore. Our winters can be bad, but I'd feel guilty complaining too loudly when I think of what the fire fighters in those *really* cold climates face.

Thunderstorms, tornadoes, hurricanes, and floods all have a special meaning to fire fighters. They mean danger to the fire fighter and to those that he or she is sworn to protect.

Indeed, the weather is of more than passing interest to fire fighters. To us the weather is not neutral. It is always something to be considered and frequently something to be reckoned with.

"Winter storm warning for today and tonight," was the weatherman's prediction as I listened to the morning radio on my day off. Maybe this time the snow would be something I could enjoy rather than something I would have to deal with at work. With two young kids and a dog who loved snow, the storms that fell on my off-duty days were a lot of fun.

The woods behind our house are particularly beautiful when snow decorates the trees and bushes. In the field next to our house it would be fun to play in the fresh snow, build snowmen, or just look for the tracks of the first animals to wander out after the snow had ended. Mixed with the pleasant anticipation of the fun that the snow would bring was the knowledge that the next morning I would be on the road driving to get to work. I hoped the snow wouldn't be too bad.

Throughout the morning and the early afternoon, the snow fell and the neighborhood traffic slowed. The occasional cars moved much more slowly up the road, and the snowplows tried to keep up as the snow accumulated rapidly.

By early afternoon the predictions of snow had included increasing amounts of accumulation, blowing and drifting snow, and eventually the word "blizzard" crept into the weather report. Now the fun part of the snowstorm gave way to the concerns of the implications of the deteriorating weather. The forecasts were getting more ominous as the storm stalled over our area and intensified.

Sense of duty is one of the things that makes me proud to be a part of the Baltimore City Fire Department. It would never occur to a fire fighter to just not go to work because of a snowstorm. Night shift people were already making their way to their stations. Those of us who were due to report the next morning were already formulating plans. The forecasts didn't make it sound like the early morning commute would be a picnic. Heavy snow and wind would likely continue much of the night. Conditions were going to get worse before they got better.

Years of being a fire fighter's wife had prepared my wife for the decision. She understood when I announced that I was heading in early—about fourteen hours early. The only problem was how to get there. I knew that neither our Mustang nor our van with its light rear end would have a chance in the deep snow. Fortunately, my friend and neighbor, Pete Fiset, thought it a great opportunity to go "four wheeling" and jumped at my petition to take me to work. Loaded up with extra clothes and food, we soon found ourselves on the Beltway headed towards the city. We were one of the few vehicles on the road during what would normally be the evening rush hour. Even the snowplows had given up the impossible task of trying to stay ahead of the storm. They would now wait until the storm subsided to begin again to clear the roads.

When we got into the city we were amazed at how deep the snow was. Usually the city doesn't get quite as much snow as the suburbs, but the roads were almost impassable, even with Pete's four wheel drive vehicle. Cars stuck hopelessly in the drifting snow littered the streets where they had been abandoned and forced us to try route after route toward the west side of town where I was stationed.

The fun of driving in the snow gave way to the realization that this was not your ordinary storm. This had become a dangerous, crippling blizzard. The snow fell hard and the wind howled as we reached the end of the line. Finally we had exhausted the possibilities. Abandoned cars, trucks and even busses blocked every street we tried. "You sure you'll be alright?" Pete asked sincerely as I gathered my things for the long walk ahead.

"I'm fine. I just hope you can get home OK," I replied as

I left the warm jeep and felt the bitter wind.

Mondawmin Mall looked eerily silent. Normally bustling with shoppers at this hour, the vast shopping center parking lots held only a few cars transformed into snow-covered blobs. The street lights that normally illuminated the parking lot were little specks of light as the blowing snow nearly obscured them. I pulled my stocking cap down over my ears and began the trudge through the snow that was already well above my knees.

A mile and a half doesn't sound like a long way—unless you're walking in a blizzard. The battle through the snow, wind and cold carrying my things was no stroll in the park. Determined to make the best time possible, I plodded through the nearly deserted residential neighborhoods. No traffic moved and only a few times did I see anybody outside. The silence was broken only by the wind and the snow. No traffic noises, no kids playing, not even the distant wail of sirens so common to the large urban setting.

Once I reached the commercial area on North Avenue, though, the picture changed. Groups of bundled-up people were on the sidewalks in front of the stores. Here and there the voices exchanged heated words, muffled by the blowing snow. It took me a few minutes to realize what was going on. These folks had realized that the police department was immobilized and decided to take advantage.

The sound of breaking glass was muted by the weather, but it was a sound that I instantly recognized. Looters braved the bitter weather to smash the store windows, dash inside, and remove the clothing, food, liquor, furniture, and televisions. There weren't the large crowds that cities saw during the riots of the late sixties. The weather made it darned hard to have a party atmosphere. Determined people got what they wanted and trudged, head down, into the bitter wind. I felt uneasy as I walked through the area, not knowing whether to expect violence this night. Fortunately, the residents were more intent on doing a little free shopping that on causing harm to anyone.

North Avenue was clogged by cars and busses abandoned

in the deep, blowing snow. No traffic at all moved on this major street. Whole intersections were blocked by mounds of pristine snow that vaguely took the shape of the vehicles underneath.

A sense of relief accompanied the warmth and light of the firehouse as I shook the snow off me just inside the front door. *Safe*!

I could see the melting snow dripping off the bottom of Truck 18, my company. The soggy clumps of half-melted slush and the wet coats hanging on the side of the truck told me that they had just come back in from the storm. The chief's car sat alone in the other bay. Engine 20 was nowhere in sight. The department radio was squawking as I wound my way up the black, metal, spiral staircase toward the noises of the upstairs.

"Hey, Cap" came the greetings as soon as I hit the top step. The promise of warm coffee tempted me, but first I sought out the on-duty truck officer. John O., my very sincere and dedicated lieutenant, reluctantly agreed to go home early after I convinced him that there was no sense in our both staying. Bundled up against the elements, he soon headed out into the night, and I joined the other on-duty members in the warm kitchen.

"Second alarm," the speaker in the kitchen announced. Down on Fremont Avenue other companies were battling the weather and a lumberyard fire. Fires in that type of facility are dangerous, fast-spreading events on the best of nights. Tonight's weather would make the job even worse. We all listened intently, hoping that the fire would not get worse. Two alarms would not get us in town that far, but any more and we might be headed out into the cold. I was just starting to warm up.

The truck guys quickly filled me in on their night so far. They hadn't seen the engine company for hours. Each company had been on the street almost constantly, fighting the weather and the congested streets more than fighting fire. Fortunately, the runs had been for relatively minor calls.

Automatic alarms, power lines down, and similar calls had kept the companies on the move. So many stranded vehicles littered the streets that moving from one area to another was a real challenge. Detours around the blocked streets caused response times to grow dramatically. So far it had not made any serious difference.

In a few short minutes we were headed to the fourth alarm on Fremont Avenue. On a good day this response would take less than ten minutes. This was definitely not a good day. North Avenue was completely blocked at Dukeland Street by three transit company busses that had tried unsuccessfully to defy the growing snowfall only to become hopelessly mired.

We traveled down to Lafayette and another possible route to take us into town. Again, we found the street completely blocked by huge snowdrifts and abandoned cars. Again and again we detoured and encountered obstacles at every turn.

Finally, we found a street we could use but the snow was over the truck's running boards. We plowed through the best we could, but even this powerful, massive fire truck was no match for the snow. Stuck hopelessly in the snowdrifts, we got out our shovels and struggled to clear some of the snow from in front of the wheels to get some forward movement again.

My earlier anger with the residents of the neighborhood gave way to a new appreciation as neighbor after neighbor joined us in the struggle to free the fire truck. Soon we had a dozen shovel-wielding people helping us yard by yard down the street. When we could get up a little momentum, we would be able to go thirty or forty feet before we were bogged down again. Then the shovel workers dug furiously to get us free again. It was a great feeling to have the crowds jumping in to help, and slowly we made progress toward the fire.

For over an hour we fought our way through the streets that way until finally we were unable to go any farther. Four blocks from the fire we had exhausted all options and decided to trek the rest of the way on foot. We grabbed our tools and set off toward the smoke. I felt satisfied that we had given it our best shot. The vehicle that now lay as the insurmountable obstacle was one of the truck companies due on the first alarm. This was as far as they had gotten. I didn't feel quite as bad.

At the fire, the companies had been able to overcome the difficulties presented by the storm and had the fire contained. When we reported finally to the chief and briefly explained our delay, he gave us an assignment to relieve some of the guys already working on the fire. What had been a pretty serious fire was now just plain old "bullwork." We had missed all the excitement and challenge and the satisfaction of doing a good job on a difficult fire. Not only did we miss out on the action, we had to endure the kidding of our comrades.

"What'd you guys come on, the twelfth alarm for Christ's sake? We could've walked barefoot from Twenty Engine faster than you guys got here."

We shot back some smart answer about their needing the practice or something, and we all had a good laugh. Each of us knew the true story, but in the fire service you never miss a chance to needle someone.

The fire was good for another laugh as well. At the time, my friend, Mike Moritz, was a lieutenant on Truck 13. We used to get mistaken for one another all the time— though he claimed to be much better looking. In those days we were both young, blonde curly-haired truck officers. Today we're both officers.

I noticed that the deputy chief's aide kept looking at me a little funny, but I figured that came from being old or something. "Old" in those days was a lot different than today. Finally he couldn't stand it any longer. "Didn't I just see you on the other side of the building?" He paused with a quizzical look. "And weren't you a lieutenant?" My guys got a huge laugh from that one and retold the story for weeks. I'm not sure anybody ever told the deputy's aide the true story.

Back through the snow covered streets and toward the warmth of our station we headed. At least this time we had an idea of the streets to avoid. The snow had given way to flurries, but the biting wind made it a miserable night. We were all delighted when we made it all the way back to the station without picking up another run.

Once again there was no sign of the engine company. This led one of the guys to suggest that we throw some of the spare hose on the truck "just in case." A quick search of the hose tower turned up only two sections of one and a half inch hose—not much to work with but maybe it would come in handy. Since the changeover to synthetic hose that could be loaded back onto the engine without drying there was no longer any need to keep spare hose in station. No spare nozzle was available either but a phone call to nearby Engine 36 secured the promise of one. "We'll see you before the night's out or we'll swing by if we're in your area," I told them, not putting any real priority to the acquisition of a nozzle. The chances of a truck needing one were slim.

It didn't take long before we were headed out into the cold again. "Ellamont and Normount," yelled the man on watch as we slid the pole. Someone had pulled the street box in a residential neighborhood south of us. We could be headed out to anything. The snow was so deep that I knew we would never be able to get the truck into the small streets. A couple of blocks from the box we dismounted and began the process of wading through waist deep snow to get to the box. The wind blown snow tore at us as we made our way slowly towards—what? Part of me was miffed that some slob was actually out pulling a flase alarm on a night like this. The other part was relieved that there was no fire. I had no idea what we would do if we had encountered something serious. The closest we could get apparatus was several blocks away. Back to the truck we headed, cursing the weather and the guy who brought us out into it again.

"OK, Truck 18, you respond..." came the dispatcher's instruction as soon as we got back to the truck and went in service. In a minute we were headed back north again passing within a block of the station. "Building fire at Windsor Mill and Chelsea Terrace" had been the information. We all hoped that it wasn't going to be serious. The weather meant that we couldn't see any smoke ahead. In front of us we could just make out the chief's car as Battalion Chief 7 headed for the same fire.

One set of tire tracks led the way as we followed the same route as the chief. Nothing else was moving on the streets tonight. We could see the smoke when we were a couple of blocks away. The white smoke could mean anything tonight. When it is bitterly cold, smoke frequently turns white regardless of what is burning, and man was it cold.

The chief's car slowed in the one set of tire tracks that led up the street and we caught up in time to help move the debris out of the street in front of us both. Looters had emptied the grocery store that was now burning ferociously. The discarded items, including the vending machines they had dragged into the street and ravaged, were strewn in the snow covered street. Apparently satisfied with their work, the looters had left. Not a soul poked a head out as we pulled up to the blazing corner store.

Fire had heavily involved the store and threatened to spread in the wind. Fortunately, the building and the apartment building adjoining it were brick. Unfortunately, the only things on the scene were the chief's car and the truck company. And as the engine guys always smugly remind their truck company counterparts, "You can't beat it out with ladders."

We quickly set about doing the things that truck guys do. We got ladders into place where we could, careful not to put them where they would be damaged before an engine could arrive and get water on the fire. We entered the apartment building next door and routed the people inside. Some were reluctant to leave at first, but when we pointed out the smoke already seeping through the walls in the hallway they quickly cooperated. Nobody wanted to brave the elements tonight, but when the fire department tells you to get out, you go.

Bob Williams, the battalion chief, stood patiently in the front street watching the situation and contemplating the next move.

"Well, is it in there yet?" he inquired as I approached him to report.

"Not yet, but it's only a matter of time. We can see the fire through the cracks in the wall where the floor joists go through," was my pessimistic reply.

Uncharacteristically calm for Bob, he just shook his head resignedly. We all knew the situation was not good. With no engines on the scene we were very limited in the actions that we could take, and the fire was threatening to spread. Flames churned throughout the store feeding on the combustibles still left inside and on the building's walls, floors, and now its roof. Flames blew from every window leaping into the night and lighting up the whole neighborhood. With the terrible road conditions and the high level of activity in the department, there was no telling how long it would be before an engine company arrived.

With the fire threatening to take the apartment building next door, we decided on an unusual approach. Duff, the tillerman, hooked the hose that we had thrown onto the truck "just in case" to the hydrant on the corner. We stretched it as far as it would reach and charged the line. We looked a little foolish standing there with no nozzle on the hose, lobbing water the best we could at the front of the building where the wind bent the flames toward the apartment building. Adapting to the situation, Duff put his hand over the coupling like you would do to your garden hose. That gave him just enough reach. Strange as it seemed, the water was helping a little to delay the spread of the fire.

Through the darkness came the welcome sight of apparatus warning lights as the arriving company made its way up the single set of tire tracks as we had. What a disappointment when we realized that the help that had just arrived was Truck 8, another non-water carrying company. We continued with the only attack method that we had, hoping that an engine would arrive in time.

Fortunately, Engine 30 arrived shortly after the truck, plodding through the deep snow in the single file that we all formed on the street. Because we could only form a single file on the street, they would be behind the chief's car and two one-hundred foot tractor trailer ladder trucks. When we looked down the street we could see that they had stopped a block away to lay hose from the next hydrant. Before we could get the message to them they had already laid about two hundred feet in the snow. They were unaware that we were using the hydrant on the corner near the fire for a stop-gap holding action and that we had planned to shut the hydrant down so that they could use it.

With the message communicated to them, the plan went into full swing. They drove the rest of the way up the street and positioned behind Truck 8 as guys carried and dragged the hose already trailing behind them. Then, the guys dragged the hose up toward the hydrant we were using and the switch was ready. Even though our pathetic stream of water wasn't much, it was helping a little, so the plan was to keep that going until the last minute. Then a fire fighter would shut the hydrant, we would disconnect our small line, put the cap back on that opening on the hydrant, remove the cap on the big opening, attach E-30's hydrant connection, and turn the hydrant back on. This would give the water to Engine 30 and we could make a real attack on the fire. Sounded like a good plan to all of us.

Snap. The operating nut of the hydrant now spun freely, controlling nothing. The operating stem had broken due to the frigid temperatures. The hydrant was on and was going to remain on. There was no way for us to connect the supply to E-30 now. Instead, we were relegated to using our pathetic "thumb-over-the-end " hose stream.

Down, but not out, we quickly assembled all the available fire fighters to drag the hose all the way back down the street to that hydrant that Engine 30 had first started to use. Much farther away, it still offered the next best solution. Through the waist-deep snow, the fire fighters struggled with the heavy three inch hose, looping it over shoulders, across chests, under arms, however they could use their body weight to drag it through the drifts. Finally, the end of the line reached the hydrant and was connected. The other end of the line was attached to the pump panel and . . . *nothing*. The hydrant was frozen. There would be no water coming from it without major work to get it thawed.

The bad situation just kept getting worse. Plan B had just gone down the tubes and the fire continued to engulf the store. Flames burst through the roof into the night sky and reflected off the snow-covered trees and cars. It seemed as though the fire would never go out. Still, at the front of the building, the fire lapped at the wall separating the store from the apartment building and the wind forced it ever closer, but the little stream of water thrown in its way was holding at the key spot. Incredibly, the fire had not yet moved into the adjacent building.

On Gwynns Falls Parkway, a very long block to the North, we could make out the lights of another engine company who had finally been able to negotiate the blocked streets and was at another hydrant. The street between them and us was virgin snowdrifts. No person, no vehicle had been up that block where the winds had sculpted the snow into a most formidable obstacle. The snow was so deep that there was no way that the engine would be able to drive down the street and lay hose, so Chief Williams quickly formulated Plan C.

Once again all of the available manpower assembled to hand-carry the heavy hose through the waist deep snow. Assured that this hydrant was working, the men dragged and carried the hose until the water supply was finally established. While all of this was taking place, the fire continued to burn furiously and the weak stream of water directed at that one key spot kept the fire from wrapping around the wall and forcing its way into the building next door. It was to be a long, bitter night for all of us as ice coated every ladder and tool, and each piece of hose froze as soon as the water stopped flowing, but as we say with typical fire service insight, "They all go out eventually." This fire was yet another tribute to the effectiveness of brick construction. Thank heavens these buildings were not wood frame.

Many areas of the city had experienced similar problems with looters and arson that night. The police commissioner even took to the streets on horseback in a rather symbolic attempt to reassure the public that the police were in control. The city learned some valuable lessons from this blizzard. The police and fire departments looked at their troubles in getting around and began to equip the forces with four-wheel drive vehicles. Four years later, when a similar blizzard hit Baltimore, the departments were better prepared, and there was no repeat of the lawlessness.

Shortly before daybreak, we finally made our way back to the station, bone tired and bitterly cold. We had been on the streets almost constantly for the last twelve hours, and the end of the shift was a welcome thought. As I took off my frozen turnout coat and hung it on the apparatus door to thaw, one of the day shift guys walked by with a cheery "Mornin', Cap." And then it hit me. This was *my* shift arriving for work. My ten hour day shift was just about to start!

9

Another Niche

Chief. The very word connotes a powerful, wise leader. To a new firefighter a chief is like a god. The fire department's paramilitary structure carefully details the chain of command so critical to everyday functions and to emergency operations. Down at the bottom of the food chain, the fire fighter deals directly with the other non-officers and his company officer. Being around and talking with the lieutenant or the captain becomes a normal part of everyday firehouse life. That company officer is the boss, but also a member of the operating crew at each incident. He's there helping on the hose or the ladder, carrying the oxygen at a medical call, or operating the tools at a rescue. On the other hand, the chief officers, the ones with the crossed bugles on their collars and the white coats and helmets on the fireground, are more removed from the firefighter. The lieutenants and captains, the company officers, report directly to the battalion chief. My early dealings with my battalion chief were pretty positive, but not all fire fighters are so lucky. "Going to see the chief" rarely means good things to a new fire fighter. Hardly what you would term a social call, such a visit usually resulted from an infraction of some fire department regulation.

As a new recruit at the fire academy, I quickly determined I didn't want to go visiting. Being singled out by an instructor and called down was bad enough. Being dragged before the chief was a step far more intimidating. I tried very hard to limit the number of times I ever heard my name called out loud. "Wil-*son*!" was the resounding call that punctuated my class' daily fire academy ritual. Finding new ways each day to frustrate the instructors and buck the system, this same recruit seemed to spend an inordinate amount of time parading into the secretive and unsettling confines of the chief's office. We were all amazed he graduated with the rest of us. Not for me, I didn't care if the chief even knew my name.

Once we had graduated from the fire academy and were assigned to companies, the situation changed and my battalion chief, Pete O'Connor, became the first chief I actually got to know. Each day of the day shift he would arrive in the morning, driven by his popular and friendly aide. In Baltimore, whenever a chief officer enters the station, the person on watch trips the large gong once signaling all to assemble near the watch desk for line up and inspection. During his visits Chief O'Connor sometimes briefed us on recent problems or developments in the battalion or the department. Afterwards, as we non-officers made our way back to the fire station duties, the chief frequently consulted further with our company officers. Things always seemed to be handled pretty professionally, but I idly wondered what all the discussions were about.

Battalion chiefs may have seemed divine to me, but even the chief gets days off. When the battalion chief is off sick or on vacation or is away on some other duty, the job doesn't go unfilled. Captain Klossman, the captain of one of the battalion's truck companies, was the first acting battalion chief on our shift. If Chief O'Connor was away, this Archie Bunker look-alike would assume the role of acting battalion chief. Perpetually grumpy and on edge, the captain's personality and demeanor were quite different from our chief's. Things were never quite the same when the captain was "in the car." He swore we saved up all of the trouble we could cause until he was in charge. I don't think that was true. For example, I'm sure there was no ill intent that autumn as we decorated the fire station for Fire Prevention Week.

Each year, around the anniversary of the Great Chicago Fire and another tragic fire the same time in the forests of

Wisconsin, fire departments all over the country observe Fire Prevention Week. Painstaking efforts are made to get out the word of fire safety and to reinforce the lessons preached all year. Firefighters visit schools, supervise fire safety poster contests, conduct fire drills, put on demonstrations of their equipment and skills, and encourage citizens to visit their local fire stations. Many fire stations display signs touting fire safety slogans. Some of the fire fighters are pretty creative in decorating the outside of their stations with eye-catching, thought-provoking fire safety messages.

It seemed like a good idea. This year there would be none of the mundane, big, thermometer-type signs indicating the total fire deaths in the city. No dummies made up to look like victims of a home fire tragedy would do. And a downscaled house with fake smoke and fire coming from the windows lacked imagination. No, this time the guys at Engine 45 and Truck 27 thought they had the perfect Fire Prevention Week display. They'd put the whole firehouse on display—or the lack of it. "Wouldn't it be great if the fire prevention was so good that there was no need for a fire station in the neighborhood anymore?" Sounded like a terrific goal and a great idea.

Armed with 2x4's, hammer, nails, and a saw, some of the guys started the work at the front doors. Others fashioned the big sign that would adorn the front of the fire station with the wonderful news. What a great display. Wouldn't the department officials be proud?

Whenever the chief's car rolled to a stop in front of the station in the middle of the afternoon there was a sense of foreboding, especially when Captain Klossman was in the car. *Bonnnnggggg* reverberated the gong, sending everybody scrambling to the poles and sliding to the apparatus floor below. "Why me? Why me?" the captain slowly muttered as we all assembled into a straight line. His hanging head told us all that once again this wasn't a social call. And if that weren't enough, the red face that signaled his repressed anger gave the next clue. "What the hell is wrong with you guys?" he began.

"Have you lost your minds?" Dumbfounded, we listened as he related the phone call he had just received from a very irate deputy chief. Our best intentions had backfired. One thing was certain, we had definitely gotten the community's attention. The great idea had indeed been noticed.

On the two apparatus bay doors at the front of the station—doors that swung outwards to allow the engine and truck to exit—were 2x4's in an **X** shape. The wood appeared to be holding the doors as though they were nailed shut. In reality, of course, the wood was cut at the point where the doors met to allow them to swing open and closed unobstructed. But the key to the effect was the big sign that adorned the front of the firehouse: **CLOSED FOR LACK OF BUSINESS**.

Needless to say, in order to stop the barrage of frantic phone calls downtown after neighbors passed the station we were immediately ordered to remove the fire prevention display. The poor captain had the responsibility of investigating and responding to the flood of complaints. The story of the "closed" fire station soon spread throughout the department and was cause for more than a few laughs, though not many of them seemed to come from downtown. The story of the memorable Fire Prevention Week display would be funny enough, but the strangest part wasn't the citizens who were fooled by the sign. Headed in with his wife to pick up his paycheck was Jim Polankowsky, one of the ambulance guys on the shift. Jim had been off duty for quite a while due to injuries he had received in an accident. We missed Jim not just because he was a nice guy, but because he was the kind of guy who was funny without trying. All of us laughed at the incredibly stupid things the man did and said with the utmost sincerity. It probably shouldn't have surprised anyone when we found out that Jim had turned around and gone home when he had seen the sign saying the firehouse was closed. His phone call later in the day seriously inquiring where he should pick up his paycheck was the crowning touch.

Captain Klossman was an unexpected visitor on a number

of occasions when he was acting battalion chief. Another of his most livid moments involved the mysterious weather front. At that first station of mine long ago the day's non-emergency activities were well planned. Each day the battalion schedule clearly indicated which companies would do building inspections, which companies would have in-station training on prescribed topics, and which companies would go out into their districts to inspect their fire hydrants. Other companies would go to neighborhoods and ask residents if they wished for fire fighters to walk through their homes with them pointing out potential fire problems. Still other sessions were allocated for driver training, training not only in the skills of actually driving, but in the procedures for operating the pumps on the engines and the aerial ladder on the truck companies. Time slots in the morning and afternoon were determined at the battalion office and pretty much non-negotiable.

The unofficial activities of the day were much more flexible, depending greatly on who happened to be working. While some guys liked to read, others would rather watch the soap operas. Some of the guys enjoyed the pool table while others just tinkered and talked. But it was the card players on the shift who were the most dedicated recreationalists. No sooner had the housework been completed than the cry went up for the players to assemble upstairs at the card table. If left alone, the card players would sit for hours hooting and hollering and having a great time. Any response, or even a telephone call for one of the participants, was viewed as an unwelcome interruption to the very important work at hand.

One memorable day, a frequent visitor to the firehouse, Mort, was the fourth card player for the day. Not actually a member of the department, Mort was an older man who was a devoted fire department buff and former auxiliary fire fighter. His amazing knowledge of the fire department's history, gained over a lifetime, easily surpassed all of ours. During the Second World War many of the Morts in Baltimore helped staff the fire department as many of its regulars went off to serve. Now Mort was relegated to playing cards with the guys, recounting fascinating stories—some might even have been true!—and trying to impress us with the "pull" he purported to have.

The usual afternoon of cards had begun and the players were engrossed as the time for building inspection approached. The only events that would cause the department to postpone all of the non-emergency activities scheduled for the afternoon would be an additional alarm fire somewhere in the city or inclement weather, in which case an announcement would be made canceling all outdoor activities. The bells were quiet; no distant fire would save the day. A few clouds dotted the sky, but no rain promised to save the card game from a premature ending. Since the day's card game was a particularly hot one, talk turned to performing a rain dance or conjuring up some other miracle to avoid going out on inspection. In the spirit of the card game underway, somebody decided to call Mort's bluff: "Hey Mort, if you know so many important guys downtown, why don't you call down there and get us out of building inspection so we can keep playing?" The challenge was irresistible. It was Mort's turn to deliver.

However, Mort's influence didn't seem to run quite as deep as he had portrayed. The captain at our communications office was a little skeptical of Mort's request. According to Mort, the truck lieutenant was a little reluctant to call downtown to report this since no announcement had been made, but it was raining. Out here on the outskirts of the city, light rain was falling and the guys really shouldn't have to go out in the rain. That was Mort's plea to his "buddy" at communications, the one with whom he had all that drag.

The cynical captain called Engine 44's station, the station east of Engine 45. "How's the weather out there?" he innocently inquired. Informed that it was sunny and pleasant, the captain checked the station to the west.

"Red car!" yelled the man on watch as he threw the gong at the unexpected sight of the acting battalion chief pulling to a stop at the front of the station. Soon, we were all lined up listening attentively as Captain Klossman once again shook his head in disgust. "Jeez, Cap, those guys downtown must have misunderstood. We were just trying to help. We said it looked like it might be gonna rain. We didn't want the lieutenant here gettin' in any trouble by going out when he shouldn't," Flockie offered with a sincerity in his voice that would have made Lyndon Johnson proud.

"Boy, and that's the thanks you get for try'n to help," added another terribly offended card shark.

Crimson-faced, the acting battalion chief stared disbelievingly before he began his trademark headshake. "Why don't you guys ever pull this crap when the chief's here?"   P o o r Mort was banned from card playing at the firehouse for a spell, but worse for him was the tarnished image he suffered that day. His stories were never the same after that.

It was many years later that I had a chance to experience the frustrations of an acting battalion chief. As a captain, I had received the training that allowed me to qualify as an acting battalion chief. Eventually the opportunities for me to act as the battalion chief rolled around. I experienced some rather troubling moments, becoming involved in some serious disciplinary matters. And I was acting the day that one of my stations allowed the neighborhood drunk to sleep it off upstairs. Unfortunately, he decided to set the firehouse attic area afire. The guys were pretty creative with that story. It was years before I found out the true version—if even that is the true story!

Progress in any occupation brings with it a new set of problems, and the fire department is a great example. The firehouse apparatus bay doors of my early career were sets of massive, wooden hinged doors that swung outward leaving one door on either side of the opening. Once the last piece of apparatus had cleared somebody had to close the doors. A fire fighter had to grab one side and throw it towards the center, leap to the other side and push that side toward the closed position, then try to stretch wide enough to grab both sides and bring them together at the middle. Then the fire fighter had to secure the doors closed from the outside by releasing a steel rod that sank into the concrete or by moving some kind of bar arrangement into place. Only then could the fire fighter run back to take his place on the waiting apparatus to begin the response.

Push button-controlled overhead doors gradually replaced the other arrangements. The doors were easy to open, quicker, and more secure from unauthorized entry while the company was out. The fire fighters loved them because they only needed to stand by the button controls at the opening to hit the "down" button to close the door. As soon as the time was right, they could hit the button that would begin the descent of the big overhead door. These guys got pretty good at the timing, so good in fact that the apparatus barely had to pause to allow the person to jump on and they were off on their response. Therefore, the new doors improved response times.

The new doors would probably have been a lot more economical too if the department hadn't had to repair or replace them each time a piece of apparatus and a door competed for the same space. Add the cost of repairing the damage to the apparatus and this "progress" became pretty expensive. After excusing a few accidents, the department instituted "foolproof" guidelines. Nobody was to touch the down button, not even to put their hand up at the control box, until the fire apparatus was completely clear of the door opening. But "foolproof" and "firefighter proof" are not always synonymous. Anyone found at fault in another of these accidents was subject to official departmental charges that could lead to a loss of vacation days or to suspensions. In Baltimore any damage to a station or to the apparatus requires an on-scene investigation by the battalion chief who determines any negligence involved and determines the appropriate disciplinary actions that will result. Suspending someone, in effect taking possibly hundreds of dollars out of their pay, is not something to take lightly, so the chief is cautious to explore all possibilities. I was constantly amazed by the explanations offered to me each time I responded to investigate an overhead door incident. My own single experience had not prepared me.

Sitting in the front seat of the long, tractor-trailer ladder truck, I was far removed from the back end of the truck. Busy pulling the map book out to look up the address to which we were headed, I wasn't paying much attention to anything else. As the Engine Company disappeared around the corner, we sat stopped in the middle of North Avenue waiting for the guys to close the station doors and jump on the truck.

"Duff just came through the doors, Cap," blared Rick as he entered the jump seat behind me. Duff was our tillerman.

"OK. You ready?" was my automatic reply. Stupidly, I thought Rick meant that the back end of the long truck was now clear of the door opening.

"Cap, I don't think you understand. Duff just came *through* the doors."

The splintered wood that littered the alcove of the fire station doorway and the sidewalk helped me understand. At least these doors weren't heavy construction and didn't do anything to Duff except give him quite a scare. Some of our tillermen had been injured that way as they raced toward a door that suddenly lowered in front of them. A few inches of descent was all it took to catch the poor tillerman perched up so high on the vehicle. There was no time to react.

As it turned out, John, one of my other fire fighters, readily admitted that in his haste to get going he had hit the down button a little too soon. Then he watched with his heart in his mouth as the tiller cab of the truck smashed the bottom third of the door into pieces. He was greatly relieved to see that Duff was not hurt. That investigation was easy. I found out as acting battalion chief, however, that those involved were not always as forthcoming as John with explanations. Still others offered explanations that stretched the imagination. Most frequently, the explanation for why the door came down too early was some sort of magic: "I swear, Cap, nobody was even near the buttons. Ain't that right, guys?" That makes for a tough investigation.

More creative explanations sometimes accompanied over-head door accidents. Power surges at the most inopportune times, neighborhood kids who dashed in and hit the door button to screw with the fire department and most conveniently escaped, "defective" parts, mixed wiring which apparently caused door #1 to come down when the button for door #2 was pushed—but just this once—lightning in the area, increased solar pulses from sun spots. I heard my share and eventually became very creative myself at writing the investigative reports. With each new situation I felt myself turning into the cynical Captain Klossman. Maybe he had had good reason to shake his head.

Being an acting battalion chief was interesting, but the job of chief didn't interest me very much. I loved being the truck company captain. I had found my niche. When the time came, however, the chiefs in the battalion where I was working encouraged me to take the promotional examination for battalion chief. I had been lukewarm on the idea, but had continued to study as much as possible. Studying was a tough habit to break, but as my children started coming along it had become increasingly difficult to find the time. I figured correctly that studying would become more difficult in the years ahead. This was probably the peak of my game.

The test for battalion chief would be a killer; we all knew that. All new material, no way to learn anything from the questions asked on the last exam. Plenty of new sources of material for this exam. Just the NFPA handbook alone would take at least a year to read thoroughly. And all of the questions on the fire prevention code, leadership and supervision, firefighting tactics, departmental rules and procedures, treatment of medical emergencies—the possibilities were endless. A part of me was a little scared as well, scared I might not perform as people would expect me to perform. With strong showings on all the exams I had taken, I seemed to have a sort of reputation to uphold. I couldn't imagine being fortunate enough to do well on my first battalion chief's exam. Most guys never even passed on their first attempt.

There are a number of ways to approach a promotional exam. Some of those taking the test go just because they happen to be working day shift on that day and are granted time to go. They're not the serious competition. Others put in a little reading in the few weeks prior to the exam and hope they have enough general knowledge and carryover knowledge from previous studying to carry them through. This requires an element of luck. Sometimes these people are lucky enough to have studied the right things or see topics they know well. Some of the guys who test go there only with the hope of passing, hoping that circumstances will be right for a flood of promotions to be made from this eligibility list. But the guys who form the real competition are the ones who walk into the room shooting to be #1 on the list. I didn't know how to do anything else. Little wonder I drove everybody around me nuts with my incessant reading and studying. But "luck" does seem to come to those best prepared. I hadn't given too much thought to making chief at such a ridiculously young age, but I figured it was worth a try.

As luck would have it, two vacancies for battalion chief already existed and I made battalion chief immediately after the results were released. It all happened so quickly that some of the guys who had been off on vacation wondered what was going on when I came around the stations in the same battalion on the same shift, but this time with the crossed bugles of a full-fledged battalion chief. I was designated one of the floating battalion chiefs who would work wherever the regular assigned chief was off.

The enormity of the accomplishment was overshadowed by the enormity of the task ahead. Each battalion used its own system of paperwork for many of the daily functions; however, I figured I could learn them all in time. At least I would be working with an aide who could give me the guidance I needed. And all those various parts of the entire city to learn—one day in the Fourth Battalion, one day in the Fifth, two days in the Eleventh, then all four nights in the Tenth. Darn good thing the aide would know where we were going. I wasn't even sure where all the fire stations were, let alone all the responses.

I should not have been surprised that the department's next cost saving measure was to eliminate the position of battalion chief's aide only a few months after I made chief. The chiefs would drive themselves and have no assistant to help with all of the non-emergency duties. On the fireground, that other set of eyes and ears the chief relied upon was gone as well. Now it was definitely sink or swim time.

Actually, I floated for five years and worked every one of the shifts and every single battalion at one time or another. It was a great way to learn the city, though I'll readily admit to living with a map stuck in my boot for five years. Working everywhere also gave me a great chance to meet many of the guys throughout the whole fire department. Floating was also a terrific way to learn which battalions I liked best so I could chose a permanent spot wisely when the opportunity arose.

My time as a floating battalion chief was enjoyable and challenging. One of the things that helped me learn was the "black cloud." It didn't take very long before the guys all over were telling me that I must have one. Everything could have been relatively quiet in their battalion until I rotated through again. Then, it seemed all hell broke loose. Inevitably, wherever I worked we were busy with serious fires and screwy events. No matter where I worked the guys would joke when they saw me come in, "Aw chief, meaning no disrespect, why don't you go work somewhere else?" At least I think they were kidding. One particularly bad winter in Baltimore, back when the death rates from fire were much worse than today, I personally had ten fire fatalities, not in big groups, but in ones and two's in different parts of the city. And the serious fires that seemed to follow me around wore us all out. It got so bad that the investigator on my shift told me that when fire communications called him on the phone to inform him of a fire where he was needed they often started the conversation with "Kernan's burning down another one." Even I didn't realize what an impression I must have made until many years later, though. At the Firehouse Expo in Baltimore I was talking with Pete O'Connor, who had retired as the Chief of the Fire Department the year before. We walked up to Leo Stapleton, retired Commissioner and Chief of the Boston Fire Department, whom I had met briefly before. When the two friends greeted one another, Chief O'Connor looked over at me and commented, "You know Mike, don't you, Leo? He's the guy who burned down half of my city."

"Gee thanks, Chief, " I managed.

As with other positions in the fire department, any respect that I would earn as a battalion chief would come gradually. The majority of the battalion chief's job is of a non-emergency nature. Preparing daily staffing schedules, reviewing and approving or initiating routine departmental paperwork, and supervising the companies in the battalion are typical duties. The chief serves as the conduit through which information flows up and down the chain of command. Interpreting and explaining such information are an important duties. Enforcing the department's procedures and exacting the proverbial "pound of flesh" are less popular but necessary jobs of the chief as well. The chief is a manager, but the chief had better be more. Being one of the guys is definitely out of the question, but being there for your guys is an important distinction. Eventually, people learn who is trustworthy and fair, who is wishy-washy or self-aggrandizing, who is all talk and who can and will do the job. All the pomp and pageantry of rank can't buy an officer the true respect of those who work with him. But in the fire department there's the added element of operating under fire. An officer who is great in the office, but who proves incompetent when the chips are down is not the kind most firefighters would choose to work with. A battalion chief's abilities and deficiencies quickly show under stress. When things are the worst, situations the most tense and dangerous, the chief had better be at his best. Cool, calculated, methodical, effective management of emergency operations is critical to any chief officer's success. Little by little, fire by fire, the other young chiefs and I were earning our places among the chief officers of the department. They dubbed us "the kiddie crew." Never before in Baltimore had there been young chiefs like us. Our work was cut out for us. It would take each of us time and experience to gain full acceptance as equals.

Deputy Chief Charles E. Jones was an example of the more typical chief officer in the department in those days. He had served his time as a battalion chief and had gained promotion to one of the handful of deputy chief's positions. A proud, professional, serious-minded man, he carried himself with dignity and spoke with authority. At that time two deputies were always on duty, one over each division. Each, therefore, commanded half of the city and their offices were on either side of the second floor hallway at headquarters. In addition to all of their non-emergency responsibilities, one of them would respond on any second alarm to assume command of the fire.

I had only been a battalion chief for about eight months when the almost unthinkable situation developed. My divisional deputy chief was off. Through a combination of vacations, sick leaves, and whatever, all of the other battalion chiefs in our division were also off. I had been trained to be an acting deputy chief and had received the official approval, but never dreamed it would happen for many years.

Suddenly, there I sat that night in the first division office, the acting deputy chief. I was in charge of half of the city. After everybody else had left it was just the two of us—Chief Jones, in charge of the second division, at his desk, I at mine. For a long time we sat and did routine things, mixing paperwork with idle conversation until he could stand it no more.

"How old are you, chief?" he said in his most serious tone.

"Twenty-nine, sir."

"Uh huh."

I knew there was still a long way to go.

Going to work every day, driving the same familiar streets, by the same familiar intersections, past the same familiar landmarks makes us all creatures of habit. Most of us have had that experience where we find ourselves at our destinations and couldn't really even recall the details of our trip. The subconscious mind allows us to stop at the red lights and to go when they turn green. I was definitely on "auto-pilot" that morning as I headed in to work. Having worked the first two days of the shift in the Sixth Battalion, I had been doing some active thinking as I made sure I headed for the right place. Floating chiefs lived out of their car trunks, lugging their turnout gear and everything else they would need from station to station. I mulled over what would be worth carrying in from the parking lot and up the long steps to the office that morning.

Going downtown to the Fifth Battalion for the next two days meant going back to the huge Steadman Station where I had served as a lieutenant. I still knew most of the guys and always enjoyed seeing them. Fighting the downtown traffic, especially in the afternoon, wasn't much fun, but there was always the chance of catching a big fire. All in all it was usually pretty decent working a shift there.

The city was finally back to normal after the nasty blizzard that had us reeling a week earlier. The streets were deserted at the early hour; hardly a soul stirred anywhere as I drove through the central business district. Before long it would be bustling with activity, but not this early. Sitting at the red traffic light, listening to the soft music my kids hate, I casually took in the empty streets, the traffic lights ahead that seemed to change for no one, the newspaper boxes that would soon supply a city hungry for the overnight news, the reflection of flames against the windows. It took a few seconds to sink in. I must be imagining it. I inched forward and craned my neck to look up the street to my right. Beyond the fancy brick walkway that had replaced the street so pedestrians could stroll the shops were the unmistakable tongues of flame from a window. Only a short block away, the fire was located on the other side of a blocked off pedestrian-only area, so I drove down and around the next block. The approaching fire engines from Steadman station dispelled any doubt that there was a fire, and one glance up the street indicated it was a serious one at that.

No sense going to the office now. My relief wasn't going

to be there; he was pulling up as I drove around to Eutaw Street to park my car. I've seen enough serious fires to know you don't put your car anywhere near them. My quick glance at the building was only enough to tell me it was a big building with fire coming out of about three or four windows. Looked like it might be the second or third floor. I quickly dragged my turnout gear from the trunk, threw my shoes into my trunk, and headed up the street to the fire.

Uh oh! The fire was spreading with terrible speed. The eerie, dancing orange lit the morning darkness. In the couple of minutes since I had first seen it, the fire had jumped several floors and was spreading laterally along the Howard Street side of the building. Engine companies had laid hose from several hydrants and were positioning lines to throw large caliber streams of water against the fast-growing blaze. The snorkel was taking a position on the corner of the building, the spot that gave it the most flexibility in projecting the powerful streams of water that would soon be coming. Fires of this nature require streams that can be applied from above ground level as well as those from below.

Something didn't look right from the rear, where I stopped at Rescue 1 to grab a portable radio. From the rear we could see the fire very well—too well. It was like looking into the back of a dollhouse. The whole building was there except for the back walls that had all been removed to make it easier to do the extensive renovation work underway. From this vantage point it was immediately obvious we had big trouble. A swirling inferno was already beginning to create its own winds within the building, winds which shoved the fire left, right, and up. Growing clouds of dense, black smoke punctuated by burning embers shot skyward. At the front of the building, my classmate, Joe McKenzie, the night shift chief I never quite got to relieve was also observing the fire's progress. Positioning the companies on the scene where they could do the most good, Joe had immediately seen the need for help. The second and third alarms were already on the way, another eight engines and four trucks along with various specialized pieces and chief officers. We met at the corner as Joe tried to get a feel for the rest of the scene.

"How's it look in the rear, Mike?"

"Bad, Joe, real bad. The fire's going both ways and has already spread up a few floors. It's going all the way to the top."

"Yeah, I've already got a third alarm in," Joe replied. "I think we're probably gonna need more."

"I'll be in the back."

The fire wasn't likely to stop any time soon. Faster than the companies could stretch their lines into position and fill them with water, the fire would roar past. The flames were feeding on the ancient wooden floors and innards of the former Hochschild Kohn department store. For decades, the store had helped shape the history of downtown Baltimore. Christmas-time especially was magical at Howard and Lexington Streets. Hordes of people of all ages, bundled up against the cold, eagerly lined the sidewalks to gaze at the beautiful window displays of the elegant department stores. Shopping downtown was a ritual for many Baltimoreans before the suburban shopping centers and malls changed our shopping habits forever. As a child I had often ridden the streetcar downtown to this very spot. And now the once majestic landmark was rapidly being engulfed. Sirens of the companies summoned to help echoed through the downtown area as the flames devoured the once beautiful rooms that had given pleasure to so many. Falling chunks of flaming wood carried the fire to the lowest areas of the structure, and in just a few minutes the entire building was ablaze. Blistering radiant heat caused everything nearby to smoke; hoselines in the street, buildings, even the turnout gear of firefighters exuded ghostly halos.

Fourth alarm. Fifth alarm. More engines were needed. More firefighters to position additional hose streams to protect all the areas now threatened by the dangerous fire. More ladders were needed to allow the firefighters to throw streams of water high into the upper reaches of the burning building. Falling pieces of plywood and other debris threatened to ignite the acetylene tanks along the side of the building at its rear. Firefighters fought to keep the tanks cool to prevent even more problems.

As each company arrived, the officer threw his apparatus and crew into the battle. The fate of Hochschild's was already obvious, but the surrounding buildings were now seriously in danger of burning. Angry sheets of flame shot from many of the building's windows along the front on Howard Street. The powerful streams of water seemed puny as the fire continued to grow. Across the street stood more buildings of similar construction. Their windows reflected the inferno, but the companies in the street were hard pressed to protect all of the threatened areas and put water onto the fire itself. Both were critical needs.

On the side of the building, across narrow Lexington Street, the situation was even more grave. On the sidewalk opposite the fire building firefighters huddled in small groups holding down the hoselines which poured tons of water onto the fire. Truck companies jumped the hoses in the streets to maneuver into positions from which they could operate their ladder pipes. Truck 16, with its brand-new, sparkling one hundred foot aerial truck took up the fight to keep the fire from jumping Lexington Street. Truck 6 nosed into the street as well. High above the firefighters, the flames continued unabated and threatened to spread the fire to all of the stores across the narrow street.

Deputy Chief Ticha arrived to assume command and advised fire communications of the serious situation that we faced. We talked briefly at the corner and I told him how bad things were in the back. Back there, where the walls had been removed to facilitate the renovation, firefighters were having no problems finding places to direct their streams of water. The problem was that streams that propelled 500, 750, even 1000 gallons of water every minute toward the mass of flames were swallowed up long before they even touched the heart of the burning building. The demonic swirls took the pitiful streams into them as though they were gasoline, undeterred by the firefighters' best efforts. Because the entire mass of flames was unobstructed by any walls, the radiant heat in the back was unbearable. Firefighters tried to position behind the building portable monitor pipes that throw large caliber streams of water. They couldn't approach anywhere near the back of the building without the furnace-like heat driving them back. Even with streams of water trying to keep them cool, they soon retreated with their turnout gear steaming. The unbearable temperatures now made everything close by begin to smoke or steam or even worse.

On the sidewalk on Lexington Street I stood with George McKnight, Acting Battalion Chief 4, as we debated where to best use the forces we had. Even with yet more alarms on the way we were still faced with fire beyond our ability to control. The situation looked grim indeed as the fire threatened to become a full-blown conflagration. *Thud!* went the first of the big plastic storm windows from above. The heat of the raging fire was melting the outer windows of the Hecht Company department store we were trying desperately to protect. They began falling to the sidewalk below, indications of a battle we were losing. We looked up the side of the building from below. Steam and smoke seemed to come from the entire face of the building. Unless the fire could be brought under control, and real soon, the windows would shortly fail altogether and the fire would enter this huge building as well. The consequences of such an occurrence were spine chilling. Even with additional companies arriving constantly there weren't enough fire fighters or hoselines to go to every area of every floor inside the buildings. Wetting the outside of the exposed buildings, attempting to keep them cool enough to prevent their ignition, was the only practical option. Even the sprinkler system, usually a great protection against a serious fire, offered us little hope. We feared it would quickly be overwhelmed. The water in the mains feeding the system was already being poured onto the huge fire through dozens of hoselines. The limited water that remained would never supply the many sprinkler heads that would operate if the fire jumped into any of the large buildings so seriously threatened.

Alarm after alarm brought more help to the scene including Chief O'Connor, the Chief of the Department. It had become obvious to all that the fire had quickly grown to become the worst fire to strike the city in a very long time. There weren't many words of encouragement that we could give to those battling the huge fire; we were not winning. About forty-five minutes into the fire, the building fought back. The sturdiest construction can survive a fire only so long, and this building was being eaten alive. "This wall's gonna come down. Get 'em all outta here," instructed Deputy Chief Ticha. The battle to keep the fire from jumping Lexington Street was important, but the lives of those in the narrow street were more important still. Especially without any rear walls to support it, the side wall of the building was now a serious risk. If the massive walls were to fall, the street would surely become a tomb for the crews positioned there. No firefighter likes to withdraw; it just goes against our nature. I figured not to be very popular as I approached each crew and gave them the word. Faced with the huge fire that still raged with impunity, most of them saw the wisdom in such a change in tactics.

Soon the word spread among all of those on Lexington Street that we were pulling out and the crews began the withdraw. Firefighters shut down their lines and scurried from their vantage points in doorways and alcoves. Officers scrambled to make sure that they had all of their people as some headed toward Howard Street in the front and others of us headed further up Lexington Street past the back of the building. The guys assigned to Truck 6 and Truck 16 saw the imminent danger as well, but jumped to save their ladder trucks parked in the narrow street. The collapse was horrifying. I've watched the conventional wisdom on wall collapses evolve over the years. Walls usually begin falling apart as they come down so that the horizontal reach of a falling wall is somewhat less than the height of the wall. One-third the distance, two-thirds the height of the wall, a distance equal to the height of the wall—the authorities have all weighed in.

I've always tried to be beyond the reach of the brick that bounces the furthest.

Lexington Street provided no safe haven that morning. The thunderous collapse caught few by surprise, but it was still startling. The Lexington Street side of the building was the location of the fire escape. The heavy black, metal fire escape zigzagged up the entire height of the building. When the building was occupied, the fire escape promised those inside a way out in case of fire. Ironically, the fire escape, installed as a fire protection feature, now made the wall collapse that much worse. The entire massive brick wall leaned out into the sky and, held together by the fire escape, crashed in one gigantic piece into the street below. Six stories of heavy brick wall fell, exposing the fire's full fury. As soon as the wall was down, firefighters began a renewed effort to quench the flames. Hose streams now pounded into the fully exposed, furiously burning building. But the real drama on Lexington Street was under the bricks.

In trying to extract their apparatus from the street, some of the firefighters had been caught by the collapse. The falling wall had crushed the brand new Truck 16 and knocked the tillerman from the tiller cab atop the back of the truck. Before the dust from the collapse had even settled, firefighters struggled to reach their injured comrades. The captain of Truck 6 lay injured as well, struck by the falling bricks. Another of his men threw himself onto the captain to shield him from further injury. The situation was fraught with danger, but the desperate fight to contain the fire was still on. Immense columns of heated smoke spiraled skyward carrying thousands, maybe millions of burning embers. The collapse of the side wall had invigorated the inferno. As more air rushed in, the fire burned even more furiously, sending yet more flaming debris into the hellish sky. As the wind bore the embers toward Eutaw Street, they began to fall from the sky threatening to carry the fire into yet another area. Under the falling threat stood the famous Lexington Market, another Baltimore landmark and another important member of the business community.

I was now given the task of protecting the market and told that all the tenth alarm companies were being directed to me. Up on Eutaw Street I stood there looking down the hill at the surreal scene. The fire was still huge, but from farther away it was no longer noisy. I stood in the usually busy intersection totally alone awaiting the companies that would soon be coming. No traffic moved in the area, long ago stopped by the police. For the first time I could stand back for a minute and take it all in. Unbelievable! The elevated master streams thrown against the massive fire looked like garden hoses trying to water Yankee Stadium. Along Lexington Street, businesses continued to smoke and steam, signs disfigured by the tremendous heat sagged. Even hoselines in the street still steamed. Even the fire apparatus itself, parked a full block away, was smoking. Despite the efforts of most of the city's firefighting forces, the outcome was still very much in doubt. But the most amazing scene was the torrent of embers raining down on me and onto the intersection. I hunched my head down into my shoulders in an attempt to keep the embers from going down my neck. My helmet resounded with the plunk, plunk of the scarlet storm. Removed from the noise of the fire, I was struck by the strangeness of the moment. The only sound was that of the falling brands, a sound exactly like a sleet storm. The street was littered with the red glowing chunks and I kicked them with every step. Tremendous clouds of smoke with thousands of dancing fireflies filled the sky. Burning embers fell unopposed onto the long, hard, plastic awning that stretched across the front of the market. Some rolled down the slippery curved surface and bounced to the sidewalk below; others burned holes right through. From the dark sky, the embers came relentlessly, fed by an inferno in the distance.

On all fronts the fire was being denied by the tenacious fire fighters. Eventually the battle was won, the threat to the downtown business district removed. The damage was terrific. Several millions of dollars of property had been destroyed or damaged. But that loss, extensive as it was, was a small percentage of the potential loss. The damage to fire apparatus was significant as well. Truck 16 sat seriously damaged, crushed by the falling wall. Other pieces bore scars from falling bricks and embers. Still others lost windshields and warning lights to the terrible heat. Hose was lost, some buried, some burned. Ropes sitting on apparatus three-quarters of a block away from the fire caught ignited. Even front seats and tiller seats of the apparatus had burned. Scorched paint was the order of the day. But not a single life had been lost, and the firefighters hurt by the falling walls would recover fully.

Hours had passed before the enemy was beaten back. Finally, the night shift chief, Joe McKenzie, gave me his radio, briefed me on the other battalion business, and headed home for some well deserved rest. I stood out front with Chief O'Connor and the others as we discussed the difficult job still ahead. It would take days and heavy cranes and equipment before the last of the fire was completely extinguished. I hadn't yet begun the task of determining all the information we would need regarding the many buildings damaged by the fire. But a certain satisfaction settled over me, even faced with the massive destruction. The challenge to the department and the danger had been great, but I felt truly proud of the job that our department had done. I was surprised and honored when I was invited to attend a little "thank you" luncheon at the Lexington Market. Thankfully, we had been able to save it. My most satisfying moment came a few weeks later, however, when I was talking to Sam Miceli, the aide to the deputy chief on my shift. He reported to me the results of an earlier discussion at headquarters. Talking to a group of his deputies, Chief O'Connor informed them that he'd put "his kiddie crew" up against any of his other chiefs anytime. Maybe being a battalion chief was a pretty good job. I finally had found my real niche.

First due units arrive at a heavily involved dwelling in East Baltimore.
(Photo by Robert Carter)

Fire fighters go to work on vacant building fire near downtown.
(Photo by Paul Novak)

With ladders to the roof and to the second floor,
fire fighters attack through the first floor.
(Photo by Robert Carter)

Apparatus of all types crowd the street at multiple
alarm fire. (Photo by Geoff Donahue)

(Photo by Paul Novak)
Engines looked much different in the author's early career.

(Photo by Mark Platek)

Fighting fires in the harbor and on the waterfron requires
special equipment. (Both photos by Paul Novak)

Rescue 1 in front of Camden Yards, home of the Orioles.
(Photo by Mark Platek)

Fire fighters taking a break. The Department's most important
resource is its people. (Photo by Paul Novak)

Modern Engine 45 sits on ramp of author's first station. Engines have sure come a long way! (Photo by Paul Novak)

The modern Truck 7 from Waverly.
(Photo by Paul Novak)

Fire lights up the night sky as fire fighters arrive on the scene.
(Photo by Michael Parr)

Numerous hoselines carry water into and from the engine at this
warehouse fire. (Photo by Michael Parr)

Fire fighters at fire in frame dwelling dig out the fire inside the walls.
(Both photos by Paul Novak)

Fire fighters swarm over the building, attacking from
numerous points.

Fire fighters often encounter heavy fire conditions
in the rear of row houses on fire.
(Photo by Robert Carter)

Smoke from this vacant warehouse fire filled the afternoon sky.
(Both photos by Ed DeLottinville)

Fire fighters attack the fire using stream from ladder pipe
on the tip of aerial.

Smoke pours from typical Baltimore row house fire
as fire fighters begin the job of ventilation.
(Photo series by Jim Keefe)

Deadly poisonous, the superheated smoke vents as
a line isadvanced and more ladders are placed.

Instant death would result from inhaling atmospheres like this. Fortunately, this house is vacant.

A battalion chief coordinates the attack as flashover
ignites the superheated smoke and gases.

Fire fighter repositions ladder as others join the attack inside.

Nobody can survive an inferno of a fully involved area.

10
Death on Location

In recent years a growing number of movies have been filmed in Baltimore. The diverse architecture of our public buildings and museums has provided the backdrop for numerous scenes portrayed as New York or Washington or a host of other cities.

Our beautiful, new stadium recently appeared as the home of the Cleveland Indians on movie screens across the country. In *Tin Man*, Danny DeVito and Richard Dreyfuss fought their aluminum siding war right here in Pimlico. The fire department has even been involved in some productions. Off-duty fire fighters and former Baltimore City Fire Department apparatus helped stage a huge waterfront fire scene in *Avalon*, reminiscent of the scenes of my youth.

My parents' home, the place where I spent my teenage years, was even visible briefly in the *Accidental Tourist*.

One of the many reasons film makers frequently select Baltimore is the support from local government. The city fathers and mothers always look for a chance to have Baltimore immortalized—or at least hi-lighted—by Hollywood. Certainly the boost to the local economy is always welcomed.

Todd Walspen was glad to get the phone call inviting him to help work on the filming of the new movie. Todd was a "local." The enormous cost of making a movie would be even greater if everyone involved were to travel across the country. Instead, the production company employs "locals" to supplement their entourage of technical people.

At thirty-five, Todd was already an experienced special effects man who enjoyed the chance to work on movies when the opportunity arose. He jumped at the chance to drive the fifty miles to Baltimore for this job. Several days of extra money would come in handy.

I knew that the fire department was providing an engine and a pump operator to assist in the filming just a few blocks from my station, but I didn't give it too much thought. Being pretty much "movie illiterate," I didn't realize that if it was clear outside and the scene called for rain, somebody has to make the rain. I just figured they waited until a rainy night to film that scene. It's good that I have a job.

On Reisterstown Road that night Jim Gorham did what comes naturally to fire fighters—he waited. Lighting people tested and adjusted their lights. The sound technicians positioned microphones on funny-looking long-armed carts. Cameras were placed, then moved, then placed, then moved. Through it all Jim sat behind the wheel of his engine, idly watching and waiting.

Todd, on the other hand, was quite busy. That night's scene called for a couple to exit a car and scamper across the dark street in the pouring rain. Above, the stars shone brightly in the clear night sky. Todd, along with others, was to create the illusion of a heavy rainfall.

As the other crews readied their equipment, Todd and Bill Spiter, his friend and co-worker, assembled the tall metal framework. In the parking lot they pieced together the tower into which Jim Gorham would pump the water that would become Hollywood rain.

So much activity was taking place that hardly anyone noticed the tower start to move as Todd and Bill began to wheel the monster over to the street. Curious onlookers, held behind the police barricades, focused primarily on the street beside the Giant Food Store where soon the scene would be shot. Families watched and pointed, fascinated by the preparations that had taken two hours.

Standing over twenty feet tall, the tower was heavy and awkward, but the wheels started to roll in response to the shoves of the two men. With their shoulders and arms providing the needed force, Todd and Bill negotiated the parking lot and headed for the street. In the shadows neither saw the crack in the sidewalk that grabbed the wheel.

Suddenly the tower pitched forward and to the left as the front, left wheel dug in. Natural reaction caused Todd to grab harder and try to steady the tower. Bill's grasp was broken as the tower fell away from him.

BAM went the violent, brilliant, explosion as the metal tower contacted the uninsulated power line in the darkness overhead. So intense was the electrical arc of thousands of volts that the entire street was bathed for a brief instant in the eerie blue-white light.

Jim Gorham, behind the wheel of the parked engine, recognized the flash more quickly than most. Instinctively his eyes followed the tower downward. Todd lay crumpled near the base of the tower which still teetered above. Immediately, Jim radioed for help and for the power company.

Gradually the impact of what had happened spread throughout the crowd. The buzz of excitement turned to the realization of horror. Bill grabbed Todd and pulled him away, all the while feeling a tingling in his feet and legs. Smoke lifted from Todd's lifeless body as Bill feverishly cried for help for his injured friend. "Todd! Todd!" Bill screamed. Todd did not answer.

Jim rushed to help as did others. Soon Medic 8 arrived and, assisted by other fire fighters, the paramedics continued the CPR. Consulting with the hospital by radio, Laurie Dausch, one of our finest paramedics, administered drugs and attempted to defibrillate Todd's quivering heart.

Sadly, the powerful surge of electricity had caused massive damage to Todd's internal organs as it passed through his body before exiting out his penis and ankle. The young lady who had recruited Todd for the job sobbed on my shoulder as we watched Laurie and the others attempt to revive Todd. I knew that the smell of burned flesh that filled the street when I pulled up did not bode well for his chances.

Bill was inconsolable as he was being treated by the other

medic crew that had arrived. It would be a while before he realized how lucky he was to be alive. The soles of his shoes had completely melted.

Because the people involved with the movie were unfamiliar with the area we hastily arranged for a guide to lead them to Sinai Hospital. In the emergency room parking lot the looks on the faces of Laurie and Joe Beal told me that my hunch was correct. The paramedics and the doctors had been unable to revive Todd.

No shooting was ever done that night, and I never heard any more about the movie being filmed. It didn't matter. That's one I wouldn't want to go see.

11

Kids Trapped

The cool, gray, spring evening brings more rain to the city. Lately we've been in a wet stretch. Maryland's farmers are grateful for this early rain. Soon summer will settle in to our area and the rain will again become scarce. Crops burning in the blistering summer sunshine have become common sights in our region in recent years.

What a year it has been! The winter has finally ended in answer to our prayers. Seventeen storms came up the east coast this winter, pummeling the area with frequent snows, bone-chilling temperatures and, worst of all, ice. Not in a generation had Baltimoreans seen ice so treacherous or so tenacious. Week after week we slid, slipped, fell, skidded, and cursed our way through fires and accidents. Snow removal equipment and crews proved useless as salt, then sand, then slag from area steel mills failed to end our misery.

Emergency rooms everywhere were jammed with fall victims. Streets, parking lots, sidewalks, and steps made fools of us all. Some people wore spikes to walk on the ice. Others literally crawled from their cars to their houses or offices. Imagine trying to carry an eighty-five pound stretcher plus a patient under those conditions. It's a wonder we have any paramedics left.

Even fire apparatus with tire chains played pinball with parked cars and curbs. Our very best drivers found times that they could not even move until sand or salt trucks could arrive to rescue them. Many responses were taken at a snail's pace.

With the dreadful winter finally behind us, the topic of

conversation has shifted to the Orioles' chances this year. They've strengthened the team with some key, off-season trades. This promises to be a great year for the "Birds."

It's evening at the shift commander's office and the nightly ritual is underway. Each evening all the battalion chiefs deliver the day's reports downtown and obtain the latest orders to be distributed throughout the department. Tonight I have brought the customary collection. My briefcase holds fire reports and medic unit response forms. They will be reviewed at headquarters. Bills for medic unit service will be prepared and sent out to those who have been transported. The monies collected help the city maintain and upgrade the medic service.

The Fire Investigation Bureau will review the fire reports and do follow-up where necessary. Baltimore will file and retain a copy of the report. Copies of reports of certain types of incidents will also be sent to the State Fire Marshal's office. Eventually adding information to a nationwide data-base, these reports may help identify certain trends or patterns and result in corrective action being taken. For example, if a particular model television or automobile frequently appears in the fire report with a certain problem, this could be an indication of a defect that needs to be addressed. Some interesting and helpful information has surfaced in this way.

Tonight, I also bring reports from our company officers describing violations of the Fire Prevention Code, the Building Code, and the Housing Code that they have observed. These will be forwarded to the correct inspectors who will visit the sites of the violations and take appropriate measures.

Fire departments, like most government agencies, thrive on paperwork. Tonight's package also includes the usual assortment of repair orders, hydrant maintenance requests, court case appearance reports, requests for overtime payment, etc. The day shift battalion chief has spent a good portion of his day gathering, reviewing, correcting, sorting, and approving these reports. Others were returned to their originators for corrections or additional information. Some days the chief feels far more *secretarial* than *managerial*.

The distinctive "all call" tones that precede the announcement of a full box alarm interrupt our baseball discussion. One of us here is probably going.

"Engine 52, 46, 40, Truck 12, Truck 10, Battalion Chief 7 respond—remainder of the box being struck out...."

As I head down the rear steps of the Oldtown station for my car I switch channels on my portable radio. On Channel 1 the dispatcher advises Engine 122, "We now have a report of a dwelling fire at that location. Remainder of the box being dispatched."

The crew of Engine 122 is rapidly approaching the "discarded mattress fire" that is obviously more. Clouds of gray smoke bank down into Park Heights Avenue, held down by the heavy mist and drizzle. As they lay their five inch supply line from the hydrant at the intersection to the front of the building, Lieutenant Britcher strains to see which house is on fire.

Shouting groups of civilians hysterically point the way. This very long block is filled with two story brick rowhouses so common to Baltimore. Tucked within the block sits one three story frame apartment house, and, of course, this is the one that's burning.

The traffic is heavy with the evening commuters leaving downtown as I head onto the Jones Falls Expressway. Some cars move over, some do not; some cannot—they have nowhere to go.

"Engine 122, we've got a three story frame apartment building, heavy smoke and reports of children trapped. Give us a task force."

The lieutenant has seen the size and construction of the building and the seriousness of the situation and requested help. Two more engines and an additional truck company respond. We'll need their personnel to help search the large building and to stretch more hoselines to the building, which sits up an embankment and is recessed from the street.

Numerous civilians scream to the fire fighters to rescue the children. Even knowing that such reports are often erroneous, every fire fighter feels the adrenaline flow when faced with the plea "My kids are in there!"

One man hurriedly explains to Lt. Britcher that he had entered the building and heard the children screaming from a second floor room, but the fire and smoke prevented him from getting to them.

The crew quickly stretches 200 feet of one and three-quarter inch hose past the parked cars, across the sidewalk, and up the concrete steps to the front yard. No fire is visible from the front, but heavy, dirty smoke pushes out of the second and third floors. Since Engine 122 was already almost here when the rest of the companies were dispatched, the crew realizes that they will be on the scene by themselves for a few minutes. No truckies are on hand to ladder and vent the upper floors, so the job will be that much more difficult and dangerous. The crew pauses at the front door to put on the facepieces to their air masks. With water now filling their hoseline, the lieutenant and fire fighter on the line enter the hallway and seek the stairs that will take them to that second floor room. The hose is much heavier now and the men struggle to pull it around the hall and up the stairs. As soon as the hydrant man has charged the supply line and gotten an air mask he will join them. But for now it's just the two of them in there—and whoever might be trapped.

The heat now greets them as they reach the second floor landing. The heavy smoke robs them of the little visibility they had on the stairs. Between breaths on their noisy air masks the men hear the crackling of the fire.

"In the back, on the left," the lieutenant prompts the nozzleman as they pull the line toward the glow now visible down the hall. The heat and smoke keep the crew pinned down to the floor. On their hands and knees and turning to pull the hoseline, they near the area the would-be rescuer described.

Like a blowtorch, the fire from the involved apartment roars into the hallway just ahead of them. Flames fill the ceiling above them as they inch forward into position. Through their protective gear they feel the deadly heat on their shoulders. Before they open the nozzle the men shout muffled cries several times hoping in vain for a reply. They know that once the water hits the fire and turns to steam the visibility will be even worse.

Water explodes from the nozzle as the pipeman opens up. One hundred and twenty gallons of water each minute, broken into thousands of tiny droplets, stream from the nozzle. The fog pattern strikes the fire expanding 1700 to 1 as it converts to steam. Smoke, steam, embers and ash boil ahead of the nozzle as the crew pushes the fire back into the apartment. The atmosphere around the crew changes instantly. Swirling clouds of the superheated maelstrom envelope the men and drop the visibility to zero.

Outside, the other units are arriving and going to work. Engine companies lay additional lines to bring water from other hydrants. The truck company crews begin their job of placing portable ladders around the building to the upper floors. Because the building sits well off the street and trees block the way, the aerial ladder can't help. Normally this would provide access to the roof. Now the truck crews must lug the heavy, longer ground ladders up the embankment and into position. It is critical that they get to the roof promptly to ventilate the structure. Heavy smoke obscures the top of the building. The rain-slicked, steeply pitched roof adds yet more danger as the crews work their way up to the peak.

In the rear the fire has hold of all three floors of the building and has entered the space underneath the roof where the fire fighters now work. Working quickly the men chop a hole to allow the fire, smoke, and hot gases to escape. By drawing the fire to this hole they attempt to keep the fire from spreading horizontally throughout the rest of the building.

I can see the brownish clouds of smoke billowing over the building as I park my chief's car out of the way. As I drove to the scene I have been monitoring the companies' progress reports on the fireground channel. So far the companies have been unable to locate the trapped children.

Captain Phil Janson from Engine 52 meets me in the front. He has been in charge since he arrived as the second due company. Phil is a fine, capable officer and I'm confident he has managed the incident well. Quickly he briefs me on the conditions and situation before I assume command of the fire. Together we decide on where to place the extra companies we have coming on the task force alarm.

Reassigned to the rear of the building, Phil will now become my eyes and ears there. From his vantage point he can observe the progress of the fire back there and determine our need for additional companies.

My portable radio crackles with reports from the interior crews as they continue their search of the apartments. No victims located so far.

"Are you absolutely sure those kids are in there?" I ask of the neighbor.

"Mister, I'm telling you they were screamin' and hollerin' somethin' terrible. I just couldn't get in there!" he almost apologizes. "I tried, I tried."

"Park Heights Command, fill out the second alarm." My decision is made. We just don't have enough people on hand. Hoselines are needed on all three floors and in the attic space. The fire continues to burn stubbornly in the walls and ceilings and threatens to extend further toward the front of the building. In each of these threatened areas we will need fire fighters with ceiling hooks and axes to tear open the concealed areas to expose the traveling fire. Hoselines must be moved from room to room hitting each place that fire is discovered.

The sirens of the second alarm companies sound in the distance as the shift commander and his aide arrive on the front sidewalk. They were almost here when I requested the second alarm.

"Mac, the man who tried to get the kids is right there. He swears they are in there. Nobody can locate the family who lives in that apartment."

Shift commander Carl McDonald, long-time friend and thirty year veteran, relieves me as the incident commander.

Reassigned to the interior, I can now enter and personally check on the progress of the companies. Armed with the exact location of the children that the neighbor has given me, I proceed immediately to that area.

Hoselines crowd the only stairs as hot, filthy water trickles from above and smoke lingers in spite of the ventilation.

Down the second floor hall to the rear I follow two of the hoselines. The area the man described is completely incinerated. Fire fighters with hoselines and tools fill the area. One look at the destruction confirms my fears. We will find no *live* victims in here.

"Nothing, Chief," is the greeting I get from Lt. Britcher.

"Keep looking," I reply.

Above us the fire continues to eat at the structure. Sounds of air masks and tools crashing into the plaster walls and ceilings fill the third floor. The roar of the gasoline-powered circular saws continues on the roof as fire fighters cut more holes.

Finally the fire is almost extinguished. Only small pockets of hidden fire remain to be discovered and extinguished. The whistles of low pressure alarms on the air masks make talking difficult.

Chief McDonald has assigned some of the fresher second-alarm companies inside to replace the crews who have been engaged the whole time. Even though they are exhausted, some of the crews resist my attempts to rotate them out. Until we find the kids, the job seems unfinished. None of us feels the need to state the obvious. We all know that if the children are indeed in here they are burned beyond recognition.

Fortunately, this time there are no charred corpses to discover. Only hard work lies ahead of the crews—no body removals tonight.

The rain is torrential now as Shift Commander McDonald and his aide, Roman Clark, fill me in on the latest information. The family who lives in the apartment where the fire began has been located—safe.

The kids that the would-be rescuer had heard had been

screaming outside in the side yard. He had heard them through a window and misjudged their location.

To complete the picture, the cops and our investigator have a witness who saw these same kids set the fire in a mattress on the back steps at the second floor level. Because the witness can't positively identify the kids that she observed from across the alley, the kids will not be arrested.

The *best* our investigator can do is take their names and addresses and enroll them in the juvenile fire setter program. **JERKS!**

12
The Value of Life

My mind drifted back and forth as I approached the firehouse to report for night shift. After all these years some of the excitement and anticipation of reporting to work has worn off, but I still wonder—*What will our night be like?*

The yellow flashing traffic lights in front of the station turned to red as I came up the street and I sat behind two cars waiting to see what was responding.

Without emergency lights or siren Truck 12 appeared through the overhead doors and passed me heading into town. With change of shifts at hand it would be unusual for the company to be going out in the district to train or do inspections, so my curiosity was piqued as I parked in the rear parking lot and entered the station.

The buzz in the station indicated something was up. Derek, one of the young men in the neighborhood and our "housecat", scanner in hand, quickly filled me in.

"Truck's transferring to Truck 10" he started. "They've got four alarms in on Twenty-fifth Street."

The engine and the chief's car were still in the station. Four alarms isn't enough to get us that far downtown, but four alarms catch the attention of the whole department. Anybody could be going anywhere as units are moved around to cover the vacant areas of the city, and other fires could require companies to respond to areas they normally would not run. Until the fire is declared "under control" the potential exists for more equipment to be summoned, so ears are tuned to the radio in engine houses all over the city.

"Old Board of Education building," the day shift chief, Bill Langan, informed me. "They sounded the evacuation signal a little while ago and asked for the fourth alarm."

That meant that they had pulled all the fire fighters from the building because of safety concerns and were attacking the fire with master streams from the exterior only. While this is safer for our crews, it usually means a prolonged attack. This could be an all-nighter, we agreed.

Fire continued to eat away at the roof of the old building. The elevated streams pouring torrents of water into the building had a difficult time reaching the fire above the heavy metal ceilings. With the help of an additional aerial tower the fire was eventually contained.

Shift Commander Don Heinbuch had made the decision to withdraw the crews to the outside. This is rarely a popular decision among fire fighters. Since the very beginning of their career, these people have been taught to "Get in there—go get it." Every fire fighter knows the best way to fight most fires is to fight through the heat and smoke and get "personal" with the fire. The guys who were battling this fire were giving it everything they had in an aggressive interior attack. The thought of giving up that interior attack and admitting defeat is distasteful and usually results in "If they'd just let us have a few more minutes, we'd've had it!"

While the crews on the hoselines lament the change of tactics, the incident commander breathes a little easier. On his shoulders rests the safety of those crews.

Don Heinbuch saw the big picture. Fire had been burning a considerable amount of time, weakening the building. Tons of water being applied to the fire added new weight the building was never designed to carry. Soon this building was to be demolished anyway in the name of urban renewal. No civilian lives were at stake. The decision was clear. No fire fighters would die for this!

This is the constant balancing act we are required to perform. Does the risk we are taking make any sense considering what is to be gained? While some of the younger fire fighters may not understand, those of us who have attended too many fire fighter funerals strongly desire not to attend another. The job of fighting fires is very, very dangerous. Many risks are unavoidable. More fire fighters will be hurt. More will die. Unfortunately, that is the nature of the beast.

In recent years the fire service has taken great strides to improve safety. While controversy on some of the changes still prevails, the improved equipment and procedures have benefited many of us.

No fire fighters at this fire will lie under a headstone reading, "He died trying to save a building they tore down the next week!"

Arnie has come in tonight and we talk about the fire. Arnie Scher is an auxiliary fire fighter, a dying breed in our department.

During the Second World War the fire department found its ranks thinned as men went off to battle. Citizens in the community were trained and equipped as part of the Civil Defense effort to assist the fire department. Long after the war the auxiliary continued as a way for citizens to train in firefighting and supplement the regular force of fire fighters. For no pay, these people would ride the apparatus and assist at fires. That extra set of hands was frequently a terrific help. Over the years some true characters have served in the auxiliary. There have been lawyers, business executives, clergymen, teachers, and some politically influential types.

As funds dried up for training and gear, and interest waned, the auxiliary shrunk. Today many stations have none. We are fortunate to have two very fine auxiliary fire fighters at my station, Bob Burch on the truck and Arnie Scher on the engine.

Bob is a regular on Friday nights. Arnie usually spends a couple of evenings a week with us. They always take the ribbing "You should have been here last night" quite well.

With Arnie's visit tonight comes the guarantee of a meal. He thoroughly enjoys sharing the kitchen duties of planning, buying, and preparing dinner.

"Can we have some real meat in the chili tonight?" is usually the first question asked. Arnie's desire to eat healthier (read **turkey**) is not always shared by all the guys. Then, of course, there are the guys who beg off the hot, hot variety of chili. They get their own pot we dub the *wuss* chili!

Regardless of what the meal is, we always enjoy the chance to sit together in the kitchen and talk. Invariably the meal is delayed or interrupted by emergency calls, but we manage to salvage most everything. The pot of spaghetti noodles that cooked for three hours one busy night was one exception!

Actually, runs add to the fun of dinner. When the engine gets a medic assist, the truck guys laugh and vice versa.

One night we all went out on a fire and one of our local police officers took our hospitality a little too far. She managed to eat an incredible amount of our bushel of steamed crabs. She gave us a cute smile and a thank you as we stood gawking at the pile of shells in front of her when we returned. That was the last invitation she got!

No crabs tonight. It's some of Arnie's and John Boblits' mystery chili. The only ingredient readily identifiable is HEAT!

Storytelling is the inevitable accompaniment to dinner. It's the same everywhere. Each time the stories get told, the fires get a little bigger, the rescues a little more dramatic. Memory is a wonderful thing.

The mix of guys gives us great opportunities to exchange cultures. Black, White, Hispanic, Jewish, young, old (we say more experienced.) We laugh and share the camaraderie of the firehouse.

Both company officers on my shift came through the same fire academy class that I did. We've been friends for twenty-four years.

"Geez, that was before I was even born!" is the response to one of our stories of the heroics of our early careers. To which the usual retort is along the lines of "Damn good thing you *weren't* in the fire department in those days, 'cuz you couldn't 'uv made it." And so it goes until it usually ends with Boo

Boo saying, "Hey, Chief, tell us again about seeing that guy come around the neighborhood lighting the gas street lamps." *Boy am I sorry I ever told them about that!*

Tonight's meal has gone smoothly. The truck got back in a couple of hours from their transfer. The chili was a "two-soda" variety—not terribly hot. And the laughter flowed.

We had just finished the meal when the teleprinter alarm sounded.

"Everybody goes!" yelled the man on watch. The radio crackled, "Building fire in the rear of 6615 Reisterstown Road" as we headed out the door.

Calls like this could mean anything. Often such calls turn out to be a dumpster or a car fire in an alley that appeared to be a building fire.

I visualized the area as I responded. Across the street from the Reisterstown Plaza Shopping Center; commercial buildings, stores in that block.

"Attention units responding to Box 8912, also receiving calls for the 3900 block Clarks Lane," the dispatcher updated us. It would still be a few minutes before first due Engine 46 could get to this area near the city-county line. *Maybe it's only something outside that's putting up a lot of smoke.* These thoughts flashed through my mind as I headed out Wabash Avenue between the engine and the truck.

"Battalion Chief 7, now receiving reports of children trapped, medic unit being dispatched" ended my hopes for something minor.

In that apartment building lived Madya Veronyich, a Russian, Jewish immigrant. Tired from a full day, she had started cooking oil for french fries and had gone to change her clothes. Exhausted, she soon forgot about the stove as she lay back playing with her two cats. These were her "babies." They didn't care that her English wasn't great. They shared her life in this strange country and made coming home to her modest apartment a joy.

In the kitchen the forgotten pot of oil smoked and then flashed into a flaming, boiling cauldron. Before Nadya realized what had happened the fire had spread up the cabinets and was reaching across the ceiling.

Stark terror gripped her as the smoke detector alerted her and she suddenly remembered the stove and dashed into the kitchen. Her first reaction was to try to smother the fire, but already the fire had grown too big. Smoke burned her eyes and choked her as she stood panic-stricken watching the flames roll across the kitchen ceiling and out into the dining room. Panic grew to horror as she realized that her "babies" were still in the bedroom, now cut off from her by the rapidly spreading fire and poisonous smoke.

Terrified, Nadya ran to the neighboring apartment and beat on the door frantically, but nobody was home. She ran from the building screaming as dense smoke filled the entire apartment and her frightened "babies" fell victim.

"Engine 46 on the scene, two story brick apartment building, fire showing second floor," Lieutenant Randy Schmidt radioed as I headed across Patterson Avenue.

The truck guys were humping a thirty-five foot ground ladder up to the building as I parked my chief's car across the street. I could see that a hoseline had already been stretched from the engine, around the building and into the courtyard where the entrance to the building was located.

A quick glance told me that the fire seemed to be burning in only the one apartment. The smoke seeping from the eaves at the roofline concerned me, but our guys from the aerial tower had also seen it and were already moving to check it out. The smoke oozing out didn't mean that the fire was in the attic yet, but it warned us. Fire fighters realize that if smoke can find its way into the attic area, fire may follow using the same openings.

As the engine crew attacked the fire in the apartment, the truck guys pushed by them searching for the children reported trapped. Quickly, they brought the fire under control. No fire had extended into the attic space above, and one hoseline knocked the fire down promptly.

At the front door, Lieutenant Vince Green from Truck 12

emerged to report to me that no persons had been found during the search of the building.

"Chief, we got these two cats here that look pretty bad. OK if we see what we can do?"

"Sure, Lieutenant, see what you can do for them," I answered.

With the fire controlled and no human victims to care for, we could afford to extend our efforts to the pets.

Neighbors milled around the lawn excitedly and attempted to comfort Nadya who stood shoeless, crying softly. Others were not so kind. They vocalized their anger that she had started the fire that affected them as well. Still others spoke in languages I couldn't understand.

When fire fighters appeared with her two cats, Nadya's crying became wailing. Both cats were covered with soot and obviously not well off. One was completely unconscious, perhaps dead, and the other looked up weakly at her from a fire fighter's arms.

A makeshift first aid station rapidly took shape on the lawn. When I looked back a few minutes later the cats, their owner, and several of our guys were sitting on a blanket. Bobby "Bibbit" Morris, the pump operator from Engine 46, was administering oxygen to the unconscious cat.

"I took off the mask and stuck the end of the hose into its nose," he informed me as I bent down to see the cats. Nadya rocked and talked to the other cat who looked very dazed.

"I'll be back in a few minutes," I told her. "I've got to see how bad the damage is."

My inspection of the apartment revealed that the fire had burned out the kitchen and part of the dining room. Heavy smoke had filled the entire apartment and the apartment next door. Fortunately, the fire had not entered the attic space above. We could see that the fire had originated on the stove. No in-depth investigation would be required on this one.

The truck crews began the task of removing the burned debris and positioned a smoke ejector, a special high-powered fan, to help in clearing the remaining smoke.

Out front again, I conferred with the manager of the apartment complex, who assured me that he had another apartment available to house Nadya.

After a fire in an occupied dwelling the fire department must care for the occupants' needs. One of the most basic needs is a place to stay. If relatives or friends can't provide housing, the fire department notifies the Red Cross or city agencies that can provide shelter, clothing, etc.

When someone's home has been on fire, he or she has been traumatized. "What's left?" is a common question. Clothing, family pictures, money, car keys, insurance papers—the list of concerns is long. Nadya was lucky. A few more minutes and all of her possessions would have been destroyed. Instead, the majority of her things would be OK once they were cleaned.

I went to the blanket first-aid station to give her the good news. Nadya was nowhere to be found. "Gone," Bibbit told me.

The oxygen had helped. A few breaths and the conscious cat was able to move around. Even the unconscious cat had improved with the oxygen and had opened her eyes. One of Nadya's neighbors had helped in loading the cats into a car, and they had already left for a nearby veterinarian's office.

There I stood ready to inform this lady of the status of her belongings. I wanted to assure her that she would have a place to live. *These* were the material things that needed attention. Meanwhile, to Nadya, all these things were secondary. Her "babies" came first. They were what mattered.

As we packed up to leave we talked about the cats' chances. We had done everything we could do. It would be up to the vet now. At least we gave them a fighting chance.

Fire fighters never cease to amaze me. Because they see so much human tragedy and sadness, they sometimes become hardened. Sometimes people misunderstand their attitude and demeanor. It's a defense mechanism that helps them to do the things they have to do.

But, at the next fire, that same tough, hardened person could be warm and compassionate to a little animal. One of my fellow battalion chiefs once adopted a kitten that had been severely burned in a fire that he was on. And my wife thought I was a little goofy when I brought home two pigeons whose wings had been singed badly in a fast-moving downtown six-alarmer.

Strange bunch, fire fighters.

13
Where'd All Those Years Go

I don't *feel* old. At least I try not to feel old. Sure, the aches and pains are more frequent now, reminders of my years in the fire service. The job does tend to cause wear and tear. But that's not the main factor. Having three teenagers is a greater contributor toward that age perception.

Today's trip to the Baltimore Arena to see the US Hot Rod Grand Slam of Motorsports was a great example. Now, I guess I am a little out of touch with today's entertainment. When I was a kid monsters were ugly, scary things that we saw at the Waverly movie theater on Saturdays. For a quarter a kid could be scared all day.

Yesterday's monsters were Godzilla, Dracula, the Creature from the Black Lagoon, and similar images that could haunt a kid's dreams until at least Tuesday night. Not today. Today's monsters included Bigfoot, BoogeyVan, Equalizer, and Black Stallion. These monsters will also haunt me. The deafening roar of a thousand horsepower reverberating through the arena mixed with the screams of joy from thousands of kids was almost as scary as those monsters of my childhood.

"Monster trucks rule, Dad," I was educated by my fourteen year old. I hate it when he talks in that foreign language.

All the way downtown David had tried to contain his enthusiasm. I was certainly containing mine. "Dave, my shoulder's killing me. I took some pain medicine right before we left, so if I doze off don't be insulted."

"Yeah, Dad. Have you ever *heard* a monster truck?" was my son's reply.

"Boy, this place sure brings back a lot of memories," I started as we entered the building. To his credit, David was kind enough just to shake his head.

"When I was a teenager I spent so many nights here. My friend, Steve, and I used to come here all the time to see the Bullets play."

David's blank stare prompted me to explain that the *Washington* Bullets used to be the *Baltimore* Bullets. I guess that *was* a while ago.

"Uh huh."

"Most of all we loved to come see the Clippers play ice hockey. I can't tell you how many nights we spent up there in the upper deck."

"OK"

Finally, the fondest memory of all drifted back to me. "And your Aunt Barb and I came here and saw The Beatles when they came to America," I remembered proudly.

"Good Lord you're old, Dad"

"Thanks, Dave."

I felt a little bit more at home when the show started. The announcer began the introduction of the day's participants. He called for music and the speakers responded with the familiar introductory piece from "The Tonight Show."

"*No, no, no!*" he yelled toward the stage. "That might be fine for Johnny Carson or Jay Leno, but I want some *music*," he shouted emphatically.

Uh oh.

The young crowd screamed with delight as "The Unforgiven" by Mettalica reverberated off the walls at a dangerous volume. Now it was my turn for the blank stare.

For the next two hours and eighteen minutes—I counted—we were treated to the sight of grown men and women in gaudy, noisy, jacked-up trucks with huge wheels crushing cars that didn't look much worse than the ones I drive. Intermixed with the sessions of destruction were races of motorcycles doing suicidal leaps and hairpin turns in the dirt. Other similarly concocted competitions and displays of bravado rounded out the day's delights. The display made *Dracula* seem pretty tame.

Today certainly wasn't the first time that my kids helped me to feel old. That seems to be one of their favorite pastimes. The kids delight in pointing out my receding hair line. Actually, disappearing hair line might be more accurate. A while back David thoughtfully sent away for information on Rogaine for me. I need to keep him away from that late-night TV.

And they just hate the music that I like. "More geezer music" usually follows my change of radio stations to something more sedate than the intolerable noise that invariably assaults me when I start the car after the kids have used it.

It seems I'm always a little too slow to pick up the vernacular my kids are using. It took me two years to say something was "dudical." Then I was immediately (and not too gently) informed that *nobody* says that anymore. Nice try, dad.

I'm not sure when I got old in my children's eyes. I guess parents are naturally perceived as old. What really hurts are the other little signs that accumulate.

Not long ago, the entire family was returning from a trip to the ocean. We stopped at one of our regular "rest" stops in Denton, Maryland, a fast-food restaurant that serves a great barbecue sandwich. After a week at the beach I felt terrific. Suntanned and happy, and dressed in my favorite vacation outfit, I'm sure that I looked young and attractive as I bounced up to the counter. The cute, young lady who took our order had a beautiful smile. I couldn't help but notice her other attractive features. "Have a seat and listen for your number," she said sweetly. For just a second I thought how nice it would be to be, well, a good bit younger.

I joined the family at the booth that the kids had gone ahead to claim for us. While we talked and waited for the food to be prepared, I decided to check the receipt to make sure that our order was correct. Two barbecue sandwiches, one with cole slaw. Those for the adults. Two cheeseburgers for Tim. A steak sub for David. Robin doesn't eat meat, so it was french fries only for her. And then I saw it: *Senior Citizen's Discount—10%*. Ouch!

After what I was thinking about that cute, little gal, how could she do that to me? My wife and kids laughed so hard they nearly fell out of the booth when I showed them the receipt. I was mortified. My first senior citizen's discount at forty-four. We laughed about that incident for weeks.

When I think of some of the changes I have seen in the fire service during my career I think that maybe the kids aren't too far off.

When I first began in the Baltimore City Fire Department all of our apparatus was painted red and white. Fire engines in most places in this country were the traditional red. Then research took the fire service by storm. Scientists intent on improving fire fighter safety determined that the color of the fire trucks could be changed to improve visibility. The rationale was that if the public could see the fire trucks more easily there would be fewer accidents. Since many fire fighter deaths and injuries each year occur while responding or returning, this was of more than academic interest.

Bright yellow, lime-green, greenish-yellow, the new colors appeared all over the country. Not every fire department changed, but many did, in a sincere desire to improve safety. The Baltimore City Fire Department adopted a new paint scheme as well. Our red and white engines became orange and white. We actually tried a couple of colors before the orange took hold. Undoubtedly, the worst combination was the "rust and white" that was dubbed "babyshit and white" by some of our more eloquent members.

For any large fire department to change over to something new usually takes a considerable investment of time and money. The department decided that all new vehicles would sport the new color scheme. The apparatus that we already owned would be repainted only if it had major repairs or had major bodywork done that led to a need to repaint the vehicle. The transition to a fleet that was all the same color would take a long time.

Each year the number of the department's orange and white vehicles increased until finally the big day arrived. The oldest truck still in first line service was replaced by a brand new Truck 27, a gorgeous one hundred foot, orange and white, Seagrave ladder truck. It had taken almost twenty years, but now the transition was complete. I had witnessed history in our department.

Anyone familiar with how government functions may have already guessed the next chapter. As luck would have it, the time had come for a new fire chief to assume the top spot in our department. Chief Herman Williams Jr. was a man fond of the "old fire department" traditions. As such, one of his first decisions was that fire engines should *look* like fire engines. In a decision that was very popular among the members of our department, the chief announced that all new apparatus would be—red and white.

Years of evaluating the effectiveness of yellow fire engines had failed to yield any conclusive evidence that the color significantly improved fire fighter safety. In fact, many argued that the public did not quickly perceive yellow vehicles as emergency vehicles at all and, therefore, did not yield the right-of-way as readily. Today the trend is back toward red. Red and white fire engines again fill the stations of the Baltimore City Fire Department.

Another trend that I may have outlived concerns the protective gear that fire fighters wear. When I first entered the fire service, fire fighters were wearing the traditional fire helmet that most people could readily identify. On the front of the helmet a leather shield displayed the rank and the company of the wearer. The back of the helmet was adorned with a large brim that kept water, debris, and embers from going down the fire fighter's neck. And fire fighters' helmets were almost universally black.

Research surrounding the nation's space program yielded new materials. Drawing on this new technology and the experience of motorcyclists, the fire service radically changed helmet design. Metal helmets gave way to leather, to various plastics, to fiberglass. The distinctive shape changed as well. The brim disappeared. The leather frontpiece yielded to identifying stickers and hinged faceshields of impact-resistant plastic designed to improve eye protection. Black helmets became scarce as safety concerns dictated the use of the more visible yellow.

Today the Baltimore City Fire Department is in the process of issuing new helmets to all its members. The new helmets are fitted with a brim at the back. The large fold-down eye protector has vanished. A leather frontpiece adorns the front of the helmet. And the yellow has given way to the newest color—black. Déjà vu!

Anyone fortunate enough to be in the fire service long enough inevitably sees many changes. We tend to be hard on ourselves when we claim that things never change. The changes that do occur in the fire service have aptly been described as evolutionary rather than revolutionary, but the changes have really been substantial during my career. I can't even guess the changes that tomorrow's fire fighters will see.

It doesn't seem like I've been around that long, but maybe time gets away from me. Last year I had the opportunity to visit the Fire Museum of Maryland in nearby Lutherville. It is a wonderful place full of pictures, equipment, and memorabilia of the fire service's yesterdays. I found it a little unsettling that so much looked so familiar. It was fun to be able to explain much of what we saw to my much younger fire service friends who accompanied me.

"Hey, Mike, you've got to see the antique Baltimore City engine in the next aisle," I was told excitedly.

The guys loved it when I stood there with my mouth agape. "I used to drive that."

<u>14</u>

Sunrises

I love sunrises. I'm not sure when it was that I grew to truly appreciate them. To me, a sunrise is so much more than the beginning of a new day. It's a reality check, a time-marker that reminds me that life is too short.

One of the benefits of my job's crazy hours is that I get to see the sun come up a bit more than the average sane person. Sometimes I look back and wonder where they have all gone—the sunrises that is. I wish I could say that I had appreciated every one of them, but like most people, I've taken too many of them for granted. Some days it just seems like it's dark, and then it's light, and I never even noticed. What a shame.

Sunrises have special meanings in my life. I love the beautiful ones, the ones with some layers of clouds around to capture the first few rays and bring the sky alive with pink and light blue, and then brilliant orange even before the sun is actually visible. I can't remember my science well enough to separate the stratus clouds from the cumulus clouds. It doesn't matter to me. I love clouds.

But it's not really the scientific aspects of sunrise that touch me, it's the psychological and emotional aspects that make my sunrises important.

I've learned to take that time to be introspective, if only for a few moments.

Anyone who starts their day before 5:00 A.M. certainly has the opportunity to appreciate sunrise, but I'm particularly blessed. Depending on the time of year, I get to see the sun come up on my way to day shift or on my way home from night work. How ironic it is that what makes those commuting sunrises so spectacular isn't even part of our natural world. No matter how pre-occupied I am, no matter what my mood, the intersection of Providence Road and Interstate 695 grabs me. From there, I look south at the eleven story building originally occupied by Blue Cross and Blue Shield. Now it is the headquarters of the Baltimore County Police and the Baltimore County Fire Departments.

The faces of the building must have been oriented for other reasons than to catch the beauty of the sun, or maybe the architects were true geniuses. The entire building is made of those modern windows that reflect the light during the day and let you see right in at night. When the early morning sun gets just to the correct angle, the building is aglow in a spectacular reflection of golds and pinks and fiery reds that I can't possibly ignore. What a fabulous way to start the day.

Sometimes, though, it's not optimism that sunrise gives me. Sometimes it's relief. Night seems to bring out the ugliest side of fire.

Sleeping people are particularly likely to fall victim to its ravages. Most of my cruelest fires have occurred while the victims slept. There's an unwritten rule about being safe at home in your own bed that fire delights in violating.

Many nights when I'm working, the first signs of light bring a sense of relief to me, especially when I'm alone in the chief's car, returning from an incident. I've made it through the night. My co-workers have made it. And now the citizens start to wake. It seems trite to say that danger stalks the night, but any fire fighter will tell you so. Fourteen hours we've stood guard. Soon it will be time for us to go home, and a new shift will assume that role of guardians, of protectors.

We don't linger on those thoughts of the awesome responsibility entrusted to us, nor on the danger that duty could bring. We couldn't. The stress of firefighting is tremendous. The decisions we face, the actions we are required to execute flawlessly, could determine whether someone lives or dies. We are all aware of it, but we never talk about it. Sunrise is a sigh of relief for me.

At other times it is sadness that accompanies the dawn. Too many of my sunrises have occurred on the fireground. Those early morning tragedies often drag on into that time that should be beautiful. Instead, with the light comes the realization that something terrible has happened.

The daylight literally sheds new light on devastation. Burned out homes and buildings look different under the artificial lights at night. It's only when day breaks that the full impact of destruction can be appreciated, and for the victims the sense of loss deepens.

A particular sadness accompanies the sunrise when we are on the scene of a fatal fire. I hate the false hope that the sunrise offers. As the day begins and the community comes alive, the sunrise seems to mock us. The promise of a new day is empty. Someone didn't make it through the night. We've witnessed the end. I've gotten used to witnessing death over the years. I stopped counting a long time ago. And yet, I *never* get used to death. I hope I never will. Seeing how tentative our claim to life really is makes me appreciate it much more deeply.

I've heard people say that there's a reason for everything. Part of a great plan, I've been told. I don't know. I don't understand. I've seen people of all ages die. The youngest ones hurt us all the most, but *nobody* deserves to die like that. The unspeakable horror of a death by fire is best left undescribed. Most fire fighters already know. The rest of you don't want to.

No, sunrise doesn't undo the horror that night has brought. It reinforces my feeling of helplessness and of vulnerability. No matter how hard we try, people still die. It took me a while to learn that lesson. It's a tough one.

But even after those worst of nights sunrise serves a purpose for me. It brings me back into focus with my life.

Everyone has problems, and certainly I'm no exception. My wife's health hasn't been good for several years. The teenagers try my patience. There's never enough money. My shoulder is a mess. I need a sunrise to help me keep everything in perspective. When I take the time to marvel at God's handiwork my problems don't seem quite so big. I've seen people with *big* problems. I'll keep my own.

This morning's sunrise was a great example. For five months I've been off duty following serious shoulder surgery. For the last ten years my shoulder has caused me misery. Several fireground injuries and a bone-jarring accident in the chief's car have added to the problems.

Cortisone shots, numerous rounds of physical therapy, and two previous arthroscopic surgeries have failed to resolve the problem. In October, I consented to major reconstructive surgery, aware that it threatened to end my career. The perpetual pain and the loss of motion left me no other choice.

Now here I am, five months later. Rest, physical therapy, rest, medicine, rest, ice, heat, rest, x-rays, CT scans, rest. None of them has brought my shoulder back to working order. I'm so rested I could scream. Finally, yesterday, I came to the ocean for a few days. The uncertainty of my future weighs heavily on me, and I need restorative surgery—the mental variety.

And so I found myself at the inlet in Ocean City, Maryland this morning, a familiar place that holds pleasant memories for me.

The pre-season emptiness of the resort guaranteed me a private viewing. The unobstructed horizon of ocean lent a panoramic aspect to the sunrise.

As the chilly darkness relented, I detected an almost imperceptible lightening of the sky. Above, the stars shone brilliantly. And the sounds of the surf crashing on the great, stone jetty provided the rhythmic, soothing music that I sought. The seemingly incongruous intrusion of the automatic foghorn at the tip of the jetty actually enhanced the pacifying melody. I stood on the beach and reflected that even the foghorn of my youth had evolved into a piercing electronic "beeeeeep." Off for thirteen seconds, on for two, off for thirteen. I wondered how many boaters have been warned by it.

A metal, fifteen foot high tower at the end of the jetty held the other sentry. A white flashing light blinked its warning on and off at three second intervals.

Even before it was light enough to make them out clearly, a few commercial fishing vessels plodded their way through the inlet, ocean-bound. I could see only their running lights and their dark outlines as they bobbed their way within fifty yards of me. The rumble of their powerful diesels soon faded and they shrunk quickly as they headed offshore. The parfait along the horizon was a blend of pastels. The white sand of the beach in the foreground and the green of the ocean dissolved smoothly into the bottom layer of dark gray sky. In ascending order were swatches of lighter gray, then deep pink, then light pink, and finally the brightest portion of the rainbow-like picture, the light blue-gray that merged with the still dark blue sky above.

Against this backdrop the seagulls began to stir. Their silhouettes silently moved right to left, left to right, over my head, as they started their day of doing whatever it is that gulls do. The birds drifted effortlessly on the ocean-bred breeze that satisfied my senses with the taste and smell of salt.

Soon it became obvious where the sun would peek above the ocean. That spot became a brighter pink.

Then the whole sky was lighter. All the stars but one had disappeared and it was daylight on the beach. The day had started in earnest, but the sun still was not up.

For a long time it seemed as through the process of sunrise had stopped. For a full half-hour I meandered the water's edge. The high-tide mark was strewn with bits of sea grass, shells, and hundreds of crab legs. Obviously something shares my affinity for the blue crab.

And then a red point appeared. Just one brilliant spot at first, then a little bigger. It seemed to take only a minute for the whole fiery sun to leap up. It happened so quickly I almost missed it.

The brilliant red-orange ball didn't hang onto the horizon as I had hoped it would—obviously showing who was in charge.

It was still cold, but the promise of a sunny, mild day filled me with hope as I headed back to the car.

I know I'm alive. God just reaffirmed it for me.

I love sunrises.

15

Reading Signs

I spend much of my time in the fire department reading signs. Not *sign* signs. Other signs. Over the years, I have read so many accounts of tragic fires where fire fighters have been killed because "the roof collapsed without warning" or because "they had no time to escape before the wall fell outward, burying them." I can't let that happen.

As a chief, my job is to see that "warning," to give them that "time to escape." It's a part of my job that I take very seriously, and I learn everything that I possibly can to help me read the signs correctly.

In fire department training classes, we learn to recognize the signs of an impending backdraft (a type of explosion that can occur during a fire when certain conditions are present). We spend much time learning to analyze a fire's behavior and to predict its next step. We learn when and where to ventilate a fire, based on those observations. Only with correct ventilation can we reduce the heat and smoke to more manageable levels that will allow us to make a prompt and effective attack.

Our textbooks are filled with descriptions of various colors of smoke and flames and with explanations of their significance. Understanding what is burning helps us to determine what extinguishing agent to use and the proper method to fight the fire.

Certain noises, we learn, can be clues to imminent collapse of a burning building. A rumble above, a creak in the floor, a change in the noise of the fire—missing these signs could be disastrous.

Signs abound on the emergency scene. We all study them... and still fire fighters die.

Fire is a terrifying, dynamic force that is unforgiving. If I miscalculate on my income tax, the IRS may punish me. If I miscalculate on the fireground, my co-workers or I may not go home tonight.

Since the day that I came into the fire service, even before, I have been an avid reader. I've read and studied just about every fire service textbook around. Each month, I read the fire service journals cover-to-cover. The hours that I have spent in the classroom, as teacher and student, are mind-boggling, and still there is so much that I don't know.

I do not believe enough can be said about the value of experience. Coupled with reading and training, experience prepares the fire fighter for the next emergency. Even after all these years, I still try to learn something from every significant incident. Sometimes it can be dramatic, such as what can happen when you rely on one water source at a serious fire. Sometimes it can be more mundane, like learning to make sure that there are *two* gloves in your turnout coat pocket when you put it on the apparatus. But they all add up.

All the little bits of information become experience. Some things just can't be taught in the classroom. No amount of study nor reading can bring the intangibles, the "sixth sense" that experienced fire fighters seem to possess. Experience is difficult to quantify, maybe impossible, yet it is a very real attribute of the best fire fighters. The fire service, like most fields, has its share of those filled with the "book-learning," the theorists who can regurgitate verbatim endless formulae and technical jargon. Those who fit this description may "razzle-dazzle" some outside the fire service. They might even succeed in duping some within the service.

Unfortunately, fires are not fought in the classroom. Real emergencies happen in real time, with real people, and with real consequences. The stakes are high, and the margin for error is frightfully slim. It is here, in the real world of firefighting, that experience shows.

I made a decision early in my career to work in busy stations whenever I possibly could. I firmly believe that you don't learn by sitting around listening to the other companies run. From my observations, it seems the most energetic, reliable, and talented individuals gravitate to the busiest stations, for it is here that they can best learn. There are exceptions, of course, but generally the busier companies perform more efficiently.

I've been fortunate to have spent most of my career in busy areas. I've learned from some seasoned veterans, and I've had the opportunity to practice. That experience has paid off frequently, and I continue to do everything that I can to learn.

Reading signs means being able to look beyond the things that everybody sees, and picking out the subtle indicators of something not so obvious. I have seen many displays of this ability that have saved our people from death or serious injury. Those who possess that sixth sense coveted by fire fighters are, in fact, the best sign readers.

Fire fighters begin learning to read signs early in their career, even without thinking about it. It doesn't take too long before fire fighters begin to learn the fundamentals.

Fire fighters learn to call on all of their senses. Before long, they can enter the hallway of an apartment building at 3:00 A.M. and immediately recognize the distinctive odor of burning food. No book or class can teach somebody the smells that become familiar with experience. Mattress fire, burning paper, overheated fluorescent light ballast, oil burner backfire—each produces a unique odor that fire fighters instinctively catalog for future reference.

Actually, I read signs all day. Emergency scenes are just one test of my sign reading abilities. Each day, I try to be alert for signs as I go around the battalion and interact with the people in my command.

Since teamwork is so critical in our job, we spend much time and effort building the team and keeping it running smoothly. To do that, I need to know what is going on. There is an axiom in the fire service that the higher you go up the rank structure, the more difficult it is for you to stay in tune with the daily activities in the trenches. Of necessity, the battalion chief is occupied with managerial activities much of the time. It is very easy to become removed from the mainstream.

Fire fighters are usually a pretty outspoken bunch, but their way of conveying messages is not always direct. Sometimes the verbal messages do not match the non-verbal, and it's time for me to play detective. Morale always needs attention, and it is constantly under attack.

"How come I've gotta ride that gut bucket again this shift? It can't possibly be my turn again." Riding the medic unit is not a favorite activity of our average fire fighter.

"When am I gonna get a callback (overtime)? I know Smitty's had two in the last month. How come I'm behind everybody else? They never call me."

"Do they know you guys are 'in service'? That was our third medic assist, and you guys haven't even turned a wheel. Buncha prima donnas."

"Are we the only shift that knows where the mops are? What do the other shifts do all day, since the bums obviously don't do housework?"

There are those who believe that as long as the guys are complaining, they're happy. I guess there's some truth to that. We obviously have some very happy guys.

Like all fire fighters who have been around for awhile, I have accumulated my sign-reading skills in many ways Actually, my ability to read signs started long before I entered the fire department.

Like most children, I learned the value of being able to read signs from my parents. When mom says *no*, it really means *maybe*. When dad says *no*, it means wait a while and ask mom.

Children learn to observe the general climate in the household. When love flows and laughter fills the room, *that's* the time to ask for something. When mom says icily, "Tell your father... " Bad sign. Not the time to ask *anything*.

When I was huddled at the top of the stairs with my brother

and sister, Christmas and Easter mornings held special anticipation. Had we been good enough for Santa to come? Did the Easter Bunny bring goodies to our house? As we waited, and mom sleepily went downstairs to "check first", we all hoped that Santa couldn't really see everything we did all year. And why were mom and dad so upset that we're up? It'll be daylight before too long. We soon learned to recognize it as a good sign when we heard, "You stay right there until I tell you. Don't you dare come down those steps." It wasn't too many years before I found myself on the other end of that ritual.

Growing up, I soon learned the little signs that foretold what was to come. Something as simple as what name was being used to address me took on meaning. "Honey..." This was a good sign. *"Michael..."*—a bad sign. And then there was the dreaded *"Michael Stephen Ker-nan . . ."*—a *very* bad sign.

When I was a kid, I learned that conversations were not always conversations. Eventually, I learned that my parents didn't really want an answer at all when they said, "And just what do you think you're doing?" Sometimes it was definitely better to keep my mouth shut.

"I know I shouldn't do this but..." generally signaled that the softening up process had been successful. Something favorable usually followed.

Conversely, "This is going to hurt me a lot more that it is going to hurt you . . . " was never a good sign and was certainly not true. Nothing favorable *ever* followed this.

Catholic school education provided many opportunities to learn signs. Now to fully appreciate the lessons, you had to know the teachers. The nuns at Saints Philip and James took particular delight in driving terror into the hearts of children. They called this process "instilling values." A good swat with a wooden pointer or ten "twangs" from a rubber band placed around a kid's wrist—these were "character builders." Learning to read signs became very important. Nobody wanted to risk incurring the wrath of the dreaded Sister Suzanne. I learned to pay real close attention to the little signs that warned the boys that today would not be a good day to mess with the girls' hair and make them cry. Slamming of books, brusque, sharp movements, and stern, monosyllabic instructions were bad signs. Good signs were harder to detect since they apparently never taught the nuns how to smile in "nun school." I once heard someone say that nuns were "God's hit men." Now there's someone who went to Catholic school.

My high school teachers, Jesuit priests, on the other hand, were actually like real people. That's probably one of the reasons that the rest of the Catholic clergy barely consider them Catholic at all. Those days at Loyola High School taught me a lot about reading signs. Father Sheridan, called "Buc" by all, but never to his face, was a master at sending signs. I never heard the man raise his voice, but there was never a doubt who was in charge. When he looked up from the book he was reading and affixed *the stare*, the message was unmistakable: "You have caused a disruption. Cease." That stare was all that it ever took to immediately send cold chills down the offender's spine.

As meaningful as the stare could be, the best lesson in sign reading was more dramatic. Father Sheridan was a wonderful teacher in freshman English and Latin. But late on a spring afternoon, after lunch had its inevitable sedating effect, a young man's thoughts turned to other things. Daydreams of fishing, baseball, and girls invaded even the most scholastic minds. Somehow, *Caesar's Gallic Wars*—in a long-dead language at that—could not compete. Undaunted by the competition, Father Sheridan maintained that low, rhythmic, approach to education that has anesthetized students forever. Being the experienced teacher that he was—he had taught my father at Loyola—Father Sheridan was well aware of the attention lapses that glazed eyes and bobbing heads betrayed. I quickly learned the tell-tale sign that "remedial action" was about to take place.

Without a discernible change in the tempo or pitch of his voice, Father Sheridan drifted slowly toward the blackboard. Intimate familiarity with the subject matter allowed him to continue reciting the lesson as he reached for the eraser on the ledge and headed toward the oblivious offender. With a remarkable precision, he lobbed the chalk dust laden eraser in an arc that terminated on the desk of the daydreamer. Invariably, the student was immediately enveloped in a cloud of choking, white chalk dust and the class was treated to the best laugh of the day. Everybody in the class thoroughly enjoyed this display, except the embarrassed victim because remedial action of this type also resulted in "jug", or detention. No baseball after school today. I learned to be always vigilant for the slightest movement toward that blackboard.

Reading signs took on new meaning when I began the dating game. Since it is widely recognized that men and women speak totally different languages, it helped to learn to read the signs that helped translate "feminine" into English. I admit that I still have not mastered this art, but I was able to learn some early lessons.

"I'm just not in the mood," or "I've got a headache." We all know what they mean. But I learned the more subtle signs.

After sitting on her porch for hours and getting up the nerve to put my arm around her, it was a welcome sign to see her glasses come off. That's the sign that a kiss would be welcome. And if she took out her chewing gum, maybe more than one kiss was possible. Good signs. If a girl laughed when you tried to kiss her, however, that was a bad sign.

"Can you come over tonight? My parents are going out and they'll be gone all evening." Great sign.

Blind dates were a part of growing up. Inevitably the question arose, "What does she look like?" Almost anything was acceptable except the dreaded, "She's really got a great personality." Look out.

Second dates were not always as easy to get, but sometimes I was a little slow to pick up on that. One gorgeous blonde I met at a C.Y.O. (Catholic Youth Organization) dance at St. Bernard's taught me a valuable lesson. After being turned down for "I have to stay home and wash my hair," I probably should have been suspicious. The next weekend she couldn't go out because, "I have to go to Novena with my Mom." Bad sign. It took one more weekend and "I have to stay home and vacuum the ceilings!" before the signs were clear.

One of the phrases that has humbled many a young man is, "I really like you as a friend." I eventually learned this was the sign to look for another girlfriend.

All of that education in sign reading that I obtained early in life has helped me to be able to accurately read my wife's body language. When she takes her body upstairs in a huff and slams the bedroom door, that means, "Don't bother hurrying up to bed tonight."

16
First Line of Defense

Yesterday was a terrible day. My day at work was uneventful. My light duty assignment kept me doing office work while my shoulder slowly healed. In the morning, I took time out to see the surgeon who operated on my shoulder six months ago. The doctor yesterday told me that he was no longer optimistic that I will regain full use of my shoulder. I headed back to work feeling disappointed and frustrated. It was a pretty good day to feel sorry for myself.

The day changed for me, however, and for all Americans when the news broke from Oklahoma City. Throughout the afternoon, I watched the story unfold. A devastating explosion, apparently caused by a car-bomb, had demolished a federal office building filled with government workers, civilians, and children in the building's day-care center. All day the screen was filled with the scenes of horror. Bloody, shocked, and terrified, the faces of Americans struck by terrorism reached out to us all. If Oklahoma City could be hit, the obvious question was "Can anyone ever feel safe from this kind of thing?"

Admittedly, I didn't get much work done yesterday. I sat in the lounge area at the station transfixed by the sight of America in pain. I frequently looked out the windows from my vantage point at the Oldtown Station and pondered the possibility that the explosion could just as easily have been in one of the many high-rises I was staring at. It was a chilling thought.

Throughout the day, commentators speculated that some group with Middle East connections may have struck. Others noted the explosion occurred on the anniversary of the storming of the Branch Davidian compound in Waco, Texas, and suggested that a motive might lie there.

These were the questions that begged for answers. Who could do such a horrible thing and why? I shared the outrage and the pain, but not the surprise. My career has provided me with a look at the worst side of people. I have seen the senseless cruelty that we try to explain away with insight into the sociological problems of the perpetrators or the psychological foundation for the actions of a madman. Fire fighters are the ones who pick up the pieces when violence rips at the decency of our society.

I watched as the government officials talked about the federal response that was being organized. I saw the politicians. I saw the President. All expressed the outrage that we all felt and each promised some sort of mobilization.

I couldn't help but watch with pride at the knowledge of what was already underway. As always, it was the fire service who was already on the scene working furiously to treat and transport the injured. It was the fire service who was searching the precarious remnants of the shattered building, risking their own lives in the process. No bureaucratic mechanism would slow the response of the fire fighters. No politicians would have to go before the public to promise the response of those who are always on the front line.

Even without a personal knowledge of the Oklahoma City Fire Department or of the surrounding fire departments, I knew for certain that the dust had not even settled before fire fighters were responding.

So many times I have watched the scenes of large scale disasters—hurricanes, tornadoes, floods, earthquakes—and listened to the reports of "rescue workers" laboring to find the missing or rescue those trapped. I doubt that most people ever question just who those "rescue workers" are. At every disaster the first to lay their lives on the line are the fire fighters. While the politicians and other officials are describing the response to the emergency, the fire fighters, police officers, and medical crews are quietly doing what they do best. Rarely do they get the credit—even more rarely do they seek it.

These weren't anonymous "rescue workers" I watched helping the injured. These weren't nameless, faceless hordes of workers who tore at the collapsed building to find those still trapped. These were fire fighters, my brother and sister fire fighters, doing what they have committed their lives to. Unselfishly and without hesitation, they threw themselves into the terror as fire fighters do.

Reports circulated that another bomb had been found. Instinctively, people ran for their lives. But I knew the agonizing decision that the fire fighters inside the building faced. Do I turn and run when people are still trapped inside? How can I leave an injured, terrified victim whose hand I'm holding so that I can retreat to safety while they lie pinned under tons of steel and concrete? I could imagine the feelings that must have torn at those forced to withdraw. Sure they were scared, but the fear was mixed with other stronger emotions.

Fire fighters don't leave people in need. That is just not in their make-up. Intellectually they knew that dead fire fighters could help nobody. Another explosion that could trap them would add to an already horrible problem. Intellectually they knew, but instinct, human compassion, and a lifetime of dedication to helping people must have made the decision to withdraw excruciating.

The entire country watched the scene as the magnitude of the tragedy sunk in. Eventually, we learned that many had died, many, many were missing. As big as the overall incident was, it was the little parts of the incident scene that touched me the most.

I watched the fire fighter climb the aerial ladder to an upper floor and bring down an injured man who had no other means of escape. The reporters interviewed the injured man shortly afterward and he told of his terrible experience. Most of his co-workers had just simply vanished as the building collapsed. I wondered if he realized what was involved in his rescue.

I looked at the huge pieces of concrete that hung

precariously above the area from which he was rescued. That entire side of the building was shattered and torn away, leaving the most unstable, dangerous environment for the rescue. I held my breath as the fire fighter ascended the ladder. What a decision that must have been to place the ladder truck up to that side of the building knowing that the rest of the building could come down at any minute. There would be no escape for those underneath. Instant death was a terrifying possibility. And yet here they were. The truck crew maneuvered into position and they went up and rescued that man. I'm sure they didn't even have time to enjoy the satisfaction of the rescue before they moved on to their next assignment. I wondered how many acts of incredible bravery were hidden from our view inside the horror of twisted steel, broken concrete, dangling electrical lines, gas lines and water pipes spewing their contents. What terrible working conditions.

The nation watched with horror as a fire fighter carried the broken body of a child. It isn't often that civilians see that terrible part of a fire fighter's job. Few things touch a fire fighter as deeply as holding the lifeless little body of one that couldn't be saved. As a parent, as a human being, as a fire fighter, I felt the pain.

Yesterday and today, I listened as the assistant fire chief briefed the country on the situation. I was impressed by how well he tactfully handled the situation. While giving an informative look into what was involved, the chief did not mention what I knew the fire fighters were facing inside. I don't think the average person could be ready to deal with the mangled and dismembered. Even the thoughts of people torn to shreds would be too horrible for many to comprehend, and so the chief compassionately didn't describe what I knew must be the situation. Unfortunately, no one would be able to shield the fire fighters from the things that nightmares are made of.

Knowing the fire service mentality, I know that I was not alone in wanting to be able to help. Obviously, I could not be there to physically help, but my thoughts and prayers were for the victims and their families. I'm sure my prayers were but a tiny part of a nationwide outpouring. I hope God was listening when I prayed for all of those fire fighters, police officers, and others who had to deal with the horror. God, help them with their nightmares.

17

I Remember

The day that I determine that I know everything I need to know about the fire service, I hope that I have enough sense to get out, for I will have lost my mind.

Those who serve in the emergency services deal with a dangerous and complicated world. To make matters worse, the rules keep changing. Only through constant reading, practice, and training can a fire fighter hope to keep up. It's that desire that has brought me to the National Fire Academy again.

Since 1981, the National Fire Academy in Emmitsburg, Maryland has trained many thousands of fire fighters from across our country, even some from other countries. It is an establishment dedicated to excellence. The Academy seeks out the very best in the fire service and other fields to do the course development and delivery.

I remember when the search was on for a campus. The National Fire Academy, newly formed to fill a void in emergency services training, needed a home. Numerous sites were considered. Finally, it looked as though the campus would be in New York or in Maryland. I remember reading that the site in Maryland had been selected.

The decision was of particular interest to me because I already knew the facility. The home of the National Fire Academy was to be the campus of the former St. Joseph's College. In high school I had attended a retreat only a half mile away and during our free time we walked the area. A college for girls seemed a natural attraction for a group from an all boys' high school. Had it not been for my familiarity with and proximity to the area, I doubt that the decision for the location of the campus would have meant much to me. In those early days, most of us in the fire service probably could not envision what the Academy would become. I certainly didn't.

The Academy isn't a place where I come to be taught. It's a place where I come to be absorbed, to become re-focused.

This isn't an academy where fire fighters learn to use hose or to climb ladders. This is an academy where fire service leaders of today and tomorrow learn how to use Nominal Group Technique, synergy, and risk assessment. These are the tools of the brain rather than the tools of the hands.

At the National Fire Academy, the emphasis is on learning to deal with the management issues that face fire departments and governments each day. Students study legal issues, financial management, community master-planning, and disaster preparedness. Interpersonal dynamics, written and verbal communications skills, media relations—these are the tools of the manager. Other students will specialize in public fire education, arson investigation, code enforcement, emergency medical services management, and educational methodology.

For the most part, this is the non-glamorous side of the fire service. These are the foundations for an emergency service that serves the citizens everyday in so many invisible ways. None of these services happens by accident. They require tremendous effort and dedication from the fire departments and the individuals who serve in them. The National Fire Academy is here to enhance the delivery of those services nationwide.

Again this time, my trip to the Academy has been rewarding. For the better part of two weeks, my classmates and I have learned how to prepare for the catastrophic incidents that challenge the best of departments. Tornadoes, hurricanes, floods, and similar scenarios have been discussed. We have studied community risk assessment, capability assessment, media relations, integrated emergency management systems, damage assessment, and emergency operations center.

Tomorrow we will have an all-day exercise in which we will all participate. Central City, the fictitious town we've been running for the last ten days, will be hit by a major disaster, or maybe more than one. We will be running an Emergency Operations Center where the representatives of the city, county, and state departments of various types will interface to handle the emergency and begin the steps necessary to restore the community to normal. Each of us has been playing a role in the days leading up to the disaster and tomorrow the full-scale exercise takes place. I look forward to the opportunity to learn something that may benefit me and my department when I return home.

So many topics, so much information flies by in the two week course. Just carrying all the notes, handouts, and books could cause a hernia. And yet the learning doesn't stop there. Much of the learning that takes place at the Academy occurs outside the classroom. With such a diverse group of fire service officials gathered for two weeks, the exchange of ideas and information is tremendous. *Networking* was a buzz word in management circles some years ago. I don't hear the term much anymore, but I see the process clearly each time I visit here. The National Fire Academy provides the perfect forum for the interaction that prevents stagnation and parochialism within the nation's fire service.

Much of the learning is jokingly referred to as "pub ed"—as in discussions over a beer in the campus pub at night. After the night's studies and reading assignments many of the students drift to the student center and pub. Over the music, the televisions, and the smack of pool balls, the discussions center on everything from the latest trends in protective clothing and current management techniques to the skiing opportunities in various areas. In this relaxed atmosphere of fun and camaraderie many seeds are planted. I have brought home new ideas every time I have come and been able to share some as well. I wonder how much the pub has changed the fire service throughout the country.

Each time I come to the Academy I come away with a new

appreciation for the commitment of the people in my profession. I return home refreshed and re-motivated. A visit here is a rewarding experience.

The beauty and serenity of the campus and the surrounding area add greatly to the overall Academy experience. Nestled in the foothills of the Catoctin mountains, the campus possesses a tranquillity that belies the activity within the walls of the various buildings.

Early morning, before classes start, usually finds me walking. A variety of little creatures scamper among the stately, ancient trees. The flowers and blossoming dogwood trees make for a great place to start the day.

Spring is my favorite season and this year again I've been lucky enough to be here at this most beautiful time. Snow-covered mountains make winter spectacular as well, but my favorite is still the spring. Part of that is because, if time permits, I can spend a little time fishing the gently flowing Tom's Creek which meanders through the edge of the campus. Over the years, I have spent many a peaceful evening there, sometimes with a new friend, most of the time alone. I love to sit quietly along the banks watching the beavers, the geese, the mallards, and the other animals who make that area their home. After dark, the stars and the lights of distant airliners lining up for their approach to Washington fascinate me. Many times I have stayed late into the night just enjoying the solitude.

With all that goes on in the two weeks, one thing is always certain. Before I leave to come home to Baltimore I will visit a very special corner of the campus. In an area so filled with history, it seems only fitting that this corner should hold such feelings for me.

History is a great source of interest for those who visit the National Fire Academy. The surrounding area is rich in native American and Civil War history. Being a native Marylander, I have spent much time at the local attractions. Harpers Ferry, site of John Brown's raid, is a frequent weekend destination for Fire Academy visitors. Gettysburg and Antietam are the other nearby Civil War battlefields that attract the most attention.

I have read the books and seen the movies. I have studied the history lessons and learned of the strategy of the famous generals. But nothing can compare to actually being there.

When I stand at the Devil's Den I can feel the eyes of the snipers poised above pinning me down. When I stand on Little Roundtop and look over the fields below, I can see the confederate troops massing for their famous charge and smell the gunpowder in the air.

I have stood silently at The Bloody Lane at Antietam and imagined the horror of the piles of fallen soldiers and the river of blood. In the Dunker Church, I can hear the screams of the men as the crude "medicine" of that day robbed them of their arms and legs. The pictures of those horrible scenes are etched in my mind.

The monuments to the various units of both sides stand in lasting testimony to the sacrifices of those who fought there.

The most vivid feelings envelope me when I walk into the national cemetery near the Gettysburg visitor center. A deep sense of history settles onto me when I stand where President Lincoln stood to deliver his Gettysburg address at the dedication ceremony. Row after row of markers touch me as I wonder how the families left behind coped with the loss of these soldiers, many no older than my own children. A terrible sadness fills this place, and I cannot escape it.

And yet there is a sense of pride and accomplishment that tempers the loss or at least strives to give it meaning. The convictions of those who fought and the struggle that resulted are part of what made our country what it is. This is a place where our country remembers. Like the Vietnam Memorial or the Holocaust Museum, this is a place we dare not forget.

The little corner of the National Fire Academy that I must visit holds the same feelings for me.

Not far from the building where the students can swim and enjoy the gymnasium and weight room is an area set aside to honor those who will never use these facilities again. The bronze plaque on the unobtrusive, stone monument reads:

Fallen Fire Fighters Memorial
Dedicated October 4, 1981
National Emergency Training Center
Emmitsburg, Maryland

Dedicated to the thousands of fire fighters
who have lost their lives in the
very act of saving others.

Ronald Reagan, President
United States of America

The simple monument is topped with a bronze Maltese Cross on which appear the traditional fire service tools. On one side is a fire hydrant. The other side holds a hook and a ladder. The middle portion of the cross displays a fire helmet—not a "space-age" helmet, but an old style, traditional fire helmet. These are the tools that say it all, the implements of firefighting for over a hundred years. There are no gimmicks, no innovations, no glitter.

At the base of the monument burns an eternal flame and the area around the base of the monument is a circle with small plants. A larger circular patio of flagstone and small stones in concrete surrounds the monument. Outside the walking space is the outermost circle. This part of the memorial area is filled with shrubs and shaded by a few trees.

Four tall flagpoles hold the flags of the United States, Maryland, The U.S. Fire Administration, and the Federal Emergency Management Agency. Thankfully, today they fly high above in the breeze. When a fire fighter dies in the line of duty, the flags will be lowered to half-staff until the funeral, and a notice will be posted listing the name of the deceased and a brief description of what happened. It's a sight I've seen too many times up here.

The most striking features on the perimeter, however, are

the individual headstones spaced around the circle. The bronze plaque on each is dated with a year starting in 1981. Each plaque holds the names of the fire fighters who died in the line of duty that year. The names are divided by state: New Hampshire, Colorado, Ohio, New Jersey, Tennessee, and, of course, Maryland. I guess every state is represented, though I have never actually checked. I don't linger here.

Most times I come in the daylight. At night the memorial is lit by spotlights directed from among the shrubs on the outer perimeter. That makes for a moving sight, but one I find even more unsettling.

I walk the circle slowly and check each plaque again. The names are still there. The names of friends and co-workers. The names of people whose funerals I attended, whose families I comforted. I still see their faces. One year in particular strikes me. In 1985, all four Maryland fire fighters who died in the line of duty were from my department. I knew three of the four.

This time the flowers left by loved ones grab my attention. There's a pot that holds jonquils and lilacs and some pink flower I don't recognize. There's a cross made of red flowers with one white flower in the center. Next to the 1992 plaque I spot the remnants of something. No longer identifiable, the flowers have shriveled to dead stalks. I wonder who has the unpleasant task of saying that the flowers should go. Who decides that the tribute left by someone who cared is now trash? I contemplate whether the dead are aware. I wish that I really knew.

This visit to the memorial always causes me pain, and yet I cannot leave the National Fire Academy until I spend a few private moments there. Maybe it's to pay my respects. Maybe it's to somehow reassure myself that the names are still there, that the fallen friends have not been forgotten.

Just a few miles away in Gettysburg, American heroes are immortalized. Thousands remember them every day. Here, my heroes are remembered by only a few. Their sacrifice was no less great.

As I walk slowly away, I recall President Lincoln's "It is altogether fitting that we should do so."

I remember.

18
Sometimes, No Matter How Hard...

Another late night reported dwelling fire brought another silent hope that the call would turn out to be someone's dinner left on the stove too long.

Here in this far northwestern part of the city, the neighborhoods have struggled to resist the encroachment of crime and drugs. The beautiful, large, two and three story wood frame houses were once home to some of Baltimore's elite. Now they stand as a stronghold battling what the community organizations have refused to accept as the inevitable deterioration that has claimed far too many of our neighborhoods.

Just a week before, I had sat in a community meeting as the fire department's representative. The focus of that night's meeting had been the effort to remove pay phones from the streets of the neighborhood. To those unfamiliar with urban life this might seem a ridiculous concern—hardly the topic for a whole night of discussion. Unfortunately, the proliferation of pay phones is often a boon to the drug market on the streets of urban America. The phones attract the sellers and buyers who loiter with their pagers and their lists, and defiantly conduct their business in full view. At one convenience store there were eight pay phones outside. They attracted quite a crowd.

"In one three-block area around Liberty Heights and Gwynn Oak there are twenty-two pay phones. You go count 'em." The words of the disgusted, longtime resident came back to me. She had described being threatened by the young dealers when she had actually dared try to use one of the phones one evening. That was the final straw. "Who the hell do they think they are?" she had demanded as she slammed her hand on the table and rallied the citizens' group to action.

This was no racially motivated reaction to changes perceived as threatening the status quo. All of the residents were black; the dealers they despised were black. This was no knee-jerk reaction to a single dramatic occurrence. This was war. This was a life and death struggle by decent, hardworking people to preserve a civil way of life. Speaker after speaker had decried the changes they had witnessed.

"I had to rearrange my work schedule so that I can walk my kids to and from school every day," lamented the young mother. She described her morning ritual that differed slightly from the one most of us parents experience. "After I get them all ready, I slip my twenty-two down in my pocket and off we go. Nobody's gonna put a hand on my babies." The police representatives looked on with resignation. Nobody dared chastise that lady for arming herself.

Life here is tough, but so are the good people who call this area home. The courage of the ordinary people had left room for optimism that night on Liberty Heights Avenue. *Courage* is a word that I don't use freely. That night I had listened as the president of the community group praised a young lady who had had enough. She had secreted a video camera and made the rounds of the neighborhood filming the many drug transactions she observed. Then, she had taken the film to the police and delivered them the faces and the crimes and challenged them to act. Some arrests followed; more were promised, as the police moved on the new information.

Among the two hundred persons at the community meeting that night, the president had warned, were sure to be some from "the other element, the one that poisons our children and terrorizes our nights." These are vicious, uncaring criminals who show no compassion for the victims of their crimes and who would not think twice about killing those who get in their way. Even knowing that they were there, this young woman stepped forward to show what she was willing to do and to serve as an example. That's *courage*.

The memory of that meeting and of those residents flashed through my mind as I responded toward their neighborhood.

As I neared the scene, I listened as Engine 40 reported smoke showing. Maybe it won't be too serious, I hoped. The dense smoke that filled the street as I turned the corner told me otherwise. The smell of burning wood hung heavily in the whole neighborhood. The smoke illuminated by the street lights looked like a fog rolling in off the ocean.

As I parked the chief's car out of the way and began to get my turnout gear on, I heard the message we all hate: "We have a report of children trapped," radioed Lieutenant Gil Wroten. The stakes immediately went up.

We consider all fires life threatening until we know definitely otherwise. But the report from someone who just escaped from a burning building that there are others still inside causes us more concern. And the report of children trapped is a particularly disturbing thought.

I could hear the screams before I could even make out the figures through the clouds of brownish gray smoke which grew heavier by the second. "Help me! Help me! Oh God, please help me!" implored the terrified voice from somewhere in the smoke. The voice came from above me, not the area to which Engine 40's crew was stretching their hoseline to make the initial attack. With the report from the family that there were children trapped in the basement, the lieutenant and his crew made that their top priority. As the engine crew prepared to enter through the side basement door to begin the search for the children, members from Truck 12 were positioning the ladders that would allow fire fighters to reach the other areas of the house that now belched life-threatening clouds of hot, poisonous gases and smoke.

As the smoke lifted momentarily, I could make out the figure lying face down on the front porch roof. "Please, help me," the man coughed, his earlier scream now stifled by the blinding, choking atmosphere.

"Go ahead. I'll get him," I assured Captain Feathers and Eddie. With so much to do, the entire truck crew was needed elsewhere. With the ladder that the truck crew had quickly placed to the porch roof, I was confident that I could easily remove the guy on the roof. That would free the others for the more urgent tasks of searching for those not able to escape the growing fire. While the guy on the roof obviously thought himself the top priority, fire fighters know well that those who are truly in the most dire straits are those who are unable to call for help. Trapped in the terrible smoke and searing heat, cut off by the spreading fire, their life expectancy could be measured in seconds. Only an immediate, coordinated rescue attempt could save those people.

The familiar sounds of the fireground surrounded me. Metal ladders clanging as they were being raised against the building, glass breaking as the truck guys began venting above me, fire fighters shuffling below as they advanced hoselines toward the other parts of the building, pumpers revving up their engines as they forced water through the hoselines toward the nozzles—the sounds so familiar to all of us barely forced their way into my consciousness as I helped the terrified man crawl to the top of the ladder. But there was something else, another weak sound, something that didn't fit.

"Is everybody else outta there?" I asked the guy as he started onto the ladder. Dazed, but not seriously hurt, the guy responded, "Oh, yeah, man, my mother's still in there." *Nice son.*

Through the smoke and darkness I could just make out the hand reaching out from the bedroom window. The thick clouds of swirling hell obscured the rest of the person at the window. When I reached her hand the woman grabbed me with a death grip. Her weak, terrified plea for help had been overwhelmed by the other noises. She had felt that she would surely die there in that window since nobody could hear her. Now that I had come to her, there was no way she was going to let go.

The lady had every reason to be terrified. Paralyzed from

the waist down, she had crawled to the window but was unable to get out. Now she sat on the floor with her head at the window gasping desperately for air. Three hundred pounds of dead weight clad only in a flimsy nightgown makes for a tricky package to lift. On my knees on the porch roof, I tried time after time to lift her from under her arms. Time after time, she slipped out of my grasp and plopped back into her sitting position. She was so big that she almost filled the window opening. I thought briefly about getting in the window and trying to push her out.

"Need help?" came the welcome voice of Captain Feathers. Fortunately, someone on the ground had seen my plight and sent a helper. Had it not been such a serious situation, it would have been an entertaining sight to see our less than "textbook" rescue. As we got the lady through the window opening like a cork popping out of a wine bottle, she fell right on top of me and both of us started rolling toward the end of the porch roof. Exhausted, and with my bad shoulder about ripped out of my socket, I pinned her to the porch roof like a wrestler going for the final count. At least she was safe now.

Down in the basement, things were not going as well. The guys from Engine 40 and others had fought their way through the heavy smoke and heat which had turned the safety of home into a death trap. They advanced the one and three-quarters inch hose and attacked the fire. As they crawled, they groped everywhere, swinging their arms and legs in all directions, looking for the children reported inside. They knew very well that the clock was running out for anyone still inside.

The basement had been finished as a bedroom, and the fire fighters searched above, below, and beside the furniture. First right, then left, the fire fighters searched. The total blackness meant that everything had to be done by touch. Heavy gloves tried to discern the differences between toys, pillows, dolls, and children. Wedged between the bed and the wall where they had tried to hide from the fire were the two little girls.

Back on the ground, I looked on as fire fighters with steam coming off their coats carried the two limp, soot-covered bundles outside. The rush of long blonde hair going by me meant that Laurie, one of the paramedics, was dashing to meet them and begin the actions that might save their lives. But their fragile bodies had taken the brunt of the terrible heat and smoke; this time the fire won.

A certain sadness surrounds the loss of any life on the fireground. When children die the loss is magnified. That night, we all knew that we had done everything that we could have done. That's the frustrating reality of our job. Sometimes, no matter how hard we try, people die.

19
Stupid Human Tricks

I have stupid children. Well, at least I have stupid sons. My daughter, Robin, seems to have inherited some intelligence from her mother. My wife claims this stupidity is a male thing. Then it becomes more clear where they got it. "And the only thing more stupid than a man, is a man who fishes." That's us!

I'll admit that sometimes we don't exhibit the finest judgment in all of our actions. Many times, though, I think we're just misunderstood by the female of the species.

"We drive one thousand miles, spend a million dollars, and come to Disney World, the most fantastic place we've ever been, and you guys want to *fish*. There's something seriously wrong with you," my wife offered her unsolicited opinion. "Why would you come all the way down here to fish when you can fish five minutes from home? *That's* stupid."

"Yeah, but these are *Florida* bass down here. You just don't understand," we replied to a disbelieving face.

Reluctantly, Diana agreed to the plan. She and my son David would go to a restaurant and have lunch while Tim and I fished. Tim and I had been out that morning visiting several fire department friends of mine in Orange County and Kissimee; during our excursion I spotted a place where Diana could drop us off and pick us up. She was irritated enough about my taking time out of our vacation for the fire department visits. This twist really helped.

The spot there on Route 192 outside Kissimee looked

inviting. The highway crossed a tea-colored creek that disappeared into a tree-lined, shaded refuge from the blazing, August, Florida sun. "Should be perfect," I assured everyone.

Actually, the first ten minutes weren't bad. A few minor snags developed. What had looked to be a serene creek when viewed at fifty-five miles per hour passing over the bridge was in fact also the entrance to a very busy boat rental business that sat in the trees on the south side of the bridge—not just a *boat* rental either, but an *air boat* rental. I'd seen them on TV before but I'd never heard one live. That huge fan that propels the boat and whips up the water hardly makes for a quiet place, but what the heck, we'd just walk up the creek north of the bridge. Looked nice.

The side of the stream I chose looked pretty interesting. Heavy brush ahead, but for about fifty yards it looked passable with a little work. I quickly learned another lesson. Swamp is hard to identify at fifty-five miles per hour. My new running shoes soon made a sickening oozing sound each time I tried to step. *Sure am glad I didn't wear my old shoes like Diana suggested.*

I did manage a few casts from the general area of the bank, though I couldn't get too close because of the sticker bushes which now tore at my exposed legs while my shoes settled in the muck. *Who wears long pants in Florida anyway?*

Meanwhile, Tim had chosen to walk the other side of the stream. It was obvious he was faring better. He was casting up a storm, between boats that is. It was obvious that his side of the stream was easier walking, but I never need "easy" to be content. And then I remembered: "I always put tape around the bottom of my pants to keep the snakes from crawlin' up." The words of the native Floridian, professional fishing guide drifted—no *slammed*—back to me. I didn't even *have* a bottom of my pants.

The trip back to the bridge went much faster even with my head rotating 360 degrees non-stop. At least the air-boaters were kind enough not to say anything to me as they watched wide-eyed my high-stepping, swamp-extrication maneuver.

After dodging the fifty-five miles per hour traffic on the bridge, I joined Tim on the other side of the stream which actually was pretty nice. The trees overhead shielded us from the blistering sun and the ground was firm. With each cast I realized what a great choice of spots I had made. The boat traffic was churning up the creek, but it was wider up here and we could avoid the boats a little.

"Hey guys, this is private property. You can't fish here," boomed the voice from the motorboat which had shot up the stream from the marina to us. "Under the bridge is state owned property; you're OK there, but no fishin' here," he added. *Great.*

Disappointed, but not yet defeated, we retreated to the bridge.

Not everybody has been fortunate enough to see modern, big, fancy bridges. The underside can be pretty roomy. Of course, this one was not big, fancy, or roomy.

On the steep rock ledge under the bridge was the only shade anywhere. Unfortunately, the steep, loose rock near the top of the ledge led to slime near the water. Neither provides the best footing for a guy with a fishing rod and a bum shoulder. Hunched down to fit under the bridge and half-crawling to avoid sliding into the water, I eased into position—and what a position it was.

The bridge prevented me from lifting the rod to cast so the little sideways motion possible resulted in a maximum cast of about twenty feet. That proved not to be a problem because at about fifteen feet out the air boats crossed under the bridge going to and from the marina. That guy must be rich! I know that there was a boat every thirty seconds in one direction or the other.

With all those boats you'd think there'd be some air movement under here—not even a hint. The dank, stale air was made even worse by the temperature, which was something approaching the "bake" setting.

Tim again chose another vantage point from the many available to us. He crawled under the other side of the bridge.

I guess we could have at least talked and spent some "quality family time." Could have—if it weren't for the intermittent noise of the airboats and the constant rumble and traffic noise directly over our heads. I never realized how busy that road is. And, you know, exhaust fumes really are heavier than air. What a great spot!

With my "fishing" confined to an area about fifteen feet by twenty feet, I sat waiting for a stupid fish to come along—a deaf, stupid fish. Eventually I realized this was about as productive as trying to deer hunt in the middle of the Daytona 500. I'm really glad that Diana and David took their time having lunch that day. No fast food today. I spent a week there that afternoon finally opting to join Tim sitting on the guard rail frying in the Florida sunshine while we lost every bit of body fluid we had.

Waiting gave us time for reflection.

"Wish we'd brought the cold drinks that Mom suggested." We were silent for a long moment before I made my final father-son cast of the day: "You know we can't tell her."

"Naw, I know, Dad. She'll think we're stupid."

We can all laugh at the stupid things we do, at least those of us who are lucky. Sometimes, though, the stupid things that people do result in the fire department being called.

Most of us have laughed about the people who get their toe caught in the bathtub spigot or the little kid with his foot caught in the toilet. These things really do happen. We've seen people's hands stuck in soda machines, fingers in bubble gum machines, and heads wedged in railings. We've had burglars stuck in chimneys. We've rescued arsonists from the very fire they've set. Once we removed a would-be thief from the top of a trailer in a fenced in compound. He apparently hadn't believed the warnings about the guard dogs. He actually welcomed the police officer's handcuffs.

Sometimes, however, stupid actions have dire consequences.

A number of years ago a homeowner in South Baltimore

decided to repair the wooden stairs leading down to his basement. One of the nails he drove into the riser pierced an aerosol can on the built-in shelf behind the step and sent it hissing and rolling across the basement floor.

Boom went the basement when the pilot light on the water heater ignited the mist. Fortunately, the would-be repairman escaped in time, but the house was destroyed.

"Careless smoking" and "unattended cooking" are the official causes listed thousands of times each year in the country. There is no category "stupid action." That probably would be politically incorrect.

The Baltimore area was entrenched in a winter that would long be remembered as one of our worst in years. The Chesapeake Bay was frozen solid. It was actually possible to walk from one shore to the other, and shipping on the busy waterway ground to a halt. To many of us it was a fascinating and beautiful sight. To others it was a very serious problem. The inhabited islands of the Chesapeake Bay, home to generation after generation of commercial watermen and their families, were running out of fuel. The barges that supplied the islands were unable to break through the ice, even with Coast Guard help. Supplies were being taken to the islands by sled from the mainland. What a winter. I was sure glad that the night had been relatively quiet as I rested fitfully in the Fifth Battalion's office in the Steadman Station.

Relatively quiet in a station that is consistently one of the busiest stations in the country is not exactly like a peaceful night at the place where "We'll leave the light on for you." One of Baltimore's two famous superhouses, the Steadman Station is always alive. Runs for the various engine companies, the truck, the rescue unit, the air cascade unit, and the very busy medic unit are intermixed with runs for Battalion Chief 5. That makes for a very busy and not very quiet setting.

Broken water pipes, alarm malfunctions, and furnace fires kept the city busy. Listening to a few serious fires around town, but nothing bad around my area, had made the night pass quickly. This was definitely a night to stay indoors. The temperature of minus seven degrees Fahrenheit and wind of thirty to forty miles per hour, with gusts and snow squalls made it feel like Greenland.

Willie Jasper could hear the winds howling, too. In his modest rowhouse in the little neighborhood off Washington Boulevard, he wanted badly to be warm again. Willie's wife had forced him from their warm bed to find out why there was no water in the bathroom. Shivering in the midnight cold, Willie traced the problem to a frozen pipe in the back of the basement. Fortunately, the pipe had not broken yet. If he could thaw it out he knew that he could get water flowing again and get back to the warmth of the bedroom. The basement was dark and cold, and Willie decided to make quick work of the chore.

Frozen water pipes are a common problem when the temperature dips below zero. Thawing them takes time and patience. Finding where the pipe has frozen can take time and often requires crawling around in basements and crawl spaces or reaching into partitions and other inaccessible areas. Finding the trouble spot is only the first step. The pipe has to be thawed before the expanding ice breaks it and causes major problems. Sometimes a portable electric space heater placed in the area will raise the room temperature enough to thaw the pipe gradually. Another relatively safe technique is to hold a hair dryer where the hot air can gradually warm the pipe and allow it to flow again.

Not exactly blessed with patience, Willie decided to take a shortcut. He quickly decided on a plan to get him back to his warm bed. Rolling newspaper into tight rolls, he began the thawing process. As he lit one roll after another on fire, Willie held them under the point where he suspected the pipe had frozen. The wooden open ceiling of the basement flickered with the reflection of the fire underneath and smoke drifted through the basement. Each rolled up newspaper burned for just a short time but it put out a lot of heat and he could hold them right up to the pipe. "I'll be back to bed in no time," he thought as he stamped out the remains of another burned roll of paper.

Content that the bathroom pipes now flowed freely, Willie gratefully felt the warmth of the covers again as the wind howled outside. In the basement, one tiny spot on the underside of the kitchen floorboards smoldered, just a wisp, unseen, waiting for life. In his haste to be done with the job, Willie failed to check everything closely before he went back to bed. Fires often smolder for a long time before gaining enough momentum to be self-sustaining. The old wood held the spark and nurtured it, allowing it to gradually build heat. Little by little the ember grew, and the glow in the wood increased.

Upstairs, Willie and his wife slept, unaware of the monster being born in their basement. Outside, the wind whipped through the neighborhood and the bone-chilling temperatures kept the streets empty. Only a few lights were visible throughout the neighborhood. It was a great night to cuddle.

At the fire stations in that part of town, some fire fighters were awake, as always. Others attempted to catch a little sleep between responses. Old fire stations eerily turn the sounds of the wind into a howl that could come out of the best Hollywood horror movie.

It was a call from the street behind Willie's that sent the first fire engines into the night. "Investigate smoke in the area" is not an unusual call in weather like this. Smoke from chimneys swirls in the wind as oil and gas furnaces churn to keep up with the demand. Wood stoves add to the smells and haze in the depths of winter.

I slid the long two-story pole to the apparatus floor below as others descended nearby. Shaking off sleep, I started the car and headed for the little street where we had just been dispatched for the reported dwelling fire. I wasn't even out the door when the radio brought bad news: "Engine 55. It looks like we've got a dwelling on fire on Nanticoke Street. You'd better strike out the box."

"We've just struck out a box for a dwelling fire there, Engine 55. We'll add your companies to the assignment," came the reply from the dispatcher.

I didn't realize exactly what had happened to put Engine 55 there so quickly, but I recognized instantly that this was not going to be a good night.

Heavy fire belched from the back of the house, lapping from the basement window and door and involving the entire back porch. Fire was already extending above the second floor windows toward the roof as the first-in Engine 55 turned the corner and headed for the hydrant. The fire was blowing to the porch of the house next door as the bitter wind forced it sideways. Fire fighters arrived to find a well advanced fire in an occupied dwelling in the most miserable of weather conditions.

Wakened by the smoke and noises from beneath them, Willie and his wife had narrowly escaped. They were able to get down the steps and out the front door just in time. Blinding, choking smoke filled the house, and the crackle of the flames and red glow from the kitchen terrified the couple as they fled into the darkness and cold. The inrush of air from the open front door brought new oxygen to the fire and instantly transformed the inside of the house into a *swoosh* of flames. Fire danced from the kitchen to the living room in seconds and found the stairs to the second floor. Racing up the open stairway, the fire quickly engulfed the hall and the bedroom where the couple had slept just moments earlier. This time the fire was a little too late to trap its victims.

As fire fighters stretched their lines into position to enter the first floor front door, the windows of the second floor bedroom blew out followed immediately by torchlike flames that lit up the street and reached for the sky. I parked the chief's car down the street and took a quick mental calculation of the effects of the wind and cold on the fire and the fire fighters. Crap!

The effects of adrenaline are well known. Fire fighters battling a serious fire work hard, physically and mentally.

Concentrating on the task at hand, the fire fighters put off the thoughts of the weather as they fought to keep the fire from spreading. They quickly pulled hose off the back of the engines and snaked it toward the front of the house. Water soon filled the hoselines and began to hit the fire. In the rear, the narrow alley prevented any apparatus from driving up to the area of the fire. Instead, here fire fighters carried and dragged the hose up the alley extending the lines to the proper length—one line at first to cut off the fire's spread, more lines to attack the fire as other companies arrived.

The truck company crews wrestled the metal ground ladders in the wind. Without the ladders the fire fighters could not fight the fire effectively. They would need to stretch hose-lines to the second floors of the fire building and the ones being threatened. Fire fighters would need to enter the second floors to search and to ventilate. The roof, as always, was an important part of the firefighting operation. Water spray from the hoselines instantly glazed the metal ladders with a film of ice, making a dangerous job that much worse.

I felt some relief when I talked to a shaken but unhurt Willie on a neighbor's front porch and was assured that everyone was out of the house. My initial size-up from a half block away had told me that anyone still inside was surely dead.

The concern now was that the wind-driven fire would extend down the block. I stood in the front street and counted ten houses with smoke showing at their roof lines. If a common cockloft (the area between the top floor ceiling and the roof) connected the homes, the fire would be quickly traveling laterally. Until we could position fire fighters with tools and hoselines to check from underneath, we could only hope that the roof ventilation would draw the fire straight up and slow its sideways progress. Putting a hole in the roof directly over the fire is a difficult job on a good day. In gusting wind with heavy fire conditions directly underneath, the danger was severe. I watched as the swirling clouds of smoke nearly obscured the fire fighters on the roof. Fire belched from the front second floor windows reaching above the roofline, and the fire fighters were visible behind it as it reached into the sky. The danger had become an unacceptable risk, and the truck crew scrambled to the safety of an adjoining roof as fire blew through the roof. The fire had done the roof venting job for us.

The high winds threatened to spread the fire across the roofs, and crews stretched additional hoselines up to stop the spread of the fire. Portions of the roof collapsed as the fire ate away at the top floor and cockloft area. Eventually, the fire fighters won the battle. The fire didn't spread beyond the original home and the back of two adjoining homes. The fire fighters were able to keep the high winds from pushing the fire down the block.

Heartbroken, but thankful to be alive, Willie explained to me that he had been thawing pipes in the basement earlier. He shook his head slowly as he recalled the method he had chosen. Later, when the investigator was able to examine the remains of the house, he determined that the point of origin was indeed right where Willie had used the burning newspapers in his hurry to return to the warmth of his bed. Now Willie and his wife sat shaking in the living room of a neighbor, wrapped in borrowed blankets.

For us, the night was not nearly over. Now that the excitement of the fire died away, the reality of the long overhauling job ahead sank in. Wet with perspiration and water from the firefighting, the crews began to feel the cold in earnest. Over the next few hours everybody on the scene would curse the weather. Ears burned. Noses ran. Eyes watered. Feet and hands ached with the bitter cold. It seemed like time had stopped.

The condition of the burned out house would make for very slow going. The roaring fire had burned away the stairs. The floors were weakened and had gaping holes where fire had broken through. Worst of all, the damaged roof sagged and hung precariously in places. The companies would have to do all the work very slowly and carefully. Ideally, the fire fighters would not have to enter the inside of the house and could wet down from outside, but that was impossible. All the interior partition walls remained, and the only way to complete the job was to tear apart slowly the remaining walls, door frames, furniture, and anything else that could conceal any remaining embers. The fire fighters would have to uncover every hiding place for sparks and wet them down. The burned out house was right in the middle of a block of occupied houses. There was no way that we could leave without making absolutely sure that no rekindle could occur. Whatever it took, we were here for the duration.

Working in the dark, broken building was even more dangerous because of the ice which quickly coated everything. Portable electric lights stretched by the truck companies and powered by the noisy generators outside brightened parts of the area and created weird shadows. Icicles hung from debris and from the roof above. Illuminated by our lights, they might have been pretty under different circumstances. Tonight, they only served as reminders of how cold we all were. At least here the burned out building provided some shelter from the wind.

Inside was miserable. Outside was unbearable. Frigid winds instantly froze anything that got wet. Sidewalks, streets and alleys, hydrants, hose couplings, ladders—everything was at risk of freezing solid. Fire fighters slipped often as they went about the task of undoing all that had been done earlier to fight the fire, but now they were tired and extremely cold.

As they prepared to shut down each hoseline, fire fighters took up positions at every coupling. Once the flow of water stopped in the line, the hose would freeze instantly, so an immediate, coordinated effort was the only way to uncouple the hose so that it could be retrieved. Sometimes, the fire fighters had to drag the frozen couplings up underneath the engines and hold them up to the exhaust pipes to get enough warmth to free them. Others used powerful quartz lights to provide enough heat to disentangle the lines and uncouple the sections. No reloading of the hose was possible. The fire fighters looped or bent the frozen hose however possible to get it on top the vehicles. Only after it could be thawed out back in the station would it be possible to drain the hose and re-pack it. And even so, it seemed to take forever. Some of the hose was frozen so solidly to the street that the men had to chop away blocks of ice to take with the hose.

Fire fighters are accustomed to operating in lousy conditions, but tonight was beyond lousy, beyond miserable. Tonight was dangerous. Frostbite was a very real threat to everyone involved in the operation. Even the complaining about and cursing of the weather stopped. Talking was too much trouble. A quiet resignation replaced the usual chatter amongst the guys.

The wind gusted and the snow squalls continued. At times it would snow and blow so hard for a minute or so that we couldn't even see each other. The snow didn't accumulate. It just blew away like a great dust storm. Even rotating the crews so that half worked while the other half sought some relief in the cabs of apparatus was not enough to relieve the misery. Frozen hands, feet, and ears painfully reminded us all of the perils of wintertime firefighting. Our turnout coats were stiff with ice, and even moving and bending became difficult.

One by one the companies got all of their things together and were released. The operation had lasted hours. Before too long it would be time for the day shift to replace us. All of us thought about that, though nobody said anything.

Early in the incident I had made a conscious decision to show my support and appreciation for the efforts of everyone by staying with the crews the entire time. When half rotated to a place of relative warmth for a break, I stayed with the other half who then came out to resume working. For all those hours I had stayed in the cold and wind. Now that the last company was almost ready to leave, I decided it was time to go.

At my chief's car I realized just how cold I was. My turnout gear was frozen so stiff that I couldn't bend. The clasps that held my coat closed were frozen solid and covered with ice, and my hands absolutely refused to work. I needed help.

Fortunately, the pump operator saw my plight and used a spanner wrench to break away the ice so that we could get my coat open. Still my hands refused to cooperate. I couldn't get my car keys out of my pockets, so the pump operator retrieved them for me and opened my car door. His reaching into my pants pockets and rooting around would normally have guaranteed some smart quip, but tonight we were all too cold and tired to bother.

Still dressed in all my frozen protective gear, I sat behind the steering wheel and started the car, but I was too cold to drive. That's when the shivering really set in. My teeth actually chattered as I sat waiting for heat to come out of the heater.

"Darn it, Willie. I'm glad you weren't hurt, but did you have to do something so stupid?"

20

Routine—A Word We Hate

Summer rains are always welcome in Baltimore. In Maryland's rural areas the farmers struggle with drought conditions too often. In the greener parts of the city and its suburbs the rain means nicer lawns and healthier gardens.

Summer rains in the built-up asphalt and concrete world of Baltimore bring summer smells familiar to anyone who has ever lived in the city. The heavy downpours temporarily cleanse the streets and sidewalks before the process of human contamination begins again. And so the rains are usually welcomed.

The heavy rain pelted my car roof, and the windshield wipers had trouble keeping up as I began my trip around the battalion. Each morning the battalion chief makes the rounds of the stations under his command. I look forward to it.

At my seven stations I would follow the morning routine: distribute the orders that came from Headquarters last night. Return any of the reports that the companies sent in yesterday that have now been acted on, or that need corrections; pick up today's batch of incoming reports—the great paper-shuffle.

Each day, the battalion chief is supposed to inspect each member for cleanliness and proper attire. The condition of the station is always a concern, and once each week the chief thoroughly inspects the apparatus.

The part of the routine not mentioned in the official instructions is the part many of us consider the most important. This morning time provides the opportunity for the battalion chief to talk with the troops. It is here that the fishing stories, accounts of last night's softball games, and general talk find their way into the exchange of departmental information.

At Engine 40, my first stop, I'll talk horses with Bob Gamber, carpentry projects with Lieutenant Gil Wroten, the latest computer advances with Paul Howard. Pete Bogetti and I will talk union issues. And always we laugh about the things that make us all the same—family, co-workers, and life.

My second stop will be Truck 12. Captain Al Feathers and I will talk about restoring antique cars or his latest course in law enforcement at the community college. Frank Corasiniti and I will share kids' stories. I'll talk with Eddie Arthur about the truck, his "baby", and the chances of Truck 12 being in line for a new one. John Newmuis, "Newmo" to us, will quietly and shyly listen mostly. And again we'll all share a laugh.

And so the routine goes each morning. To Engine 20 and Truck 18, to 52, then 29, to Engine 45 and Truck 27, and finally back to Engine 46, the battalion headquarters, and the isolation of the office as the paper shuffle begins in earnest.

My time with the members of my companies is treasured, special time that makes even a rainy morning pleasant. It is a vital part of building a team, a valuable activity in this job where teamwork is so important and our lives depend on each other.

"Engine 40, Engine 20..." the radio blares and my visit to my first station, Engine 40, is cut short. I head out to my car as the crew of Engine 40 makes their way toward the pumper. It's a dwelling fire not far from where I am. Person reported trapped.

Bonner Road is a typical Northwest Baltimore residential street of identical two story brick rowhouses and small front yards. Flowers, azalea bushes, and birdbaths allow the residents to show their individuality. Front porches, great evening congregation points, serve two houses at a time. Running the length of the row, green terra-cotta tiles three deep provide a look of continuity to the roofs as they form a block-long shelf-like protrusion just below the roofline.

"Truck 12 on the scene. Two story brick, heavy smoke showing." I hear the calm report from Captain Al Feathers. In a few words he has told us the incident won't be a "nonsense run," a pot of food or a chair smoldering. We all know the implications of the report.

The job will be tough for the truck. As the only unit assigned to their station, the crew of first due Truck 12 is accustomed to arriving before an engine, and having no hoseline makes the job of search and rescue more difficult and more dangerous. The truck crew must be skillful and resourceful to accomplish the rescue.

The team knows what has to be done. With just a few words the captain sets the plan into motion. Frank and his partner don their air masks and gain entry into the house. Bystanders scream that a man is trapped in the basement. The clouds of smoke billowing from the whole front of the house don't bode well for his chances. Heavy smoke hangs in the front yard as the rain and humidity work against the natural tendency of heated smoke to rise. Everyone recognizes the challenge to the ventilation operation.

I can see the ladders going up as I walk to the front yard. The engines are arriving and laying hose up the street from the hydrant as the captain pauses to tell me of the reports of the person trapped in the basement.

"We're going to get the place opened up, Chief," he informs me as he and Eddie Arthur begin the ventilation process so critical to the rescue attempt. Any chance the occupant has is tied to our ability to find him quickly and remove him. As the engines position their hoselines to attack the fire and truck members begin their search, other truck crew members draw the heat and smoke away by opening the roof scuttles, skylights, windows, and doors in a planned, systematic approach toward improving conditions inside the building.

The process begins at the top where the heated smoke and gases have met their vertical obstacle. Remove this obstacle—take off the "lid"—and the conditions will begin to improve.

To get to the roof the truck crew has used a familiar tactic. A ladder is placed to the porch roof. From here fire fighters can vent and enter the second floor windows to search the bedrooms. Another ladder from the porch roof to the house and the roof is in reach. The house sits too far away from the street for the aerial ladder so this is the next best procedure.

I can hear the glass breaking above me as the smoke pours from every opening of the house and fills the yard around me. Fire is raging in the basement, front to back, and the heated smoke and toxic gases fill the house and push outside. Removing the second floor windows will provide some ventilation until the guys can get to the roof. The crew on the first hoseline has made it inside to the top of the basement stairs and is preventing the fire from coming up to the first floor. Their position is the chimney for the raging fire. No descent of these stairs is possible. Meanwhile, crews in the rear are in position to attack from the rear outside basement entrance but only on command. If the first crew has entered the basement down the interior stairs, a line from the outside will endanger them as it forces the fire and heat ahead of it. Coordination is essential for the attack to be done properly.

In the last few years, two of our lieutenants have been killed fighting basement fires in this type dwelling, and we are all well aware of the dangers. Each crew knows its role.

Captain Feathers knows the need to vent the roof openings is great. Heavy heat and smoke conditions hamper the interior crews in their search of the building. The rains come even harder as Eddie holds the bottom of the ladder steady on the porch roof while his captain ascends.

The protruding, decorative terra cotta ledge means that the ladder doesn't sit flat against the building at the top, but the captain scrambles safely onto the roof surrounded by clouds of noxious, billowing, brown and gray smoke. Now he holds the ladder from the top, and Eddie begins to ascend the ladder to join him.

Fire vents through the front basement windows, and the flames blow upward and outward. Any chance the man trapped in the basement may have had is gone as the flashover involves the whole basement. We've been on the scene only a few minutes. Lines are inside through the front door. Other lines are ready to push in from the back if needed. Ladders are up. Ventilation is underway. Crews are searching on the first and second floors. Everything has gone according to plan.

I give the OK for the crews out back to attack the fire from the rear when the inside crew has informed me that they can't make it down the interior basement stairs. Their job now is to hold the fire in the basement while the other lines push the fire out toward the front.

Routine is a word we hesitate to use in the fire service. The nature of our job dictates that considering any fire as routine could lead to serious miscalculations.

As Eddie nears the top of the ladder the center of gravity shifts. The terra-cotta ledge has created a pivot point, and the bottom of the ladder kicks out and heads toward the edge of the porch roof.

Eddie lunges; the captain tightens his grip. The ladder starts to slide down away from the roofline as Eddie gropes for a handhold on the roof's ledge. The captain sees what is happening and realizes that Eddie needs that extra second to reach something firm. Twenty-five feet above the ground, Eddie is in mortal danger. Years of training and instinct result in the only course of action. Crouched on the roof, the captain strains with everything he has to hold the top of the ladder.

As Eddie lunges for a spot to hold onto, the ladder tip slides down the face of the building and pulls the captain head-first from the roof. It's all over in an instant.

Now it's Eddie's turn to react, and again the instinct to protect a co-worker takes hold. With a precarious one-hand hold on the edge of the roof, Eddie reaches out to grab his captain as the captain falls past him. Each in his turn has imperiled himself to protect his partner. The captain's momentum plunges him headlong past Eddie.

Five seconds after I move to my left to assess the fire lapping out of the basement windows the crash above startles me. Again, instinct and training take hold, and I react by hunching in my head and arms and preparing for the impact rather than looking up—the natural reaction. Fire fighters are taught early of the dangers above and how to react properly to minimize injuries from falling glass and other objects.

A sickening thud results when the captain hits the porch roof and continues down the metal awning to land in the rain-soaked yard right where I had stood not ten seconds before.

Suddenly the focus of our efforts shifts to the care of a critically injured comrade. "Dispatch a medic unit. Injured fire fighter," I call into my portable radio. Even before I can finish the message, I look up and see Scott and Laurie, our paramedics from Medic 8, rushing toward us. They were standing-by in the front street and witnessed the whole thing.

"Help me get up," come the dazed words that reassure us that Al is alive. Semi-conscious and critically injured he attempts to move, but nothing happens. Nothing will happen. The fall has damaged his spinal cord to the point where Al will never walk again. Months and months of hospital stays are ahead, then rehabilitation. Frustration and agonizing pain, infections, depression, and despair lie ahead for the injured captain, though none of us would know it at that instant. Saving his life and preventing further injury were the immediate concerns.

Above, almost unseen and unheard in the smoke and confusion, Eddie Arthur clings to the edge of the roof. An alert pump operator, Steve Ferragamo, quickly realizes his plight and gets to the porch roof to reposition the ladder in time to keep Eddie from falling. Other than an injured knee and getting the scare of his life, Eddie would be OK. Feelings of responsibility and guilt—"survivor's guilt" the medical professionals call it—will stay with him long after his knee heals.

While the paramedics care for the injured captain, the other fire fighters continue to battle the fire, many unaware that the injuries have occurred. There is still the job of firefighting to be done and the search for the missing civilian.

When the fire is out, I find myself again entering a hospital to check on one of my guys. Dirty and wet, I walk into Shock Trauma wanting to know...but not. Deputy Chief Ticha meets me with the somber face that reflects our moods. "He's alive, but he'll probably never walk again." He skips the formalities, the greetings, and gets right to the point. We've worked together for a lot of years. We both know the routine.

Again, I greet a grieving shocked family and offer the words of sympathy and comfort that always seem so insufficient. At least this time the fire fighter is alive.

I was there. I'm his boss. I know what happened. It's logical that the family looks to me for answers, but I can't offer much. It would be a couple days before we actually piece together the small factors that all combined—the heavy rain, the slippery, metal-clad porch roof covered by the tar coating, the terra-cotta ledge. How much does it matter? This morning their lives have changed forever. I feel so inadequate when I produce Al's glasses that I found in the front yard. It seems so little.

There's no way that I can leave the hospital until I know more, so the family and I wait. Anyone faced with a similar situation knows the gut-wrenching feelings of waiting helplessly to hear the news of an injured loved one. Shift change comes and goes. My relief can use the spare car to get the battalion back in service. My place is here with the family. Nervous talk fills our time together as the hours pass, mostly because the silence is worse.

Finally, the doctors allow Al's wife to spend a few minutes with him, and her report that he is alert and able to talk with her sends me home. Before I leave the hospital, I call Truck 12 to relay the information that they all await. Tomorrow, we'll sort out all the emotions. Tomorrow, we'll begin the investigation into what happened. Tomorrow. For now, I'm suddenly exhausted, and I know the experience has just begun. The ride home seems terribly long tonight.

And the fire—the companies handled it without further incident. The "trapped person" had already escaped before we had arrived. It wasn't the first fire that he had started while intoxicated and smoking. I'm glad that I didn't meet him.

Another basement fire—just *routine*.

21
Some Nights....

The plain one-story building on Belvedere Avenue was the kind of business that had adapted to the changes in the community. Filled with bargain clothing and household items, the business had survived because it served the needs of the community. For a few bucks a customer could pick up a dress or a coat, maybe even a pair of shoes. A little money could go a lot further here than at the mall.

We had been there on a few occasions, most recently for an odor-of-smoke call that turned out to be an overheated fluorescent light ballast. I talked with the manager and warned him of the need to keep the back door clear as an exit. Those chains that secured the doors were illegal while the store was occupied. The owner and I understood each other. He knew that I couldn't let him keep the exit doors chained shut; I knew that his security problems were his major concern. And so he just smiled and humored me and removed the chains. We both knew they wouldn't be off long.

Life here on Belvedere Avenue is tough. The bars on all the doors and window openings and the Lexan (a tough, almost impenetrable, unbreakable plastic) windows provided the best guarantee that the contents of the building would be there in the morning. In a neighborhood where few can afford insurance, even if they could find someone willing to write it, self-protection takes on a heightened importance.

When we are responding to a fire we try to visualize the neighborhood, knowing the type of construction we are likely to find when we arrive. Sometimes we don't know exactly which building is on fire until we arrive. At other times we are responding to a place we know well. The call for the building fire that night immediately set my mind to a mental review of the Thrift Shop. Heavy fire load, no sprinkler protection, difficult entry and ventilation problems could be expected—my size-up, my mental picture of the fire, began even as I followed Engine 46 down the street. *Maybe it won't be anything serious.*

My wife's last instructions to me before I left for work came drifting back: "And make sure you get some sleep tonight. Remember, you *promised* David that you'd go on that field trip to the zoo tomorrow with his class, and it's all day."

"No problem," I assured her. It was the last of four nights of night shift and we had been relatively slow the first three. I didn't need to take off tonight like she asked. I'd get some rest at work and be bright-eyed and bushy-tailed for the kids tomorrow, just me and the rest of the moms.

No sweat, I thought. It's only 10:30. I'll be back before the late news comes on.

Wrong again. I took in the view as Engine 46 laid their supply hose from the hydrant across the street and positioned the engine in the front of the building. No fire was visible from the building as I drove by to view three sides before I parked the chief's car. That was a good sign.

Pitch black smoke oozed lazily from around the roof line at the corners of the building and the show windows were as black as night—definitely *not* a good sign. Nobody stood outside to meet us. The light traffic and the deserted sidewalks meant that at least we could operate unimpeded. But the lack of people meant that the fire could have been burning a good while before someone had spotted it.

From the front sidewalk I could see the only obvious opening. The bottom half of one side of the front doors had been broken out. Visibility inside the door was zero, but the smoke was not blowing out at us under pressure. This meant that either the fire was not very hot or that it wasn't near this part of the store.

As the engine companies began to place their hoselines into

position at the front door, the truck crews started the forcible entry and ventilation procedures that we would need to fight the fire. Before we could advance the lines to the seat of the fire we would have to find it within the large open area filled with bins of clothing and other merchandise. The whole inside of the store was now filled with dense black smoke, but there was no heat as the crews began to push deeper into the building. Fire fighters have gotten into bad situations on occasions like this because the high ceilings in this kind of building can hide the fact that a serious fire is underway. The area up at the highest levels of the building can indeed be very hot and burst into flames at any moment, catching the unsuspecting fire fighters below. It is a time for caution and for ventilation.

The security bars and the Lexan windows made for slow, difficult work for the truck crews, and the smoke got heavier. Still the seat of the fire was not obvious. The large building and the amount of work involved meant we needed more help.

"Battalion Chief 11. Dispatch two additional engines and another truck," was my response to the situation. The additional help would speed the efforts already underway and provide us some reinforcements if the fire did prove to be serious.

On the roof the truck crews found that the only opening was the scuttle that was secured from inside by chains and locks. The scuttle itself had been reinforced with steel so that burglars could not easily cut through it. Fortunately, fire fighters are better equipped than the average burglar and eventually the roof hatch gave way.

Slow going it was, but the guys finally located the fire, and one line easily controlled it. Heavy smoke still filled the store and would for awhile. The polyester clothing and other plastic and fabrics that had burned created the thickest of black smoke which hung in the store. The truck companies and Rescue 1, which I had special called, used their smoke ejectors to clear out the large store as our investigator began his search for the cause of the fire. This time it would be easy. The broken out front door had been the entry point for the arsonist or arsonists. Once inside the store, they had ransacked and vandalized, then set the store on fire.

When the owner arrived, we stood on the sidewalk in front of the store and talked. Earlier in the day he had caught two shoplifters and had quite a confrontation with them. Trying to give the kids a break, he didn't have them arrested. Now he wondered aloud if they had come back to seek revenge. Someone interested in more than just burglary had caused the damage within the store before setting it on fire. When the smoke cleared and we could walk through the store with the police and our investigator, the owner and I looked at the damage together. With some cleanup and repairs he would be able to open for business in a few days. That was good news. The bad news was that there was no insurance to cover his losses.

I felt bad as I finally left the owner there and headed back to the station. His determination and spirit impressed me. Even with all that he had just been through, he had thanked us for not doing more damage to his store, and with a smile commented to me, "I see you guys cut my chains." We both got a little laugh.

"If I wait until I come back on day shift to write the fire report, I can still get some sleep," I thought as I backed into the station. *Remember*, you promised David. . . . No problem.

Sleep in a fire station usually doesn't come easily. Knowing that at any minute you might be called upon to go instantly from resting to a fully alert, thinking emergency responder frequently makes for light, fitful sleep. Under the best of circumstances a night's sleep in the fire station is not like a night's sleep at home. After most significant incidents I have always found myself thinking about and reviewing, analyzing the incident for awhile before I can drift off to sleep. I'm not sure that I had even drifted when the lights came on and the speaker came to life.

"Engine 46, Engine 29, Engine 40..." came the dispatch that sent us racing to the next run of the night. I thought about the 4100 block of Belvieu Avenue in our first due area as I led the way with the engine a couple of blocks behind. Three story, big, wood frame houses—we'd had numerous bad fires in this neighborhood in the years I had served in the area. Again I made the silent prayer, "Please let it be nothing."

Again, I was disappointed. As I turned the corner onto Belvieu Avenue I saw the sign that this was not a "nothing." While I was in total darkness, the block ahead was nearly as bright as day. I knew what the brightness meant for us.

"Battalion Chief 11 on the scene. Three story frame, occupied dwelling. Heavy fire showing. People jumping out of the windows at this time. Dispatch two medic units," was my message before my car had even pulled to a stop.

One woman was visible lying on the second floor porch roof in the front. From the third floor window above, another occupant dangled by his hands as the heavy smoke forced him to jump. He fell to the porch roof as I parked the car and got out to confront the nightmarish scene.

The whole left side of the first and second floors was engulfed in fire. The fire not only blew out from the windows, the walls themselves were already burning, making the whole left side of the building a mass of red-orange hell. Heavy, black smoke oozed from the other windows of all three floors. Several screaming people stood on the front porch. Others, dressed only in their nightclothes, milled about in the front yard. Some were gathered around an injured person lying in the yard. The roaring fire illuminated the whole scene, turning night into day.

As Frank Manning and Ed Stocks advanced their line from Engine 46 toward the front door, I absorbed the scene. Not only was the fire heavily involving the original building, but the fire was already threatening the large frame house next door. The vinyl siding on the house was melting, and the window sills were already smoking. Another minute and that house would be doomed. With a wave of the hand I directed Engine 29 to position their line to wet the exposed house. No words were necessary. They had seen the same threat as they dragged their line by the parked cars, across the sidewalk, and into the yard. Seeing the severity of the fire, the captain had chosen to use the larger two and a half inch line to attack the large body of fire. Though heavier and more cumbersome than the one and a half inch hose, the bigger line gave them 300 gallons every minute to attack the growing fire. Every gallon would be needed to overcome the tremendous heat.

I ran to the porch to question the occupants who had escaped. Injured and terrified people were screaming all around me as I tried to find out if everyone had gotten out of the house. It was important to get an idea where anyone not accounted for might be. Every second counted in our attempt to save those still trapped.

"Where's James?" screamed the mother hysterically. "Where's James?"

With the panic surrounding the frantic escapes from many directions, it was very hard to get an accurate picture of how many occupants might still be inside. As always, we approached the situation as a worst case scenario until we could be sure otherwise. That meant that fire fighters would need to quickly search every area where someone might still be trapped. Some areas were so involved in fire that no search there would be possible. One glance told us that anyone in those areas was beyond help anyway.

While some of the companies began their operations from the front, other companies were making their way to the back yard of the house. The report from the rear was not encouraging. In the rear yard, the fire fighters encountered even more occupants who had escaped, including one who had jumped before we had arrived. Another occupant was visible at a second floor window and the conditions in the rear were bad.

"Battalion Chief 11. Strike out a second alarm."

We needed more hoselines to get ahead of the spreading fire. We needed more ladders and crews to access all the areas of the large house and conduct the necessary search.

Fire fighters had begun the attack inside with the hoselines they had advanced through the front door. Crouched down just inside the front door, they were faced with fire throughout the left side of the house. The water gushing from the nozzle disappeared instantly into the inferno seemingly having no effect. The one and a half inch line gave them the maneuverability they would need to move around inside the house, but the fire required more than the 100 gallons per minute that the line could deliver. Another line soon joined them, and the crews moved deeper into the house. At least the fire had vented out the side and the heat wasn't as bad as they made their way from room to room knocking as much fire as they could. The stairway was the key to any rescue attempt above, so one line worked quickly to attack the fire racing up the stairs. Controlling the fire going up the stairs was necessary not only to protect any civilians still inside but to protect the truck crews who were searching above the fire.

The guys from Truck 12 had used ground ladders to gain entrance to the second and third floors. Breaking out the windows, they quickly dropped inside to the floor and began the search. The heat upstairs was worse than below and forced them to crawl on their hands and knees. Even with some of the windows broken out, it would be a while before conditions improved. The fire was still very much alive and pumping heat and smoke throughout the upper floors. Visibility was near zero in the thick, black, lethal smoke.

The noise of the fire fighters' air masks increased with their breathing rates as the truck guys tried desperately to beat the clock. Anyone left inside was in terrible danger. Above the fire, with no hoseline for protection, these fire fighters were in terrible danger as well. The large house, filled with beds and dressers, tables and lamps, televisions, toys, stereos, closets, clothes racks, and other furniture, and divided into numerous rooms connected by narrow hallways was a fire fighter's nightmare. Entangled in any of the dozens of possible traps or lost in the confusing, disorienting labyrinth of rooms, a fire fighter could run out of air and become a victim himself. The danger was real, the mission critical. Find those who might not have escaped. There is no more pressing emergency, no higher goal for a fire fighter. When lives are at stake the risk is accepted. This is what being a fire fighter is about.

"Has anybody seen James?" was the anguished plea being sent through the crowd of the injured, the scared, and now the curious who began congregating on the front street and sidewalk. As medic units came and went, and other occupants were herded into neighbors' homes, the situation became even more confusing. At least twenty people had been inside when the fire broke out. Had everyone gotten out?

"Chief, we've got one dead one in the second floor rear," Eddie Arthur and Newmo reported to me out front. "As soon as we get new bottles, we'll finish searching."

"Are you sure he's dead, guys, any possibility he could be revived?"

"Definitely dead, Chief, and it's a woman," Newmo answered somberly.

"Damn. Alright. The second alarm companies should be getting here any minute, I'll send you some help upstairs. We're still looking for at least one more boy."

The familiar figure of Deputy Chief Ticha came into view as he made his way up to me for a briefing. The consummate gentleman, Chief Ticha listened patiently as I briefed him. The forty year veteran had heard it all too many times before.

I gave him the report that would prepare him to assume command: "One confirmed dead. Companies are still searching. There's a good chance that we've got at least one more missing. We're making progress on the fire."

"Battalion Chief 7 to Command. We've got a non-breathing victim in the rear being removed by ladder at this time," came the report from the chief who had responded on the second alarm.

"Male or female, Joe?" was my reply. *Had we found James?*

The answer that it was a woman meant that we still held out hope that James might be found alive. Had he been shepherded into a neighbor's house for protection or wandered away terrified? Maybe one of the medic units had him among the many injured being sent to various hospitals.

Finally, the fire succumbed to the water being thrown from the numerous hoselines. Foot by foot, the fire fighters had fought their way through every room involved in the fire. They tore open the partitions and ceilings where fire could hide and wet down the fires they uncovered. Only foul-smelling steam and smoke poured from the house. With the fire under control, I once again sought out the mother at the next door neighbor's house. Huddled in a blanket and shaking she looked to me for answers. I had come to her for the same. Neither of us had found James.

"He was in his bedroom on the second floor, down the hall and on the left."

I knew that was a bad spot. The fire had been so intense in that area that the floor and ceilings had collapsed. Part of the third floor now rested inside of the second floor, which then sagged under the weight and damage. Holes burned through by the fire had allowed debris to fall to the first floor as well. Plaster, electrical wiring and fixtures, burned wooden laths, and the burned furnishings from the third floor now covered up the burned remains of the second floor bedroom—James' bedroom.

The painstaking process of removing each piece of debris was complicated by the unstable building condition and by the need to go slowly for the investigators. Determining the cause of all fires is important, but when the fire has caused a fatality, extra effort is required. Everything must be photographed and documented. Samples of suspicious items might be taken. Fingerprints might be retrieved. Until it is known for sure what caused the fire, the scene must be considered a possible crime scene. If the fire was set intentionally, this would now be a murder scene. The smallest detail might be important in court. Police and fire investigators worked with the crime lab personnel to determine the exact point of origin of the fire. From that first step, they would seek the cause of the fire from among the many possibilities.

Every square inch of the rest of the house had been searched. Fire fighters had methodically checked each room, every closet, every corner where someone could hide. They had overturned every bed and moved every piece of furniture that could possibly have concealed a small victim. Nothing.

"If he *is* in here, he's got to be in *there*," said Chief Ticha resignedly as we stood in the hallway looking into what remained of James' bedroom. We both knew what that meant. Piece by piece the fire fighters carefully pulled apart and moved the debris that filled the area of the collapse.

"Chief, we got him," came the voice from the room. A burned foot protruded from under the pile of fire debris. We had found James. He had never made it out of his room. Gently, the fire fighters uncovered him and the pathetic sight touched us all. Burned to an inhuman state, the body lay near the window. One of the guys came to me privately and asked that he not be assigned the job of removing the body when the time came. He had kids about the same size, and the sight of the dead child had particularly affected him. Even though fire fighters deal with death often and learn to put aside their emotions to get the job done, they are still human beings with human feelings. The violent, horrible death of a child is a particularly distressing experience for most people.

While the investigators and crime lab obtained the necessary photography and documentation, I once again performed the most miserable of my duties. There is no easy way to tell a mother of the death of her child.

Hours later, when I finally had gotten home, exhausted, dirty and wet, I was greeted by "Hi, Dad. Are you ready?"

It was a really good day to spend with my son and his classmates at the zoo. I'm sure they didn't notice that my mind seemed to wander.

22
Helping Hands

Ask any fire fighter and he or she will tell you the same story:
Firefighting is a series of ups and downs, busy periods and
slack ones, routine events and screwball occurrences. In
sports, we say that teams or individual players are in streaks
or slumps. In life, we say we're in a stretch of bad luck or,
more rarely it seems, good luck.

Is it luck? Do the stars seem to align themselves in patterns
that affect our world in strange ways? Does the full moon
really drive people to "lunacy"? Or is the hand of God at
work in mysterious ways? Who knows? People much smarter
than I struggle for the answers. I simply marvel at all the
"coincidences" and "dumb luck" that make my job so
interesting.

At the little church in northwest Baltimore, the congregation
faced the same problem so many inner-city churches face
today. Maintenance costs on the old buildings often outstrip
the financial resources of dwindling numbers of churchgoers.
Limited in their ability to meet ever-increasing costs, the
faithful sadly watch their facilities age and wear.

When the beautiful hardwood floors needed refinishing, the
choice was simple. Watch them and do nothing or pitch in and
do the work. The rental commercial-grade sander and the
solvent would cost money, but the labor charge, always the
biggest expense, could be avoided. And so the work
began—hot, tedious, and dirty. The teams of volunteer workers divided the tasks. Some ran the noisy sanding machine.

Some swept. Others poured and spread the solvent onto the floor to loosen the old finish. With each movement the powerful sander removed the old varnished top layer of the wood flooring and dispatched it as fine, solvent-saturated sawdust into the attached plastic collector bags. As each bag filled, someone would detach it, set it aside, and attach a new bag.

The work was slow going, but rewarding. The final reward was days away yet—a few more days sanding and preparing the floors, another couple of days applying the new finish. Soon though, all the hard work would result in a glistening, like-new floor, one that all could be proud of. Surely the Lord appreciated all the labor of His faithful to beautify the house of worship.

Tired, but pleased with their progress, the church members agreed to quit for the day. There would be plenty to do tomorrow. For now, it was home to dinner and the families. "I'll lock up," offered Mr. Ramsay, the semi-official caretaker and long-time church member. With only a half block to walk, he'd be home before the others were anyway.

At the dinner table Mr. Ramsay briefed his wife on the day's progress. His pride in the work they were doing was obvious. The sore muscles and fatigue were a small price to pay.

With dinner finished, Mr. Ramsay could look forward to an evening of relaxation, but something nagged at him. It was as though someone were trying to send him a message. Something or someone told him to go check the church he had just left a short while earlier.

Curiosity turned to fear when he slid the lock on the church's side door and opened it into a wall of smoke. Quickly pulling the door closed again, he headed for the phone to summon help.

Any report of a church fire causes fire fighters concern. Historically, church fires are among some of the most difficult and challenging fires to fight. Old church buildings frequently contain characteristics conducive to the development and spread of fire. Large open areas allow almost unlimited oxygen to feed the fire. Numerous void spaces (structural areas hidden behind walls, above ceilings, etc.) allow fire to travel unseen and unchecked. Extremely high ceilings mean fire fighters can't pull them down to attack fire traveling above them. Add the large quantities of wood and other combustibles, deep, confusing basements, meeting rooms, classrooms, offices, choir lofts, and the like, and the recipe for a serious fire is complete.

Outside the outlook is no more encouraging. High, steeply-pitched, heavy slate tiled roofs, which are treacherous for fire fighters, make roof ventilation almost impossible. Often, the windows, stained glass or other, are narrow and infrequent, making an attack from outside also very difficult. The L shape, U shape, or other configuration often removes much of the building from the reach of aerial ladders. All in all, church fires are often not our best success stories.

At least it was evening, I thought, as I responded to the report of the church fire. Chances were less that a fire could burn unnoticed for too long. Fires in the wee hours of the morning usually get the most time to burn undetected and often result in the most serious fires.

Nothing obvious greeted us as we arrived at the church. A quick look from outside didn't reveal any smoke or fire, but when Mr. Ramsay opened the side door for us, we met a wall of gray, acrid smoke—the familiar smell of wood burning that signifies trouble to the fire fighter. Hoselines came flying off the engines, some to the doors where they would enter the smoky church, others to the hydrants that would assure us of a continuous water supply for what might be ahead; truck crews readied their tools and ladders; and the noise of the air masks began as the search for the fire started.

Carefully and slowly the engine crew advanced down the short hallway and into the large, open room. Almost immediately, they located the fire and water quickly killed the flames. Only a small area was actually burning. As the smoke began to lift we could see what had been involved. A sanding machine, plastic bags, and some of the wooden floor had burned. Though smoke had filled the building, the fire had been confined to an area only the size of two picnic tables.

I special-called Rescue 1 to assist with the ventilation, and soon the smoke lifted. No need for us to break out any windows, no need to tear apart walls and ceilings, since we were able to locate and extinguish the fire quickly. The overall damage was relatively minor.

While we were looking for the cause of the fire, another fire started right in front of our eyes. A plastic bag stuffed with sawdust from the floor sanding operation suddenly caught fire on the opposite side of the room. The small flames were easily handled by the fire fighters standing nearby. As they removed the remaining sawdust-filled plastic bags to the outside, the fire fighters discovered several were very hot—ready to catch fire. The chemical reaction occurring within the bags was elevating the temperature to the point where the sawdust would spontaneously ignite. Had we arrived just a few minutes later, the fire would have been much worse.

Mr. Ramsay explained the day's activities to us and finished with the story of that nagging feeling that he needed to check the church. He couldn't explain the "message." He just knew that it was very real and very strong. Explain it however you wish. Had Mr. Ramsay not come back to check the church he had just left a short while before, the outcome would have been very, very different.

For almost one hundred years, St. Mark's Church has stood as a symbol of the neighborhood's dedication to the Almighty, to youth, to right in the midst of wrong. Members have come and gone. Untold pastors have led the faithful as the world changed. Once affluent, the area now stands tortured by the decay of human decency that ravages our cities. Crime, violence, drugs, AIDS, poverty, unemployment, hopelessness—these are the neighbors of St. Mark's today.

The massive stone walls and the beautiful stained glass windows stand as testament to the craftmanship of that era. The soul of any church, however, is not in its building but in its people. It's the good people of the community like those at St. Mark's who stand determined to refute the belief that decline is inevitable and resistance futile. St. Mark's exemplifies what the church means to the community. Sermons of hellfire and brimstone have given way to discussions of the erosion of the family and the epidemic of teen pregnancy. Through the worship services, community meetings, scout troop functions, and day care center St. Mark's provides a support system that assures the survival of the church as an integral part of the community. But would the church *buildings* survive the challenge of fire that bitter winter night?

The ancient steam pipes hissed and moaned as the heating system tried valiantly to keep up with the demands of the frigid weather. Year after year, the steam pipes had carried the heat to all the various areas of the large church complex. A two-story section of classrooms, offices, hallways, and storage areas formed the middle of the U shaped trio of adjoining buildings. Large sanctuaries at each end formed the "churchy" part of the church complex. Heating such a large area was hard work, so the furnace churned constantly that night.

Above the ceiling over one of the classrooms, where a steam pipe contacted a wooden beam, an almost imperceptible change was taking place. Over the years, the heat of the steam pipe had caused subtle, gradual changes in the wood. The wooden beam became drier with every passing heating season. The slow process of pyrolysis actually altered the chemical composition of the wood and gradually lowered its ignition temperature. Eventually, the wood had changed to the point that the heat from the steam pipe was enough to start a smoldering fire.

At first, just a wisp of smoke curled lazily from the charred wood. For hours, it seemed the fire would not survive, but ultimately the heat from the steam pipe proved enough to accelerate the process that would lead to a full blown fire. Smoke filled the area between the ceiling below and the floor above. At some point, the first tiny flame appeared, weak and unsure, more a flicker than a flame. The bone dry wood nurtured the infant fire. Flames began to build, not even an inch high at first, as they spread gently sideways along the beam, not yet assured of survival. Here in the darkness between the floor and the ceiling, the smoldering fire had consumed much of the oxygen. The fledgling fire was suffocating in its own byproducts, the carbon monoxide and other gases which now formed the dense smoke slinking unseen through the ancient structure. Even if someone had been inside the building, the growing fire would have remained secret, creeping now through the crevices and channels above the classroom ceiling. Following the ducts and the holes made for pipes and wiring, the fire reached slowly, yet steadily for the source of fresh air it craved. At the edge of the roof of the one story portion, the flames began to curl toward the freezing outside air. As some of the flames now tentatively poked through the edge of the roof at the back wall, the fire gained momentum laterally as well. Fire had begun to devour the underside of the floors of the hallway and other rooms. Bolstered by the infusion of fresh air, the fire headed for the main sanctuary, the one still used by the congregation, the holiest part of a holy building.

Directly across the alley from the wall where the struggling fire had found new life sat the fire station housing Engine 40, Truck 12, and Battalion Chief 7. The narrow alley was deserted on that frigid early morning; not even the street people or the drug dealers braved the cold. With no windows on that side of the fire station, there was no chance anyone inside would have seen the fire even if someone had been awake. While we rested, some fitfully, some coma-like, the fire that would soon confront us grew ever stronger.

The fire fighter on watch listened only a second to the cop who had banged on the door before he summoned the truck lieutenant. Sleepily, Lieutenant Vince Green listened as the police officer reported, "I think you oughta look out in the alley. I can't tell for sure, but I think there might be a fire."

Quickly covering the hundred feet across the front of the station, the lieutenant rounded the corner into the alley. He walked slowly examining the darkness, the haze, the...flames. Damn!

The sudden bright lights in my eyes jolted me from my semi-sleep even without the radio blaring an address. I rolled out of bed knowing the lights meant we were headed out again into the cold. I could hear the guys in the apparatus bays making their way to the engine and truck as the big overhead doors began their noisy ascent.

"What's goin' on, Boo Boo?" I asked as the pump operator pulled himself up behind the wheel of the engine.

"Fire around the corner, Chief. That's all I know."

I opened the door of the chief's car as the printer began to spew its message and the dispatcher's voice broke the silence. "Engine 40, Engine 52, Engine 29, Engine 20, Truck 12, Truck 18, Battalion Chief 7, respond to a report of a church fire, 3400 block Garrison Boulevard, Box 891."

Not knowing the "alley story," I turned the corner onto Garrison Boulevard behind the engine. Two large, stone churches, one on each side of the street, sat quietly in the darkness. Smoke that seemed to come from nowhere—or everywhere—drifted lazily in the street as the engine company laid their hose from the hydrant on the corner. Before I could decide which side of the street the fire was on, I heard the radio message, "Truck 12 on the scene. Fire showing in the rear." *Man, I wonder how they knew to go down the alley. I didn't see anything.*

Size-up is always critical to successful firefighting. The process involves assessing the size and the type construction of the building, its contents, the life hazard present, the weather conditions, and about a thousand other things. One of the first steps in converting all this information into a plan of attack is locating the fire. Sometimes that's obvious; sometimes that's extremely difficult; always it's important. The smoke that citizens see pouring from a building, even the flames they see blowing from the windows or roof do not always tell the whole story. Fire fighters need to find the heart of the fire, the "seat" of the fire as they call it. Knowing where the fire is and predicting where it is headed guide the fire fighters in positioning hoselines and selecting where, when, and how to ventilate.

Most fireground commanders agree that a quick look around all sides of the building is a good idea. Knowing the size of the building, how many stories are in the rear (not always the same as in the front), and how much separation there is between the fire building and the exposures (those not yet burning, but endangered), gives the incident commander more perspective on the overall severity of the problem.

The types of windows and doors, the pitch of the roof, the location of trees or overhead wires that might hinder ladder placement, high fences—all might be important in estimating the difficulties to be faced by the companies being placed there.

Deciding I was too old at this point in my life to run the several blocks around the entire church, I drove my car right back to my firehouse door and walked down the alley to look.

The truck guys had already begun the work of getting ladders in place as I looked at the long row of little flames curling up at the spot where the wall met the roof. *Maybe we can get the fire before it goes too far*. At least it wasn't blowing out of ten windows or leaping for the sky. That was the good news. The bad news was the location of the fire and the quantity of smoke now blanketing the alley. Fire in the concealed spaces of this type building is a nightmare, and the signs sure pointed to that.

"Don't open anything up 'til we get some lines back here," I cautioned, as I headed back to the front of the church. As I got in my car to drive back around, I could see Engine 52 already laying hose from the hydrant in front of the fire station and heading into the alley.

At the front of the building, I was pleased to see the guys had made entry into the building. Two hoselines snaked from the engine and disappeared through the heavy, oak, front doors. The first radio report from inside came back: "We've got a fair amount of smoke in the hallways and stairway and we can hear the sprinkler system running, but we don't see the fire yet."

Most fire fighters would rather have the fire blowing out at them than go through this. Crawling around in near-zero visibility dragging heavy hoselines is always tough. When the fire is hidden and you are constantly wondering where it might appear, the job is worse. Has the hidden fire eaten away the supports of the very floor we are crawling on? If so, we could drop into a boiling hell. Is there fire in the ceiling above ready to crash down onto us entangling us in wires, light fixtures, plaster and lathes, ductwork—an inescapable trap? Hidden fires are always a question mark. Unrecognized dangers like these kill many fire fighters.

Then the thought just struck me: *What sprinkler system?* I didn't remember there being any sprinklers in this place.

The sound of air masks loomed ahead as I followed the hoselines into the building for a quick look. All the contemporary management books aside, sometimes a quick look inside helps the incident commander grasp the situation more clearly. A brief conference with Engine 40's crew confirmed my suspicions—no sprinklers. The water was coming from broken pipes in a ceiling—a sure sign that's where the fire was. Unseen in the smoke, the reassuring sounds were the air masks of the guys already using the hooks to pull down the ceilings and the axes to tear open the walls. They do great work, I thought again.

Outside again, where I could see the whole picture—hate to admit they're right—the cold had mysteriously disappeared. My thoughts instead were centered on where the fire was and where it was headed. I had given the orders to place the companies in the right positions. The companies were hard at work doing the things they do best. I watched uneasily as sinister brownish-gray smoke oozed from openings all over the huge church complex.

A big part of the chief's job is knowing when to call for help. There's no magic formula. One well-placed burst of water on the fire might quickly extinguish the hidden threat once it is exposed. Then again ....

The fireground radio channel was so quiet, quiet because the guys were working—moving hoselines here and there, tearing, poking, yanking, punching, pulling. *Give 'em a coupla more minutes.*

"How's it goin', Cap?" I inquired of Phil Jansen, the captain of Engine 52 supervising the inside operations.

"Not good, Chief. We're pulling the ceilings in the back, first floor classrooms and everywhere we open there's fire," came the "tinny" radio reply. Talking through an air mask into a radio microphone makes for the weirdest sound.

The die is cast.

"Battalion Chief 7. Second Alarm."

Out on the outskirts of town, help is a long while coming, so if you *think* you are going to need help, you'd better get it moving.

The distant wail of sirens piercing the still night soon confirmed that help was on the way. Heavy smoke still drifted lazily in the street lights. It wasn't getting worse, but it wasn't getting any better either.

I was glad to see the familiar face of Joe Dillon, the second alarm battalion chief. Now, we could afford a chief inside as well as here where the overall view was.

Soon, his reports from inside reassured me. The lines were hitting all visible fire. "Making good progress," he informed me.

Bob Belluomo, the deputy chief, and I conferred and agreed that it looked like we'd be OK. Neither of us wanted to have to destroy the beautiful stained glass windows if we could avoid it. Both of us knew, however, that they would be sacrificed instantly if needed to save the building.

Heavy smoke met the companies wherever they entered the labyrinth, but the huge sanctuary at the north end was the worst. When Rescue 1 opened the massive doors, a solid wall of acrid, impenetrable smoke greeted them. The huge cavern was filled. Every pew was obscured, the organ lost in the smoky veil. It could have been anything inside those doors. Visibility was absolutely zero.

Once the fire was out, it still took the fire department fans—we call them smoke ejectors—an hour to make the interior recognizable. It was rewarding to see the undamaged areas of worship begin to emerge from the fog-like atmosphere.

Inevitably the cold returned now as the adrenaline subsided. Frozen hoselines, icy ladders, treacherous sidewalks, ice-coated streets eventually replaced the smoke and concern. At least we would leave victorious, satisfied at a "good stop."

The long, unglamorous job of overhauling and cleanup would take us all beyond the morning shift change. Day shift would relieve us on the scene and continue the work. The church officials were most appreciative. St. Mark's would survive. Indeed, they would hardly miss a beat. Disaster had been averted.

The fire fighters had done a good job. Hard work, dig it out, lines in the right places, vent. Everything had gone well.

"Look at this, Chief." The thorough investigation of a serious fire is crucial, and our fire investigators are careful to uncover every shred of evidence. This one hadn't been too hard. The heating pipe was quickly identified as the culprit, but the interesting part of the picture was farther away—over the stairway.

Uncovering the full extent of the fire's progress meant opening every wall, every floor, every ceiling where the fire had traveled. All the twists and turns in this type building can make that a chore. Some paths the fire had taken were obvious and quickly exposed; others were hidden.

Above the stairway, a small concealed area filled with ancient, bone dry wood had appeared to give the fire the perfect opportunity to spread from the classroom area into the sanctuary, the most sacred area of the church. In fact, the fire had slinked its way laterally to the little area and was headed across the void space to claim the sanctuary when "luck" intervened, probably before the cop had even discovered the fire.

A half inch diameter copper pipe ran through the area, hidden from below, hidden from above but directly in the path the fire would take in its bid to claim the sanctuary. As the fire had burned in the small area, the solder on the joint where two sections of the copper pipe met had failed. Solder melts at a much lower temperature than copper, and in failing, allowed the joint to separate and water to gush out. Not a huge amount of water flowed, nothing to compare to a hoseline. The "sprinkler" the fire fighters had heard was actually water from this little pipe running down through the ceiling. Though the quantity of water wasn't great, the location was perfect. Just enough water sprayed around within the space to prevent the fire from advancing through there.

We looked at the massive fire that would have resulted had the fire crossed that area. Century-old, huge, wooden beams, partitions filled with tinder-dry wood, the huge expanse of the roof—I shuddered at how close we had been.

"Thank you, God," was someone's cryptic comment that elicited a little laugh from all. Mixed in with all the "holy smoke" jokes and the "holy water" comments, it didn't raise an eyebrow—at least not then.

On the drive home, tired and dirty, but satisfied, my mind did the inevitable replay of the night's events. The "what ifs" are always a component of the involuntary mental critique that follows a serious fire. I wondered: What if the tiny pipe had not created the perfectly placed spray which had withstood the onrushing flames? I wondered: Was it possible this David had the same helper as the last one who faced Goliath?

Thank you, God.

23

Holiday Blessings—FD Style

One of the sacrifices a fire fighter makes is being able to spend holidays with the family. Like the police officers, doctors and nurses, and all the others who provide a 365 day-a-year service, we soon learn to make holidays fit our schedule.

The toughest times for me were the Christmas mornings when the kids were young and I was working the day shift. The choice was to wake the kids at 4:00 A.M. to open presents or make them wait until 5:00 P.M. when I'd be getting home. We got up very early those Christmas mornings.

Fire fighters' families learn to make things work out. They rearrange the family get-togethers, creatively schedule the Easter egg hunts, and hold the meals—it comes with the territory.

Many years Baltimore fire fighters have "celebrated" their Christmas and New Year's at lumber yards, warehouses, and other equally cozy places battling huge blazes. Christmas tree icicles were replaced by those dangling from helmets and mustaches. And the frigid winds and cascading torrents of water joined the whine of the pumping engine companies to provide Christmas caroling for those present.

While people at home snuggled contentedly in front of the fireplace recounting holiday tales and enjoying family and friends, many fire fighters braved the blistering heat and monstrous, roaring flames to save businesses and homes threatened by the blazes. Some years are better than others. Some years the fires are smaller. Sometimes they are particularly tragic. The burned Christmas tree skeleton, the soggy, charred remnants of presents among the debris in the front yard—too many fire fighters hold those memories.

Maybe we don't have more fires on the holidays. Maybe it's just that we attach a special significance to those fires, find them a little sadder, remember them a little longer.

The dreary morning drizzle heralded the arrival of *real* fall in Baltimore. Thanksgiving always seems to be about the time I reluctantly admit winter is around the corner. The beauty of the changing trees and the seasonal enjoyment of pumpkins and apple cider eventually yield to the cold I've grown to dislike more each year. Suddenly, the trees seemed bare as the cold rains hastened the removal of last season's leaves.

This particular Thanksgiving morning, I drove around the district collecting the reports from our battalion's stations and performing the other daily routines of day shift. Today, I couldn't be in the stands rooting for Loyola to kick Calvert Hall's butts in the traditional high school football rivalry. How many Thanksgiving mornings I shivered in the cold, concrete caverns of Memorial Stadium, shouting, clapping, stomping (partially for the noise, partially to restore some circulation) for my Alma Mater—but not today. Probably a lousy day to sit there cheering for the Blue and Gold anyway, I rationalized. Probably catch pneumonia and get the wife ticked off. Just as well.

Anticipation of a late afternoon turkey dinner at our house crept in. The whole family's coming. Diana'll work all day to make sure everything's great, as always. Dad'll rave about her cooking; Mom's never quite sure how to take that. David will keep everybody entertained again with his latest stories from school; the kid keeps us all in stitches. No doubt, we'll all eat too much and swear again that next year we won't. The smell of the turkey is probably starting to fill the house now....

The dispatcher's serious voice abruptly ended my daydreams. The address was only a half block in front of me, and I saw the smoke instantly. The big, wood frame house was typical of those in the area. Three stories, two stairways, windows everywhere, spacious front porch,   steeply-pitched peaked roofs at various angles. The numerous rooms inside had been home to a single family at one time, but like many of the homes in the neighborhood, it had found a second life. In this case, the frame house was a group home—"assisted living" they call it today—where residents unable to be totally independent could get the help they needed without having to live in a nursing home or similar facility.

Sometimes the mix of personalities and of problems can lead to conflict. This fire was the culmination of a feud from the previous day. Angry with a counselor, one of the residents had escalated her show of displeasure from yelling and screaming to slamming doors, to throwing chairs, and now to setting the house on fire.

"I think everybody's out but Mabel," the counselor reported to me on the large front porch. Above us, smoke drifted from the front of the second floor. A quick glance down the side of the house revealed much more smoke escaping from the rear.

"Are you absolutely sure she's still in there?" I asked, hoping for some doubt in her story.

"Mister, she's still in there. Please get her out," she pleaded.

Tough decisions challenge us all at times in the fire service, but for us, when confronted with a "savable" victim trapped, the decision is automatic. Faced with pretty definite information, armed with a specific location within the building and the knowledge that no apparatus would be arriving for a few more minutes, I did what we all would do—I went for Mabel.

At the top of the stairs to the second floor, I paused to assess the situation. Crouched on the top step, I could make out the familiar orange glow beneath the bottom of the layer of gray-brown smoke. The glow was visible through the doorway to the rear bedroom—Mabel's room. *No fire in the hallway yet. Fire must've vented out the back 'cause the heat's not that bad and the smoke's being pulled into the doorway.*

I found a pressurized water fire extinguisher—thank you,

fire code—and crawled closer to the open door hoping for an answer to my calls to Mabel. The angry crackling of the flames was the only reply. If I could knock enough fire just inside the doorway, I figured I might be able to get inside the room and grab her. The approaching sirens outside told me that help would be coming up those stairs shortly, but time was definitely running out for Mabel.

The two and a half gallons of water squirted onto the burning carpet and the bottom of the opening were enough to keep the fire from spreading back out into the hall, but not enough to allow entry to the room.

"Hey, Chief," I heard in a familiar, soothing voice. John "Newmo" Newmuis spoke with the same calm, quiet manner here as he would in greeting somebody at church on Sunday. The guy amazes me. Even through his air mask, his calm, calculated words came through. "Back out, Chief, I got it," and then the sounds of Engine 40's hoseline coming up the stairs told me it was time to admit defeat and retreat to the position where I belonged. The quick dash in and rescue I had hoped for was not to be, and there was still a fire to be fought.

From outside, it was immediately obvious that the fire in the back room was no longer survivable. Belching flames entirely filled the back and side window openings, and fire had spread up the outside shingled walls to the third floor and into the attic area.

Fire fighters on ladders strategically placed holes while others inside tore open all the areas necessary to get ahead of the spreading fire. Well-placed hose streams soon turned the dancing flames to wet, stinky, gray steam and smoke which blended with the drizzle outside. The fire fighters had confined the fire to the back of the house, and the inch-by-inch search of the large house revealed no victims.

Everybody had gotten out safely—even Mabel, who had escaped unobserved down the rear stairs. Part-angry, part-relieved, the counselor told me of the trouble with Mabel, and the investigator soon had her over with the cops as the companies began to "put up." Mabel would be spending Thanksgiving behind bars.

For the rest of the residents, the shock of the fire and of the damage to their home gave way to the relief that all were safe. Hugs and comforting words circulated on the big front porch.

In the corner of the porch, unscathed by fire or water, sat the big black roasting pan with the partially-baked turkey. Fortunately, someone had rescued the turkey dinner from the kitchen when the fire broke out upstairs. It was a little thing, but the boost to the morale of the residents was obvious.

"We're all going next door for Thanksgiving dinner," the counselor informed me as we prepared to leave. "We've got a special reason to be thankful this year."

The Last Chapter

Moving day had come and gone. Now the sparkling, new fire station on Liberty Heights Avenue was finally the official home of Engine 40, Truck 12, and Battalion Chief 7. Years of planning and funding and designing and building had finally produced a new fire station. New fire stations don't come along that often in a city always looking hard to stretch the available funds. We in the department sometimes joke that at our current building rate we're on the 400-year replacement schedule. Now, most people would think that fire fighters would be thrilled to leave a run down, century old, dingy firehouse for a beautiful, modern, one story station with a fenced in parking lot, a spacious, well equipped kitchen, comfortable bunk rooms, and modern showers and bathrooms. Then again, most people don't know fire fighters.

Leaving "home" was traumatic for many of the guys. Actually two "homes" were abandoned for the new place. Two sets of memories and histories, of nights spent shivering as the leaky windows beckoned the howling winds right on through. Of days spent cursing the ancient floors and walls, which defied every attempt to make them look clean. Two "homes" where the narrow, black, spiral, cast-iron staircases seemed so cruel to aching muscles, adding insult to injury after the "big one" or the seventh or eighth run of the night.

Fire fighters are a strange bunch. No matter how bad a place might seem to outsiders, no matter how much they might even complain themselves about conditions, they still become attached to their assigned station—their "home." For many, it's more like home than home. So many hours are spent there, it becomes a part of their lives as surely as their cars, or their kids. Threaten that "home" and you've intruded into their comfort zone. Few people welcome change in any way. When the change is not the fire fighters' choice, but the administration's, it's sure to receive a cool reception.

Moving to the new fire station would mean combining the engine from one station, Engine 40, and the truck company from another station, Truck 12. Put these two sets of guys from two single houses together, then throw in the relocation of a battalion chief from yet another station just to add a little spice. It looked sound on paper: No sacrifice in fire protection in the area, modern facilities to replace old stations so expensive to maintain. The true outcome would be anybody's guess.

The teamwork, the "family" so critical to the fire fighters' job takes time to build. To make things a little more complicated, the officers' union and the fire fighters' union had agreed to two different work schedules in their separate contract agreements with the city. The "shuffling of the deck" meant a different crew of fire fighters and officers worked together each shift. (Thankfully, this arrangement was reversed after that two-year contract and the permanent teams re-established.)

Nobody knew for sure how things would work out as the move approached. Some of us thought the change might turn into something positive—not just because of the new station, but because it was a fresh start. Engine 40 had recently lost a very popular pump operator to cancer. Truck 12 was still dealing with the crippling, tragic injury that had ended their captain's career. Maybe the new station would bring good luck to us all.

In Baltimore the change of shifts occurs twice each day—morning and evening—in every fire station in the city. For more than a hundred years, somebody comes in, somebody goes home. How many thousands of times we've all done it! We take it for granted. It's the way things are supposed to be.

On some of our worst days, however, not everybody who came to work goes home.

The quick cup of coffee in the morning with the oncoming shift signaled the end of my two day-two night tour of duty. *Routine*—man, how we hate that word in the fire service. Even when it best and most succinctly describes the previous shift, the connotation of "routine" seems misplaced in this job. All of us have seen how routine this job isn't.

The usual firehouse banter in the kitchen was a pleasant way to end an "uneventful" night. Eddie Arthur's son and mine both driving us crazy. Jim Bethea, so seriously asking to clarify a department policy. John Handy, so shy I've hardly gotten to know him since we all moved in together. "Good mornin', Chief," was the only exchange again this morning. And the new guy with all that long blonde hair, Lafferty. I used to have hair that looked...well, never *quite* like that. Today belongs to these guys and the others—we're outta here. A few days off and it'll be our turn again to respond to the fires and other emergencies of the city.

Fire fighters, like the rest of the world, come in all shapes and sizes and motivations. One trait that distinguishes many of the good ones is their desire to learn, learn, learn. From the day they come in 'til the day they retire, they continue to learn. Experience, reading, exchanging ideas, training—they all play a role in the learning process.

So much changes in the fire service. New tools, new strategies and tactics, new technologies challenge us constantly. The world around us changes at a dizzying pace. It's our job to keep up. It's our hope to be one step ahead. Even the skills we all have learned can go unused in the busiest of departments. Not using them means losing the efficiency so necessary in the job, and so we practice constantly.

Spending my day off in the University of Maryland Rescue Technician class was my own idea. So much to learn, so many skills I'd like to have. The opportunity to learn from P.J. Cusick and Bob Murray, two of the Baltimore County Fire

Department's instructors, two excellent rescue instructors, was well worth spending some of my off-duty time a couple of days a week for a few months. Captain Bob Murray and I go way back. Actually, his family and I go way back. While Bob chose the Baltimore County Fire Department as his career, his brother and his father had been in the city fire department. I had fought many a fire with Bob's brother, Jack.

I've never told Bob, and that's a shortcoming of mine, but he always makes me feel good to be in the fire service. Over the years, we've greeted each other in a dozen various scenarios—as attendees at events, as student/instructor, as co-instructors, as plain old fire fighters with smoke-reddened eyes and weary muscles, but always I feel touched by one of the "little things" that Bob does. It's very special to me and means more than he could ever imagine. For no matter when we see each other, often after months or even years of absence, he shakes my hand firmly, looks me dead in the eye, and sincerely says "Hey, brother." Brother. *Brother.* Never to be taken lightly or used frivolously, this is an almost sacred term fire fighters use in the most complimentary and meaningful way.

To call someone a brother in this sincere fashion is to say "I know what you are. I know what you do and how you would lay it all on the line for me. Know that I would do the same for you. Most of all, I respect you." In some departments the term is used frequently, but not in mine. Of all the fire service associates I have, Bob is the one with whom I connect in this very personal and gratifying greeting. It reaffirms my belief that what I do is important, and that somebody who knows appreciates it. It's one of those "little things" that mean the world to me.

The morning practical rescue session had gone well. Training at the county academy put me ten minutes from home. I could shoot home for lunch and back to the academy for the afternoon session with no problem. An early summer weekend—life can be good. I looked forward to a nice evening at home with the family, maybe even a little fishing in the reservoir as the sun set.

The fire department radio is such a constant companion at work that I rarely listen at home. There was a day long ago that I couldn't get enough, but time has a way of changing us all. By chance the scanner was on when I surprised the family by zipping in for a quick lunch. I long ago acquired the ability most fire fighters have. Unless the radio says something important (our company, working fire, second alarm, etc.) we filter it right out. My wife swears it's the same selective hearing I use to tune her out.

The familiar voice of Lieutenant Jim Bethea of Truck 12 broke through my inattention as he called for a medic unit. Our companies call for medic units every day, but there was something in his voice that caused me to listen more closely.

And then the words we all hate—"injured   fire fighter"—got my full attention. When the discussion quickly turned to arranging for a medevac helicopter, I knew something was seriously wrong. Being close to many major hospitals, we do not fly injured persons in helicopters very often. Something unusual was happening. Strangely, I didn't hear the usual chatter that accompanies a serious fire.

Next came the voice of the acting battalion chief who had relieved me just a few hours ago confirming that he was on the way to Truck 12's location. A few more messages, none of them good, and I knew something had happened to one of the guys—one of *my* guys.

A quick phone call to our communication center revealed only "one injured fire fighter going to Shock Trauma, some kind of training accident." That's where I belonged. "OK, I'm on the way to the hospital."

The trip downtown seemed endless driving the speed limit in my private car. Knowing the parking situation down there, I stopped at a fire station near the hospital and had that acting battalion chief drive me the rest of the way. He didn't know anything either. *Damn*. I wondered what had happened and how seriously the fire fighter had been hurt. Above all I kept wondering, who is it?

My mind went back the few hours to the kitchen. Who all

came in this morning on the truck? Jim Bethea was the one on the radio—it wasn't him. John Handy, due to retire almost any day, quiet, unassuming, a veteran of so many years—to get hurt now? The irony would make that almost unthinkable. Eddie Arthur, we go back a long way. We've been through so much together. John Lafferty, the new guy with all that hair, how terrible to get seriously injured this early in your career. There wasn't a good choice, as if I could will it to be one or the other. In times of stress, the mind plays strange tricks. Would my praying it not be one or the other affect the outcome? Would I somehow be responsible for selecting who was hurt, hurt seriously enough that he was being flown to our regional trauma center. Stupid thoughts!

Jesse Henighan, the acting medical bureau lieutenant, met me at the outside door. His sober face spoke volumes. "Chief, it's very bad. Some sort of accident; they hit a pole. His internal organs have all been displaced. He's already arrested twice. They're workin' on him now." Even without a strong medical background, I instantly grasped the gravity of the injury.

"The deputy told me to have you call him as soon as you get here. They need somebody to notify the family."

I'd waited long enough. I almost felt guilty asking, but I had to know. "Jesse, who is it that's hurt?"

"It's Eddie Arthur, Chief."

Damn!

In just a few minutes a fire department car and driver appeared to take me to Eddie's house. Nobody likes this job. Every fire fighter's family lives in fear that a battalion chief will knock on the door one day with a message that will change their lives forever.

"Is your mom home, hon?" *Christ, it just gets worse.* Eddie's daughter, about my own daughter's age, stood terrified in the doorway. *How would my daughter feel? Please, Lord, give me the guidance to do and say the right things.*

"She'll be home soon. What's wrong with my father?" The words were one quick sentence.

All I could tell her was that he'd been hurt and was in the hospital. The fire department driver opted to sit on the porch while we waited in the house. I couldn't blame him. The words never come easy at times like these. The small talk with the daughter was so strained, the silence worse. And the phone calls were the worst of all, updates from Les Helfrich, the acting deputy chief. None of them were encouraging.

"The chaplain's on the way," he explained. Each time he called I could only answer yes and no, trying not to let the impact of the conversations show to the frightened girl. I wanted to hug her, but I knew that would just frighten her more.

I talked to Eddie's son on the phone. Unable to come home, he pressed for answers, most of which I didn't have. "Is it serious?" he pleaded. I couldn't lie to him. *Please, Lord, let Eddie's wife get home soon.*

I tried not to show the brave but scared daughter how terrible the news was with each incoming call. "He's just expired," came the words I dreaded.

"I understand" was all I could say as Eddie's frantic wife rushed in and quickly questioned her daughter. I hung up the phone and turned to deliver the news that would certainly change their lives forever. I've done it before. It's never easy. No training can truly prepare you to say the right things at the right time in the right way. I heard myself, almost as another listener:

"I'm afraid there's been some sort of accident at work and Eddie has died." My heart was breaking. Many times I have had to deliver the bad news to civilians, families of fire victims, even families of our guys. But this was worse. This was one of *my* guys, a kind and gentle man with whom I had fought fires, eaten dinner, laughed, watched TV, shared private inner feelings over the career-ending injury to his captain, commiserated over problems with our sons. This time it was very personal.

For Rhondi—that was the moment that Eddie's wife became a person to me rather than just "my wife"—the news was obviously awful. And yet this lady's character, her sensitivity and considerate nature, and marvelous personal strength which would carry her through this tragedy were already at work.

Unable to tell her anything of substance, I felt so inadequate. Long ago I learned not to guess at things so important. I hadn't talked to anyone about what had happened, so I honestly didn't know. As she comforted her daughter so lovingly, I appreciated already her acceptance of my limited information and the sincere gratitude that she showed to me. In the days and weeks ahead, we would have many times together and my respect for her would continue to grow. Now I know why she could so confidently comfort her daughter that terrible day with the words I didn't fully appreciate then: "It's OK, it's OK. We'll be alright."

On the ride back that I hitched with the fire department chaplain who had finally arrived to assist, I heard the broadcast over the fire department radio in his car. Each department has its own way of announcing the death of a member to the rest of the department. In the days of the telegraph fire alarm systems and bells, there were signals reserved for the most dreaded of announcements. Whatever the method, the message is always chilling. One of our own has made the ultimate sacrifice.

"Announcing the death of Fire Fighter Eddie Arthur, Truck Company 12. Truck 12 will half-mast flag until sunset day of funeral."

"That's not right!" I told the chaplain. Before I could explain, a corrected message was announced: "Correction. *All* stations will half-mast flag until sunset day of funeral." And the message was still wrong. This would be correct if an active member had died, but not in the performance of his duty.

Eddie had been killed, his family devastated, our new station "family" touched already by tragedy, and for the first time that day I really got angry. In the presence of one of our chaplains, a man of the cloth, I let go with a tirade directed at the dispatcher, his supervisor, the department official who gave them the information to announce—I didn't care whom.

"For God's sake, Reverend, don't you the think the stupid bastards could at least get the announcement right?" I raged. "He didn't live a nice full life and die in the comfort of some old age home, for God's sake! This was *my* guy, Goddammit, and he died IN THE LINE OF DUTY and the those damn flags are gonna be at half-mast for thirty days."

Soon enough, the entire department would know that Eddie had died in the performance of his duty and, of course, the correct flag protocols were followed. Sometimes, in the midst of the dramatic and the "huge" things we deal with so often in this job, it's the *little things* that matter.

Few things are as touching or as memorable as the funeral of a police officer or fire fighter who has died in the line of duty. Maybe it's because we are surrounded by symbols of authority and "belonging", by badges and logo-filled tee shirts and patches and caps and uniforms that signify rank and discipline and camaraderie. Maybe it's because the fire service has a tradition of pageantry and parades, of pride in the condition and appearance of its apparatus. Maybe. But I think there's more.

The funeral of a member who has made the ultimate sacrifice brings out so many feelings in us. Beyond the expected sadness of those who knew him or her, there are the feelings of those who didn't even know the person involved. Members of departments often travel great distances, frequently at their own expense, to attend the funeral of someone they never met. We all take it personally.

For some, the feelings include the knowledge that it could have been them—even the fear that someday it might be. The intellectuals among us can use the occasion to ponder the meaning of life. The deeply religious can find and offer comfort in their convictions. Most of us are jolted back to the reality of life's unpredictability and cruelty. Many of us take the opportunity to re-evaluate our priorities. All of us should reflect on how short our time here really is.

Many emergency services people will be there at the funeral because it's one of those *little things* we do for each other. Call it a sense of obligation or duty. Call it a feeling of helplessness at not being able to do something more. We spend a career trying to help and protect, trying to change outcomes, trying to give good endings to bad situations. We come because it is our way of showing our compassion and support for the family and for the member's department.

We come to the funerals because we feel the pain, we share the grief, we share a bond. Though we might squabble and fight like siblings, and disagree vehemently over the dumbest of things, we understand like no outsider can. It takes a special breed of person to be willing to risk his or her own life at a moment's notice for a total stranger. These are the people who make your night's sleep a little sounder, and when one of them falls we all hurt.

We come because it is our way of showing we care. We come because it's the right thing to do. And unspoken always is the knowledge that if *your* time ever does come, *your* family will look out over the ranks of uniformed police officers, medics, and fire fighters standing rigidly at attention saluting your casket and find comfort that your sacrifice has not gone unheeded. It's one of the *little things* we do that is *huge*.

Fire department funerals don't just happen. The planning and the attention to detail, the organizing, the scheduling, the endless phone calls stagger the imagination. As the fire department officer assigned to handle this funeral, I would spend every minute for days working to make every thing just right. With the help of the other guys recruited to assist, I was determined to construct a fitting tribute.

Make sure first and foremost that the family gets the help they need. What do they need? What would they like us to do or not do? Get the uniform. Send out the notices to all the right agencies so they begin arrangements to send representatives. Coordinate with the church. Work with the funeral home and the cemetery. Get the flag lined up. Organize the color guards and the honor guard. Who will be where and in what order? Who says what and when to direct everyone smoothly? Make the arrangements for the pallbearers and their transportation. Don't forget the white gloves.

We'll need refreshments and a place for all the participants to assemble beforehand and a place to get together afterwards. We'll need the various police departments to block traffic at all the right places and times along the route from the church to the cemetery. And the route for the funeral procession—how can we make it most meaningful and appropriate? Let's send it right past the front door of Eddie's station— *our* station.

Along the procession route we'll want the family to see every single fire department unit we can standing by in honor as the procession passes. Need to coordinate it so we grab every unit we can without removing them from service in case another emergency calls. Once in the county, we'll want the procession route covered as well. Coordinate with them to have apparatus and personnel at all the right places. As always, they'll be terrific.

At the cemetery gate, we'll want the traditional fallen fire fighter's entry. Arrange for two aerial ladder trucks to have their 100 foot ladders raised and crossed to form the arch under which the procession will pass. Make sure they have the large American flag to drape from their ladders. That touch alone has meant so much to so many families. And the bagpipers, and radios for everyone to coordinate all the movements, and the seating at the church for the various department officials and the politicians, and about a thousand other things. No, fire department funerals don't just happen. But all the efforts of all those who helped put it together made the day the best we could make it. Unfortunately, we had done some before. Tragically, we have done some since. Nobody ever wants to get good at organizing a fire fighter funeral.

The day of Eddie's funeral was so painful for everyone. The large stone church was overflowing with mourners. In many of the pews family and friends, some quietly sobbing, some openly wailing, did their best to deal with the terrible grief. Others sat silently with ghostly distant stares as they too grappled with their feelings of loss. Representatives of the department in their finest dress uniforms, government officials, union officials, and members of the department who were Eddie's co-workers and friends filled the remaining spaces within the church, even spilling out onto the steps of the church and down onto the sidewalk. Each strained to hear the words that day that would bring them solace or help them make some sense of the last few days.

Two blocks up the street in the designated assembly area milled hundreds of others. The uniforms of the various departments gave a strange, quilt-like appearance as people talked in small groups. In muted, respectful voices some renewed old acquaintances while others met and shared thoughts and kind words.

From Detroit and New York City, from Virginia and Ohio and all over our fire department comrades had come to pay their respects to Eddie and to our department. The State Fire Marshal's Office was there with their distinctive garb. A variety of police department uniforms dotted the crowd. Like some bad early Civil War recreation, the blues and browns and the grays and blacks, some white-shirted, some blue, some in dress coats and others in shirt sleeves, with gold braid and badges and silver as well, the motley group waited for hours in the bright sun.

Inside the church, the tears flowed and the emotions welled as the service proceeded. A medic unit arrived at the church for a mourner overcome with grief to the point of collapse—the wailing siren a stark reminder that life does go on and the living need care.

I spoke, too, at the family's request, an honor but a daunting task indeed, for I spoke not just for myself and not just for the department. My words had to be those of all of us—of those who knew Eddie the best, those with whom he had spent so much of his life. His "other family" needed to say something and I was their voice. To Eddie's family, we gave the best present I could think of—a picture of the respect and love we all held for our fallen friend and co-worker. Eddie, a man who had risked his life so many times over the years and asked nothing in return—this man made a difference, and we made sure nobody there would ever wonder.

The transformation was remarkable. The scattered uniforms so motley earlier now formed the crisp, professional ranks of solemn honor guards and most impressive color guards. For an entire city block two rigid, arrow-straight lines of saluting men and women stared straight ahead, some with tears in their eyes as Eddie's company accompanied the coffin down the gauntlet and into the hearse to begin the trip to the cemetery. No one there was untouched at the sight.

Everywhere along the procession route cars stopped and pedestrians stared. Some whispered to the children or among themselves; others were silent witnesses as the long line of vehicles passed slowly by. At many of the intersections, fire apparatus and their crews bore witness also. As if somehow pre-ordained, the fire activity in the city dropped to nothing for that period and every single unit scheduled to be in place was there on time. The crews stood at attention next to the parked engines and trucks with their emergency lights flashing as the procession passed. For those who could not be at the church because they were protecting the city, this was an opportunity to participate.

I knew we had made the right decision to route the funeral procession past our station the moment it came into view. Draped in black bunting that stretched across the front wall, the new station—*Eddie's* new station, *our* new station—evoked the strongest of feelings. Glistening in the sunshine, the sparkling apparatus of the units sat on the ramp. Fire fighters stood at attention. Neighbors watched silently, and the traditional fire bell brought to the ramp for the occasion tolled mournfully as Eddie made his last trip up Liberty Heights Avenue.

Our Baltimore County friends made us proud as we proceeded on what seemed a never-ending journey. Even on the interstate, immaculately clad state troopers stopped traffic in both directions. Each trooper saluted in that professional way and impeccable appearance for which they are so well known. Motorists watched in awe, and at most of the overpasses yet more fire apparatus and personnel stood silent guard.

Passing into the Dulaney Valley Memorial Gardens under the aerial ladder-made arch and the beautiful American flag, the funeral procession slowly wound its way to the area we've come to know too well. In a most appreciated gesture, the cemetery years ago set aside an area where Maryland fire fighters and police officers killed in the line of duty can be buried at no expense to the families. The area houses a little memorial describing its significance and is the final resting place of too many already. I hate it and yet I love it. It's always sad to see the names of those I knew or of those whose funerals I've attended, but it is nice to know that they are remembered here.

For Eddie this would be his final tribute—to be buried among those who would have understood his sacrifice, among those who shared the bond, among those who gave their own lives to protect others, and to be remembered always by all who come to this special place.

I stood removed from but overlooking the group gathered at the gravesite, talking quietly on the fire department radio and making sure that everything would flow smoothly as we all got back into the vehicles in a few moments. For the first time in the hectic days that had followed Eddie's death, I took the time to reflect a little on all that had happened. None of it seemed quite real, almost like some bad dream that tomorrow would be only a faint memory.

I thought about the time that Eddie, the most conscientious and careful of drivers, had taken off down the street to respond to a call while the huge ladder truck had been parked in front of my then station. Hearing the dispatch for his company, he quickly ran out of the station with the other guys, started up the truck and took off down Reisterstown Road. Unfortunately, the guy who was driving the back end of the truck, the tillerman, was not quite as fast responding from the bathroom. *Smack* went the truck, sans tillerman, into a parked car after only a half block.

I thought back on the kidding that Eddie accepted so good naturedly about the guy that Eddie "had killed 'cause he went upstairs." That's how the caller to a morning talk radio show had described the incident, which had actually been a cocaine-induced heart attack suffered by an intruder into the station. Poor Eddie had wrestled with the crazed guy and then tried to save him as he died. We hated to wash away the chalk outline of the body on the floor.

I remembered how Eddie had risked his life and narrowly escaped serious injury or death trying to keep his captain from falling from the roof. And I remembered how touched Eddie had been that I had taken the time to send him a card and a note afterwards letting him know how I felt.

I pictured Eddie working on the truck in the old station as I made my morning rounds. I saw him working tirelessly on the tools and the air masks, always ensuring they would be in tiptop shape when needed.

My mind wandered to the conversations we shared over our sons and their uncanny abilities to send us to the edge of insanity. How many times we had exchanged stories and shared confidences regarding them.

I thought for a moment on how Eddie's death might affect the new station. Would sharing this tragedy so soon after moving into the new station bring us all together more quickly? I hoped so.

But mostly it would be Eddie's smile that I would miss, a smile that came so easily and naturally.

And through all the mixed emotions, I felt satisfaction for all of us and relief. Finally, we could breathe easier that the final tribute had gone well. This *little thing* we do for each other meant so much to us and to the family and friends. It was the right thing to do.

It was only two days later when I went to the next Rescue Technician class, the final night of the course. Captain Bob Murray greeted me one-on-one as I walked up. He looked me dead in the eye and said, *"Brother,* you did a hell of a job."

No words could have meant any more.